THE FUTURE OF STATE UNIVERSITIES

The publication of this book has been aided
by the generous assistance of the Ford Foundation.

THE FUTURE OF
STATE
UNIVERSITIES
ISSUES IN TEACHING, RESEARCH,
AND PUBLIC SERVICE

**EDITED BY LESLIE W. KOEPPLIN
AND DAVID A. WILSON**

Introduction by Edward J. Bloustein

RUTGERS UNIVERSITY PRESS
NEW BRUNSWICK, NEW JERSEY

Library of Congress Cataloging in Publication Data
Main entry under title:

The Future of state universities, issues in teaching
research, and public service.

Bibliography: p.
Includes index.
1. Education, Higher—United States—Aims and
objectives—Addresses, essays, lectures. 2. State
universities and colleges—United States—Addresses,
essays, lectures. I. Koepplin, Leslie, 1944–   .
II. Wilson, David, 1926–   .
LA228.F87   1985   378.73   85–11903
ISBN 0–8135–1122–4
ISBN 0–8135–1123–2 (pbk.)

CONTENTS

v

THE FUTURE OF STATE UNIVERSITIES

INTRODUCTION
EDWARD J. BLOUSTEIN

I am delighted that my role as chairman of the Ad-hoc Committee on the Future of the State Universities of the National Association of State Universities and Land-Grant Colleges provides me with this opportunity to introduce this group of essays. I hope to explain why the project was undertaken as well as why the essays were commissioned.

We sometimes entertain the comforting assumption that one or another part of the world we cherish bears the mark of eternity. Fortunately, although mistaken, it is an attitude of mind that at least nourishes not only personal contentment but loyalty and social and political stability as well.

But Charles Darwin taught us long ago to beware lest the emotional and political comfort we thus indulge be mistaken for rational and scientific appraisal. A faculty colleague of mine, George Levine, recently took the occasion to observe that Darwinism is as much a way of thinking as it is a theory of biology. It tells us that the Platonic search for eternal essences and final causes may not be as important to our understanding of the world in which we live as the study of origins and change. Darwin, said my colleague, "seems to have domesticated change" as a tool of intellectual insight.

Recall the magisterial last sentence of *The Origin of Species*: "There is a grandeur in this view of life, with its several powers, having been originally breathed into a few forms or into one: and that, whilst this planet has gone cycling on according to the fixed law of gravity, from so simple a beginning endless forms most beautiful and most wonderful have been, and are being, evolved."

In the beginning, almost a century and a quarter ago, the primal land-grant college and state university was of a simple form. But "whilst this planet has gone cycling on according to the fixed law of gravity" new forms of land-grant colleges and state universities, "forms most beautiful and most wonderful have been, and are being, evolved." The committee I chair was established to study the process of evolution at work in state universities, and the essays that are gathered in this volume attempt to study some of the "forms most beautiful and most wonderful [which] have been, and are being, evolved."

Our state universities were conceived in the Jeffersonian populist tradition of education for democratic citizenship. Although brought forth into the world in a national framework by the federal Land-Grant Acts of 1862 and 1890, they were chartered by the states in the service of local public needs. They educated, primarily at the undergraduate level, a relatively small number of each state's own young men and women, particularly in agriculture and engineering. Indeed, a distinguished historian has characterized their beginnings as a flourish of state "boosterism." Their form and finances, no less than what they did and aspired to, bespoke their local origins and intentions.

How our state universities have changed, grown, and prospered! They currently educate millions of students, from within their own states and from without, citizens and foreigners alike, in the fullest range of graduate and professional, no less than undergraduate, programs. Moreover, together with some twenty-five leading independent research universities, they conduct perhaps 80% of all the basic research in the United States— research vital to national prosperity and security. They still serve state needs and state pride, to be sure, but they do it by undertaking a national mission, with increasing amounts of their financial support coming from the national budget.

Four simultaneous and interactive conditions, operating slowly and insensibly over long years, but conspicuously and at a gallop since the end of the Second World War, have remade our state universities. Exponential growth in everything they are and do, a profound change in the other types of colleges and universities in the nation, completely new and surprisingly mixed forms of financial support, and a transformed American economy dependent as never before on knowledge, in general, and science, in particular—these factors combined have served as a powerful engine of transformation of our state universities. These four conditions, and their consequences, are described in detail in the essays that follow. Let me briefly sketch their general outline here.

First, to the fruits of the expansion of state universities: all the colleges and universities of the nation have grown markedly in the past thirty years; in the state universities, the increase in the numbers of students and faculty, in the size and variety of their programs, and of their physical facilities has been startling. In enrollment alone, from 1960 to 1980, these institutions more than doubled, going from 1,000,000 to 2,150,000 students.

More startling than enrollment growth has been the change in the character of the student population served. In the early history of the land-grant movement, students came primarily for an undergraduate education, and they came predominantly from the rural areas in which individual state universities were located, rural areas to which they intended to return after graduation.

This early homogeneity of student population and purpose has by now been completely transformed. Beginning in the aftermath of World War II, with the generation of returning veterans, and continuing through the aftermath of the civil rights movement of the sixties, with the generation of minority students and students of urban America's working classes, an enlarged and manifestly more diverse student population sought educational alternatives and programs never before considered within the province of the traditional state university. Moreover, they came from further and further afield nationally and internationally, and many intended to wander still further after graduation.

A larger, better prepared, more diverse, and more specialized faculty came into the state universities to serve this new student population and their new needs. Whereas the state universities were at one time predominantly institutions for undergraduate study, with a smattering of research, graduate, and professional programs, during the period since World War II, this emphasis has been virtually reversed. Measured by the academic qualifications of their faculty, the magnitude and sophistication of the research they undertake, and the portion of it which is externally funded, measured by published research, by the multiplication of the number of postbaccalaureate programs and students, and by the growth of libraries and laboratories—judged by any or all these factors, the state universities of the eighties must be seen as mutations, rather than simply as lineal descendants, of the state universities of the last century.

The more general environment of higher education presents a second strand of change to which the state universities have responded. In most states of the nation, there was a time when the state university was the only institution in which a poor student, or one with moderate income, could enroll as an undergraduate. This is no longer so.

The fifties and sixties saw the growth of an entirely new two-year public community college system in which a liberal arts program and many technical and professional programs became available at low cost. These decades also witnessed the transformation of the system of state teacher colleges or normal schools into four-year liberal arts colleges that provide wide access. Finally, the fifties and sixties also spawned important developments in our independent colleges and universities; new ones, with little or no endowment, sprang up with the purpose of providing low-cost education to students who formerly would have attended state universities. At the same time, the more traditional independent colleges and universities began to assume the burden of providing access to students of poor or moderate income through endowment and other sources of financial aid. The scale of what has happened is shown by these comparisons: in 1960, community colleges enrolled 400,000 students; in 1980, they enrolled 4,330,000. During the same period, state college enrollment grew from 750,000 to nearly 3,000,000, and private sector enrollment rose from 1,470,000 to 2,640,000.

This transformation of the landscape surrounding higher education has affected powerfully both the composition of the student body and the public service mission of the state university. The community and state colleges now enroll many of the undergraduates who formerly would have enrolled in the state universities. In turn, state universities now have the choice of enlarging the enrolled proportion of the best high school graduates. This more academically select student body tends more often than in the past to enter upon graduate and professional education, and increasingly, as well, these students are recruited on a national, even an international, basis.

Public service, which was once the almost exclusive purview of the state university, is now shared widely with all other segments of higher education. The community and state colleges have adopted much of what has in the past been the training mission of the state universities at the noncredit and certificate level. Likewise, large and small independent institutions, searching for state and federal financial support and attempting to maximize the benefit to be derived from their research efforts, have now incorporated into their missions many aspects of the public service role formerly almost exclusively undertaken by state universities.

Besides the new centrality of research in state universities and the marked change in other sectors of higher education, a third factor—the development of a multiplicity of funding sources—has also been at work in transforming the state university system. Large-scale federal financial support of research programs that stimulate industrial growth and undergird defense preparedness has been awarded without regard to whether an institution is state supported or independent. This catholicity of federal support has accelerated the trend toward concentration on research that was already at work in the state universities, and, as important, it has vastly expanded the nonstate resources expended within those universities. Whereas they were once supported almost exclusively by one source of tax dollars, they now have two such sources.

On the other hand, federally supported student aid programs undertaken since the end of World War II have not only expanded the proportion of federal dollars in state university budgets, they have also begun to bring a significant proportion of tax dollars into the budgets of independent colleges and universities. In 1960, the United States Office of Education made $25 million available in student aid; in the fiscal year 1980–81, the figure was $4.3 billion for Pell Grants and campus-based programs (NDSL, SEOG, CWSP), granted without regard to whether a student was enrolled in a public or independent college or university. Some large portion of that total—$1.8 billion, or 42.7 percent of it—was expended in independent institutions of higher education.

In order to provide students with freedom of choice of enrollment between public and independent institutions, many states have also provided financial aid to students at independent institutions. The vast increase in federal and state student tuition assistance programs and the enormous federal expenditure for research must be seen in the larger context of state programs of direct institutional aid to independent institutions and of the financial subsidy afforded to public and independent institutions alike by a federal tax system which provides that charitable gifts are given on, and university endowment earns income on, a tax-free basis.

To be sure, there was a time when the state universities were almost exclusively state funded, when they received little private or corporate voluntary support and few federal tax dollars, either directly or as a result of the tax benefits of private giving and nontaxable earnings on endowment. This was also a time when tuition at public institutions was low or nonexistent and when independent institutions had little or no state or federal support, directly or indirectly. But what is the situation now?

Typically, state universities now receive only 20 to 40 percent of their support from state revenues, with the remainder divided between tuition and fees—now frequently above 30 percent of educational cost—and federal or private sources. Just as typically, independent universities now receive as much as 20 to 30 percent of their support from state and federal revenues, with the remainder divided between tuition and fees—which constitute as a percentage of their budgets only some 13 percent more than they do in state university budgets—and federal indirect support through gifts and endowment, or private contract support. Have we not reached the time when the planning and financing of higher education at the institutional, state, and federal levels must begin to take account of these dramatic ways in which the income side of the higher education budget has changed?

The fourth marked break with the past that raises fundamental new questions about the future of state universities is the advent of the post-industrial age. This is obviously not the place for an extended analysis of the new economic world in which we live; it is enough to say that what is variously known as the technetronic, or information, or service economy makes demands on higher education that are lightyears removed from those of the era in which the state universities arose.

States that were once predominantly agricultural and whose state universities served that predominant interest now invest heavily in high technology. They do so partly because even the future of American agriculture is seen to turn on new developments in the scientifically advanced field of molecular biology; more broadly, however, they do so because the successful application of advanced science to agriculture has increased its productivity markedly, thereby freeing resources to support the diversification of the economic base of even what were previously our most agriculturally oriented states.

By its very nature, high technology requires an extraordinarily large investment in basic scientific research, much of which is best undertaken in a university, rather than in an industrial, setting. Very frequently the corporate structures to be served are of a national and international, rather than purely local, character. The kinds of scientific collaboration involved require links between business enterprises and universities, and between public as well as independent universities, throughout the country. And the industrial base of this development is integrally related to national defense, which in its turn has become more and more dependent on higher and higher levels of science that are frequently best undertaken in a university setting. State universities which were founded to boost local pride and serve local agriculture and manufacturing are now vital components of national economic and defense policy.

To summarize, the constantly accelerating twenty-year evolution of our state universities urgently requires that we reach informed and widely agreed upon conclusions to at least the following questions:

1. What is the appropriate role of research, graduate education, and professional training in contemporary state universities, and what implications do the changes in this role have for their planning, financial support, and accountability?

2. What kinds of students should they enroll?

3. What is the special public service role of state universities, how does this integrate into the rest of their mission, and how is it distinguishable from that of the other segments of higher education?

4. Who should pay for, and who should benefit from, this new mix of research, undergraduate and graduate education, and professional training at the state university? And how should their increasing reliance on student tuition and fees monies and tax-supported voluntary giving affect institutional planning, governance, and public accountability of, and public responsibility for, state universities?

5. What are the implications for public comprehensive research universities of the convergence of their mission with that of independent comprehensive research universities, of the increasing levels of state and federal subsidy of those latter universities, and of the relatively recent emergence of the community and state college systems?

It was in order to help answer such questions that the National Association of State Universities and Land-Grant Colleges (NASULGC) established the special study committee which I chair. The essays that follow were commissioned as part of the first major study of state universities in two decades, the first attempt to reexamine and restate the mission of these institutions since they were founded over a century ago.

The papers here published have served as the centerpieces of a series of regional conferences on the future of the state university system. The conferences have been sponsored by the National Association of State Universities and Land-Grant Colleges and cosponsored by the National Governors' Association, with the cooperation of the National Conference of State Legislatures. The study will conclude with a national wrap-up conference in the fall of 1985 in which we hope to reach a consensus of educators and state and federal legislators on the role of state universities as we approach the year 2000.

The familiar world of higher education in which privately supported colleges and universities, local and national, were sharply differentiated from publicly supported state and community colleges and universities is a thing of the past. There is now an entirely new and much more complex higher education landscape, in which is to be found a kind of state university unlike any we have known in the past, a state university that I suspect is more like the comprehensive independent research universities than like either other public institutions of higher education or independent colleges.

To borrow from Darwin again, out of what the Morrill Act "originally breathed into a few forms" of the state university more than a century

7

ago, "endless forms most beautiful and most wonderful" have evolved. Good sense requires us, as a result, to reassess their mission, their structure of planning, accountability, and support, as well as their relationship to the other institutions of higher education in our national system. I am certain the studies found in this volume will contribute greatly to this effort.

CHAPTER 1
RESEARCH, GRADUATE AND PROFESSIONAL EDUCATION: SOME OBSERVATIONS AND ISSUES

DAVID S. SAXON
WALTER L. MILNE

The member institutions of NASULGC, and especially the state research universities among them, are enthusiastically and seriously committed to research and to graduate and professional education. It is the purpose of this paper (1) to describe in broad terms the extent and character of that commitment; (2) to justify it by establishing its relevance and importance to the welfare of the states individually and collectively as they compose the Republic; and (3) to examine—or at least raise—certain policy questions that suggest themselves as we look ahead to the end of the century. We set the stage, however, by first looking back to the origins of these remarkable institutions.

THE HISTORICAL MISSION OF THE LAND-GRANT
INSTITUTIONS

Education in the United States has been closely linked with the life and progress of our society from the days of our founding, when Thomas Jefferson declared that the new nation "requires the education of her people as the safeguard of order and liberty." Later, our great public universities were either conceived by or, for those founded earlier, powerfully shaped by, the Land-Grant College Act that Abraham Lincoln signed into law in 1862. It was this act that gave American higher education its distinctive concept of scholarship as neither remote from our daily affairs nor the exclusive province of the few, but open to all and the active partner of agriculture, industry, and the broader economy.

9

The land-grant idea was a true revolution, for it represented as an ideal the first full opening of higher education to a substantial fraction of the nation's young people. Instead of a limited number of predominantly private, predominantly eastern colleges focussing on the training of ministers, doctors and lawyers, and children of privilege, America was equipping itself with largely public institutions open to the children of farmers and the industrial classes. It was a revolution, then, of access.

It was a revolution also in educational mission and in curriculum, going beyond the traditional learned professions by establishing and giving status to studies in agriculture and the mechanic arts. Accordingly, it gave meaning to the proposition that education was linked to, and essential to, the material well-being and progress of the larger society. In short, the land-grant concept of access and of practical education, and the mandate of the Morrill Act "to promote the liberal and practical education of the industrial classes in the several pursuits and professions in life," [1] extended enormously the range and diversity of American higher education. And it helped shape the character of, or influenced the development of, every public university in NASULGC, notwithstanding the differences that may mark their origins and situations. For eight decades, building on that base, our public universities grew and expanded in measured strides.

THE PERIOD SINCE WORLD WAR II

But there was a second, and more recent, phase to this educational revolution, and that is the period of great development that followed World War II. This more recent development resulted in part from the enormous growth in postwar enrollments, produced at first by the G.I. Bill, and then by the steady growth in the fraction of students seeking higher education, and finally by the great surge in absolute numbers of the "baby-boom" generation. It resulted also from the unprecedented growth of university research—predominantly, but by no means solely, in the sciences—which arose directly from the wartime experience and has been an outstanding feature of our public universities for the past four decades.

Coupled with the flood of postwar students, this growth in research transformed the universities and is central, quite obviously, to the focus of this paper on research and on graduate and professional education. The enormous change in the magnitude of our national research enterprise arose from the role of science in the Second World War. The contributions of new kinds of scientific knowledge—in nuclear physics and solid-state physics, for example—and the new skills developed by scientists working in these fields turned out to have direct, immediate, and critically important applications to the war effort of forty years ago.

Because basic science and the applications it made possible proved to be absolutely vital to our survival, many people became convinced that it was essential to the national interest that a framework for systematically encouraging support of science be established when the war had ended. The man who sketched out that framework was Vannevar Bush, who proposed in his now-famous report *Science, the Endless Frontier* that the federal government underwrite basic research—and that meant university research—on a scale undreamed of before. Bush's proposal was the first step toward the establishment of a new and spectacularly productive partnership between universities, the states, and the federal government. And it is a fact of great consequence for the strength and diversity of public higher education in the U.S. that in each of the two great federal initiatives we have recalled—the Land-Grant Act and the postwar investment in unversity research—the control and the core support of the public universities were left to the states.

THE MISSION TODAY

Out of the huge postwar increase of scientific and technical research, of discovery and of application, has come a new world with a new set of opportunities, problems, and requirements to which our universities have responded. One major feature of this new world is its technological character and the implications of that for graduate and professional education. A second is the need to provide higher education, up to the very highest levels, to an unprecedentedly large fraction of our youth. These developments have had, and will continue to have, a profound influence not only on the shape and size of our institutions of higher education but on the meaning of the traditional objectives of our public universities as well.

For one thing they have extended significantly the meaning of access to higher education and the historic goal that our land-grant colleges and state universities should be open to all on the basis of ability and talent alone. This is one justification for generous state support, and no matter how our institutions have changed and expanded, our central purpose must continue to be the education of individuals as broadly as possible and to the limits of individual capabilities.

We have fallen short of that goal. The simple fact is that to be poor, to be a woman, to be a member of a racial minority has often blocked the way to our colleges and universities—and so inevitably to our graduate and professional schools—or at best has made the way more difficult of passage. And while we have clearly made some progress, our aim must be to press constantly for more, by acting affirmatively and vigorously, until all our educational institutions, especially our graduate and professional schools, reflect reasonably and responsibly in their composition the makeup of the larger society. Higher education alone cannot solve the problem of equal opportunity and access; but higher education, including graduate and professional education, has its proper, relevant, and indispensable role, which it must play with determined purpose.

We have much to gain—all of us—from this evolvement; but the gains will not come without stress, and we must be skillful, as well as willing, in adapting to them in our graduate and professional schools. We need particularly to identify barriers to bringing women and minorities into the university's graduate and professional programs and to take effective actions to reduce the barriers. It is a matter of policy and procedure and, above all, of leadership.

Just as the meaning of access must fit the contemporary circumstance so must that of research and its relation to graduate and professional education and practical affairs. Our time, of all times past, is peculiarly and particularly an age of science and technology. Science is our great intellectual adventure. And in its technological character, our society and our world are on an accelerating and irreversible track; they will become more and more technological, inevitably. That is the dominant circumstance to which our historic concern with "practical" education and with research must be related.

And the influence of that circumstance extends as well to the social sciences, which will help us shape our technologies to human uses, and to the humanities, which relate the values of the arts and of the universals of human experience to our technological society. Surely the liberating elements of such domains of scholarship as literature and history and philosophy were never more "practical" than in our own xenophobic and nuclear age, nor ever more important.

In explaining our research activities, and in communicating with our various publics, we speak, commonly enough, of two kinds of research: basic research as the pursuit of new knowledge, pursued not for an immediate or practical end, but rather to satisfy humanity's age-old striving to understand more about ourselves and our universe; and applied or targeted research, as investigation directed toward the solution of a specific problem. The point we do not stress enough to our publics is that both basic and applied research, so different in their purposes, are absolutely essential to each other and thus to the total growth of our knowledge of the world and our ability to cope with its complexities.

APPLICATION OF RESEARCH TO PRACTICAL ENDS

Examples of the ways our universities serve their states, and the nation, through applied research are countless. The classic case, of course, is that of agriculture. University agricultural research coupled with work at the "Land-Grant experiment stations and the diffusion of the results through extension services have made deserts bloom, created new and better crops, multiplied production, brought about new industries . . . and brought science directly into the homes of the nation."[2]

While university involvement in agriculture was, in some measure, in a different mode from much of our present-day applied research, it set the stage for the later connections of university research with the economies of our states and the well-being of our people. We have added over the years many new linkages, from those that are pursued at almost all our institutions, such as medicine and health sciences, to those that are of special interest to individual states, such as schools of mines and programs of petroleum engineering.

Such local links, which are one of the advantages of our decentralized educational "system," are totally proper and desirable so long as these interests are neither transient nor expedient. While it is inevitable, and right, that in some of our applied research we set our sails to local conditions, we must be certain we are sailing with the prevailing winds and not being buffeted by the gusts and eddies of the moment. This is an important caveat, for the university, unlike most institutions in society, must not be dominated by the transitory, the short term. Equally important in the conduct of applied research in our public universities is the requirement that it have genuine intellectual content, engage the interest of the faculty, and, most of all, be intimately related to the education of students.

It is important to recognize that while universities conduct much applied research, that kind of research is also widely performed in other parts of our society, and especially in the research and development divisions of industry. Therefore, if applied research does not meet our requirements of proper fit for the university, if it is not closely linked to education, we should not accept it.

Further, it is far too narrow a concept of the benefit of university research to view it only as an instrument for attaining short-range societal goals, only as a means of immediately applying research findings to improve the quality of life or, in more dramatic examples, the chance for life itself. The research contributions of our universities are greater than that and far broader in scope.

BASIC RESEARCH AND SCHOLARSHIP

This brings us, of course, to basic research and scholarship and their special place in the university setting. That place is special because universities are the institutions society has established for the purpose of seeking new knowledge and new understanding, whether or not their discovery and transmission over the years serve immediate practical purposes. And because advances in scholarship and basic research, unlike those in the domains of application, often seem to have no immediate utility, at least not in the short run, they are nowhere pursued so constantly nor to so great a degree as in our universities.

Justification for their support—and for the support of basic research in particular—rests, in part, on the long run. Basic research provides the capital, the raw materials on which applied research and technology must draw. Without new capital, our problem solving abilities would soon be limited to better applications of existing knowledge. And while better applications are immensely useful, the limits remain.

We in the universities are generally quick to speak to this point and to the absolutely essential role of basic research in the progress of applied research and technology. And so we should be, because it is true; and it is for that reason, and in the belief that this connection will continue, that basic research is so generously supported in our society. But that argument should not be the only one, nor even the strongest one, in our justification of the research. That is bound to lead to disappointed expectations. We need to stress at least equally the essential role of research and scholarship in advancing knowledge and new understandings of deep significance to all of us.

The distinctions we have been drawing between basic and applied research are not, in reality, always that clear. How does one go, for example, from the idea of the original extension programs in agriculture, devised at a simpler time, to today's much more sophisticated work in pesticides or the biochemistry of human nutrition or the new genetic engineering? Is there a place where one would draw the line? Further, quite apart from the idea of application, there is something to the idea that when global issues, such as energy resources and food supplies and disarmament and the like, are studied and remarked upon in universities close to home, they are perhaps more likely to be heard than if they were studied only on some far-off campus, as they might be if the country had a national system of federal universities.

In summary, the message regarding research and scholarship for both the university and the broader society seems to us clear: we need each other if we are both to broaden our understanding and to look for solutions to our problems. Society, in its own interest, must continue to support the basic research and other studies the university is uniquely equipped to perform. The university, in the interests of the common good and of its own, must continue to perform applied research as well. The justification rests both on the record of the past and the promise of the future. The policy questions are those of balance and, for applied research, relevance to the fundamental mission of the university.

TEACHING AND RESEARCH

We conclude this discussion of research in the university by noting that its great growth in recent years has prompted criticism and concern from time to time about the proper balance between teaching and research. The pendulum will swing occasionally toward one or the other activity, but both will go on being essential university functions. And while we need pay attention to serious critics, the simple fact is that the creative scholar brings to his or her teaching a point of view and an understanding that simply are not possible for those who merely observe the scholarly process. We believe that this argument holds, and holds strongly, over the whole range of the arts, sciences, and professional fields.

It is a fact, well tested, that the linkage between research and education is also a two-way street. Not only does research provide a way to educate students, but our students, and our graduate and professional students in particular, contribute to scholarship and to the research process and make both more vital because they bring to them new ideas and fresh perspectives energized by youthful enthusiasm and drive. To strengthen this linkage and its benefits, we need to try more vigorously and imaginatively than we have to draw our students, and especially the brightest of them, into serious research at the earliest possible moment.

PROFESSIONAL EDUCATION

Another essential function of the contemporary public university is education for the professions. This is, in many respects, the original land-grant concept of practical education in modern mode. The readiness of our universities to innovate as they evolved, coupled with society's increasing requirements for highly educated people—requirements reaching ever more deeply into an ever greater array of fields—has created in the modern public university a broad spectrum of professional programs. These newer professional studies and their faculties, in contrast to the old established fields and faculties of law, medicine, and the arts, trace their philosophical origins in large part to the ideas of the land-grant movement.

The original practical education of the land-grant institutions, which were often in their early years highly vocational in orientation and practice, has become more and more characterized by rigorous curricula based on scholarship and thus fully converted to education for the professions, which we might define as fields for which there is a theoretical base that is being constantly refined by advances in research. The practice of a true profession is in its turn shaped and advanced by its theory and not simply by the codified trial-and-error improvements of its practitioners. It is easy to see from this perspective, and from the history of our institutions, that many of the newer professional disciplines—education, public health, nursing, pharmacy, business, public administration, and the rest—have evolved over time from vocations, focussed on practice, to true professional fields standing on proper theoretical bases supported by flourishing traditions of scholarship.

As professional studies, these newer fields inevitably became more complex, a condition that led to further professionalization and to increased specialization. These changes are seen quite clearly in the evolution of the original land-grant focus on agriculture and the mechanic arts. Thus, almost all our institutions have had from the beginning a deep involvement in agriculture, but an involvement that is marked today, as we have already suggested, by a far greater complexity and a wider array of relevant disciplines—for example, energy, water resources, pest management, nutrition. And in the original mechanic arts, the development of specialization has spawned a host of distinct engineering disciplines.

This evolution of professional subjects, and the general broad growth of professional education, is a peculiarly American phenomenon in its reach and extent. And while it has its critics, it is a natural development of the land-grant philosophy of "practical education," an orientation that has served our society and our states well. But in pursuing the land-grant idea of providing a practical education—by which we mean, in the contemporary university, a professional education—we must take into account the accelerating advance of knowledge, and the consequent accumulation of data. The pace today is so rapid in so many fields that the requirements for providing students with a truly fundamental base of knowledge on which they can build for the future, constantly change. We must take into account also the urgent requirement that we expose these students to humanistic values that will help them use their professional expertise in humane and enlightened ways. These requirements must be understood by our publics or else these very "practical" fields will seem to some as not practical enough. The pressure, in short, is inexorable for flexibility of academic programs and, even more, for liberally educated people, not least in the faculties of our own professional schools.

BALANCE BETWEEN PROFESSIONAL AND LIBERAL EDUCATION

An educational focus on the useful, practical, and professional, while it has come to its fullest flower in the American public university, has blossomed elsewhere as well. And both here and abroad, it has generated some conflict and tension between the newer studies linking learning with practical affairs and the more traditional ideals of liberal studies founded on the older arts and sciences. In his classic essay *Technology and the Academics*, Sir Eric Ashby, a British scholar, presents the dilemma this way:

> Round every senate table [the faculty senate of the British university] sit men for whom the word university stands for something unique and precious in European society: a leisurely and urbane attitude to scholarship, exemption from the obligation to use knowledge for practical ends, a sense of perspective which accompanies the broad horizon and the distant view, an opportunity to give undivided loyalty to the kingdom of the mind. At the same senate table sit men for whom the university is an institution with urgent and essential obligations to modern society; a place to which society entrusts its most intelligent young people and from which it expects to receive its most highly trained citizens; a place which society regards as the pacemaker for scientific research and technological progress. And so universities find themselves searching for a compromise.[3]

This dilemma has been with us in the universities for some time and continues to the present. Surely there is great advantage in the blending and balance of the professional and liberal strands in the university, but it is a balance to which we must pay careful and constant attention. Quite obviously, in our increasingly technological world we must continue to graduate from our universities a commensurate flow of highly educated professionals to sharpen our technological edge and to advance our society. Clearly we need our experts, experts who not only conduct their practice from a sound base of theory and proven knowledge, but who also understand, and this is equally important, the difference between knowing and not knowing. To meet this demand, our public universities have responded admirably, especially in their flowering since World War II, by providing us with a finely educated and ever-growing supply of such experts, both in the older professions and the host of newer ones. In brief, the professional schools are a crucial link between the university and the daily world around us, and as the principal provider of professional personnel universities have become an absolutely indispensable element of modern society.

A SPECIAL CONCERN FOR THE HUMANITIES

This indispensable connection between the university and modern technological society, coupled with the remarkable progress of science in our time, has tended to diminish the prestige of the humanities—and, more than their prestige, their own indigenous vigor and health. The "signs of trouble and erosion" are, we are told, all around and there is a special concern for the need of revitalization in the humanities. As Walter Jackson Bate has put it most bluntly: "The humanities are not merely entering, they are plunging into their worst state of crisis since the modern university was formed a century ago, in the 1880's."[4]

While we ourselves do not join in such cries of extreme alarm, we do believe a critical examination of the condition of the humanities is needed. At minimum we need such a review in order to make persuasive the case for their support to our publics. Too often we in the universities assume that the values of the humanities go without saying, because for us they do. Regrettably, far too often for those outside of the academy they do not. We must continue to remind ourselves, and to emphasize to the people of our states and of the nation, that a liberalizing education is in itself a worthy pursuit, that education must not be valued solely in terms of its ability to match graduates with jobs and to relate research to practical advantage. The challenge of explaining the critical importance of the array of studies encompassed by the humanities obviously requires continuing effort.

Besides this direct concern with humanistic studies and scholarship, we are concerned that it be fully acknowledged that, while we now graduate from our state universities superbly trained professionals, at least in the narrow disciplinary sense, that is not enough. Clearly our goal must be to educate our students, all our students, in ways that give us confidence that they will exercise responsibly and wisely their presently unknown and unknowable future powers. The humanities have the most fundamental contribution to make to this goal, and we believe that the relationship between the graduate programs in these fields and the undergraduate curriculum deserves serious attention.

LIFELONG LEARNING: A NEW REQUIREMENT

In educating for a society in which change is everywhere and inevitable, our curricula must obviously take into account the accelerating advance of knowledge and the consequent accumulation of data. In such a society we cannot be satisfied merely to train vocationally oriented students; that is far too narrow a goal. We must rather, as we have been arguing, provide students with a truly fundamental base of knowledge so that they will have the capacity to keep current in an unpredictable and rapidly changing technological economy and environment.

A vital corollary of this need to keep current is the increasing interest in both the university and in the larger society for building mechanisms for what some call lifelong learning. This notion of continuing professional education calls for repeated refreshment throughout a career, not as a luxury but as a necessity. It is not surprising that the need for this kind of professional education is most pressing in fields like computer science and electrical engineering, where the pace of change seems to make specific training quickly obsolete. But there is a growing similar, if not quite comparable, need in most of the professions.

We are convinced that out of this need we will have in the years ahead larger numbers of nontraditional students taught in a greater variety of nontraditional ways. That doesn't necessarily mean, of course, that they will be taught—not in great numbers at least—in our research universities. The reason is that these institutions are overwhelmingly geared to full-time students who are totally committed to full-time programs. The education of those students is the central obligation of these universities, and it must be discharged without dilution, just as other institutions already geared to part-time students must maintain their obligation to serve that population.

But we think we can also find in our research universities ways to keep professional people up to date, especially by using modern technology and thereby getting things into the workplace, so to speak. Bringing professional people to the cutting edge is the shared responsibility of active professionals and our university faculties, the people who are themselves working at the cutting edge. This is a very proper service for our research universities, for finding the right organizational and funding mechanisms for such new educational arrangements will require both time and experimentation.

STATE-WIDE SYSTEMS AND PLANS

Another most important, and radical, change that has occurred in almost all our states in the period following World War II is the development of state-wide systems of higher education encompassing a variety of institutions at different levels with different missions. As a consequence, there will be no single nor simple answer to the questions before us, for each state will have to relate each issue to its own particular plan of higher education. Those plans are not frozen, of course (or at least should not be), and it seems to us quite clear that they must be forever evolving—iterative, tentative, and difficult.

While there is great strength in our national diversity, and in the differences among our institutions, our state universities nonetheless build on a common base. In particular, the plan of any state for the provision of research and of graduate and professional education must be open and dynamic to accommodate the processes with which we are dealing, processes that are constantly shaped and reshaped by the ongoing discoveries of scholars and the consequent changing requirements of graduate and professional education. If we retard or impede this inherent evolutionary development of our public universities, we will threaten their advancement, their essential quality, their national and international distinction. In our view the principal challenge of the years ahead will be that of ensuring that the research universities in all our states continue to grow in quality even if many are not growing in enrollments and resources. The alternative is slow stagnation and academic decline. Our goal must be to maintain for our public research universities an absolutely essential capacity for dynamic change and a total commitment to excellence and to rigorous intellectual standards. They are the flagships of the fleet, and we must keep them so.

QUALITATIVE GROWTH IN THE YEARS AHEAD

Rigorous review of graduate and professional programs will be essential to qualitative growth in the years ahead. In order to meet the demand for new programs along the expanding frontier of knowledge, some older programs may need to be transplanted, reduced or even eliminated. Programs may have to be consolidated within and across campuses, and resources reallocated among campuses. It may be found desirable to cluster certain graduate programs on selected campuses. We must take a hard look, in short, at all our university programs to make sure that they are still appropriate for the university or better placed somewhere else in the system or in some other societal organization. Comparative program review of the quality of existing academic areas and the significance of their contributions to the total university mission is a principal tool in the search for resources that might shift to more productive uses. We must shoulder that task and not shrink from it.

No small part of these possible rearrangements will be cost-driven. As we look ahead, we can be reasonably certain the cost of research and of graduate and professional education is bound to increase. Even without reference to very large ventures, such as particle accelerators, the cost of doing science, and of education in science-dominated graduate and professional fields, will increase because of the growing complexity and sophistication of instrumentation coupled with its computerization and automation. While these ongoing developments extend the reach of our research and improve its productivity, they exact a price.

Moreover, the rising costs of research, although skewed to science, are not peculiar to it. Take, for example, the insatiable demands of that great core facility, the library. One solution for the easing of such costs surely must lie in the cooperative and creative sharing of resources, both among institutions and, what surprisingly is often harder, within institutions. We believe that in the years ahead universities will of necessity have to require more sharing, including that of the greatest resource of all, their faculties. NASULGC should review this issue and recommend some ways of encouraging experiments and pilot efforts that will build experience in sharing and test the effectiveness of intercampus enterprises.

The kind of cooperative sorting out we are suggesting rests on the obvious philosophical and practical base that no one institution nor any one type of institution can do all, or even very many, of the things society expects of higher education. And our institutional freedom to concentrate on a few functions—research and graduate and professional education, for example—is directly dependent upon the existence of other institutions fully able to perform other sets of functions. It behooves us then to remind ourselves of our common stake in the health of all kinds of institutions. Our diversity is, must be, our strength. Together, and only together, can we respond fully to the needs and expectations of society, and we need ultimately to search together for comprehensive solutions to our problems. We must advance according to our general plans, but we must chart that course in consultation with the whole of the academic community.

CONCLUSION

There are limits, of course, to what may be achieved by reviews and consolidations and reallocations and the like. And, at the end, one must push and push hard the proposition that our public universities, as the special seats of research and of graduate and professional education, must have a steady base of support despite the ups and downs of the economy, despite the unpopularity of new taxes, despite the possibility of fewer students, despite all. They are nothing less than an investment in the future, in ways that overused but accurate expression cannot begin to convey. We have tried, in regard to their functions of research and of graduate and professional education, to explain why.

One reason is the growing technological character of our world and the related technological and economic challenge of such rivals as Western Europe and Japan. A second is the need for research and scholarship in all disciplines, from agriculture to the humanities to sociology to medicine, as an essential way of improving human life—and each human's life—and of deepening our understanding not only of the world but of ourselves. Another is the urgent need to educate people, not just scientists and engineers, but people in all the professions and in all walks of life, for a future that will be ever more pervaded by technology. Still another is the indispensable role of a university in providing liberal learning and its value as a focus in every state of intellectual and scholarly activity.

We face some difficult and challenging times ahead to sustain in our public universities the quality of their research and of their graduate and professional programs. But our universities have faced tough challenges before and emerged the stronger for it. We believe that NASULGC can contribute importantly to these ends.

NOTES

1. U.S. Statutes at Large, 7:503.
2. *In the National Interest* (Washington, D.C.: NASULGC, 1983), p. 11.
3. Sir Eric Ashby, *Technology and the Academics* (London: Macmillan & Co. Ltd., 1959), pp. 69–70.
4. Walter Jackson Bate, "The Crisis in English Studies," *Harvard Magazine* (September-October 1982), p. 46.

CHAPTER 2
THE STAKE OF THE STATES IN RESEARCH, GRADUATE EDUCATION, AND PROFESSIONAL TRAINING

RICHARD L. VAN HORN

In the United States, and in most of the world, public universities are major centers for research, graduate education, and professional training. In every state at least one public university offers doctoral degrees, operates professional schools, and conducts externally sponsored research.

In 1983, the United States invested approximately $88 billion in research and development. The federal government supplied $40 billion search and development. The federal government supplied $40 billion and industry $45 billion (AAAS, 84). Universities performed about $7.3 billion of the work, industry $64.2 billion, and government and others $14.8 billion. Most industry research and development is highly applied to specific products, services, or processes for a firm. With respect to basic research, the major source of new ideas and innovation in society, universities probably carry out more than 50 percent of the total.

In 1982 public universities conducted approximately 63 percent of the $7.261 billion total of university research (NSF, 84). The top one hundred universities in research volume performed $6 billion of the total research, or 83 percent. Of the top one hundred, sixty-eight are public universities. (A list of the top one hundred universities and the top one hundred public universities with respect to total research expenditures appears in Appendices A and B.) Clearly, public universities are major centers for research.

Most of the support for research comes from the federal government or industry; state support for research is limited and specialized. Direct support goes largely to agriculture, engineering extension programs, and the health professions. Some states provide support indirectly to research at public institutions by paying for utilities, facilities, and general administrative costs. In return, the state may keep part or all of the overhead monies that accompany sponsored research contracts.

Graduate education, particularly doctoral education, is closely associated with research. Universities that grant doctoral degrees performed in 1982 over 98 percent of the total university research—$7.134 out of $7.261 billion (NSF, 84). This relationship grows out of the character of traditional research in a university. Doctoral students serve as research assistants to faculty on research contracts. They tend to be exceptionally bright, capable, and hard-working. The productivity of many faculty researchers depends directly on the quality of their doctoral students. As a result, the best research faculty go to institutions with doctoral programs.

As universities become more involved with applied research, some have formed research institutes to accommodate the multiple disciplines and larger staffs. The institutes hire full-time research staffs and depend less heavily on doctoral students. The trend toward research institutes appears to be accelerating, but the fundamental relations remain unchanged. The key people in research institutes are faculty members with doctoral students. For the foreseeable future, university research will occur largely at doctoral institutions.

In fall 1982, 12.4 million students were enrolled in higher education, 78 percent in public institutions (NCES, 83). Of this total, 1.3 million were graduate students and 278,000 were in professional programs. Thus, graduate and professional students represent less than 15 percent of the students in higher education. In a sample of 243 major graduate schools, 430,000 of the 566,000 total graduate students, or 76 percent, were at public institutions (*Chronicle*, 83). Note that this percentage corresponds closely to the percentage of total students and also the percentage of research expenditures at public institutions. In the sample group, 86 percent of the graduate students attended doctoral-granting institutions. While the total number of private institutions is larger than the number of public institutions of higher education, 106 of the 167 doctoral-granting universities are public. By all measures, public universities play the major role in graduate and professional education in the United States.

The impact of graduate and professional studies on public universities is larger than suggested by the enrollment numbers. For example, in Texas the total public senior college and university enrollment of 323,000 includes 24,000 in master's programs, 4,200 in doctoral programs, and 1,600 in other professional schools, or about 9 percent of the total in graduate and professional programs (Coordinating, 1983). Of total credit hours, graduate and professional studies represent 13 percent. Because of the higher payments in the funding formula, graduate and professional credit hours generate about 35 percent of the faculty salary allocations.

These numbers do not include medical and dental schools, which are funded separately.

If the state did not support graduate and professional studies, the cost of the public senior universities would not decline by 35 percent. Many of the costs of our institutions, of course, represent facilities or services shared by undergraduates and research as well. But graduate and professional programs do generate a significant marginal cost that probably is in the order of 20 percent of the total cost of a major university.

BENEFITS TO THE STATES FOR RESEARCH AND GRADUATE AND PROFESSIONAL EDUCATION

Why should states support research, graduate, and professional education? This question is a more specific form of the general question, Why should states undertake any activity? In concept, states provide services for one or both of two reasons:

1. The service is provided directly to citizens of the state who choose to consume or use it.

2. The service is an investment in the future welfare of all or many of the citizens of the state.

Highways are an example of both reasons. Citizens who drive on the highways directly and immediately benefit. By means of tolls or gasoline taxes, it is simple (again in concept) to get the users of the service to pay for it. A good highway system also attracts and enhances commerce and attracts better educated, productive, and mobile people who are sensitive to the quality of life. The resulting attractive business environment and productive work force then benefits all citizens of the state.

While educational services are more abstract than highways, the impacts are similar. Since the majority of research is supported by the federal government ($4.7 out of $7.3 billion, of 64 percent), the state benefits immediately and directly by the inflow of money to pay salaries and purchase goods and services in the state. Federal support to universities for research in 1982 went to all fifty states and ranged from $678 million in California to $4 million in South Dakota (NSF, 84). Obviously, states that encourage and support major research universities will have the most success in competing for federal research funds.

The indirect benefits of investments in research are difficult to measure, but the evidence for the existence of large benefits is strong. Studies from

27

the Brookings Institution suggest that research activities have had a strong positive effect on U.S. productivity and economic growth in recent years. The development of a large, high-technology community around Boston is deeply related to the major research programs at M.I.T. and Harvard. The San Francisco Bay area has benefited similarly from the University of California, Berkeley; University of California, San Francisco; and Stanford. Each of the above universities is in the top sixteen in the country with respect to research support.

In brief, dynamic, prosperous areas are associated with the existence of research cultures created in large part by major research universities. Companies prefer to locate in an area with a major research university. The ability of a company to attract high-quality professional employees is enhanced greatly by opportunities for graduate study and the opportunities for professional stimulation offered by seminars, conferences, or simply social contact with faculty. Faculty and graduates are major participants in new enterprises and in innovation in existing enterprises.

Strong research programs also lead to excellent education at both undergraduate and graduate levels. The long-standing myth that research conflicts with good teaching is not and never was true. Many of the strong research institutions are ranked consistently as among the best educational programs. Research institutions tend to have the most distinguished faculty members. Researchers are practitioners of the most cherished goal of universities—independent or lifelong learning. As such, researchers offer outstanding role models for students.

The future role of the United States in the world economy increasingly will be that of a generator and applier of research and development. While the United States is and probably will remain a major supplier of agricultural products to the world, our productivity results in large part from the application of research and development—or of technology—to agriculture. In similar manner, we can compete in manufacturing only where we produce high-technology products or when we apply high technology to the manufacturing process. In this environment, the existence of strong research and graduate programs at universities is essential to the prosperity and perhaps to the survival of our society.

As noted earlier, strong research programs and doctoral education represent different parts of the same process. The empirical evidence cited earlier is clear on this point. A state that believes in the desirability of research and chooses to encourage it at public universities must also encourage doctoral programs to have any realistic hopes of success.

Master's programs train professionals for the business community. Here again, the availability of trained people will attract firms that employ professionals. The fact that organizations pay higher salaries to holders of graduate and professional degrees is good evidence that these people are more productive and thus are socially desirable. The economic value of higher education is the subject of many studies and much controversy (see, for example, Douglass 1978). The movement of the U.S. economy toward a world role based on research, development, and technology certainly suggests an increasing demand for individuals with graduate and professional training.

THE ROLE OF THE STATES

What posture should a state take toward research, graduate, and professional studies? Presumably, states wish to take actions that are in the best interests of their inhabitants. The arguments for encouraging research appear clear and compelling. A majority of research funding comes from the federal government. Research universities are associated with (1) dynamic, prosperous areas, (2) excellent faculty, and (3) good education.

At a minimum, states should have policies that encourage research in such areas as allowing faculty to accept external research support, allowing existing facilities to be used for external research, and establishing purchasing, personnel, and accounting policies that are consistent with research. While these areas sound obvious, faculty at every public university can identify state policies that impede research. For example, the complex purchasing policies of many states result in months or years of delay in purchasing equipment for research contracts that only extend for one or several years.

One special area of policy deals with research supported by industry. National Science Foundation data shows industry support of academic research increasing from around $10 million in 1953 to $400 million in 1984. While this number is small compared to approximately $5 billion for the federal government, it is expected to continue to grow rapidly. It appears strongly in the interest of states to encourage industry-sponsored research at public universities. Examples of policies to encourage this research are (1) allow the use of state facilities for the work, (2) allow universities to grant intellectual property rights to sponsors, and (3) allow universities to set, collect, and retain higher overhead charges for sponsors who wish to retain intellectual property rights.

Each state in cooperation with its major research universities could review and improve state policies toward research. Such a step involves no new state funds and can have a significant impact. The major issue is for the state to decide that research at public universities is of high value and then to act accordingly. The next step is for the state to decide if it wishes to provide indirect support for research—facilities, equipment and administrative costs. Research contracts from federal or business sources often provide support only for operations. Facilities—buildings, laboratories, and the like—are presumed to exist. The state might take external research volume into account in decisions on building or renovation funds.

While research contracts provide funds for some equipment purchases, most funds for major, multiple-use equipment must come for other sources. Teaching and research equipment is widely recognized as a major need today in public universities. States might directly supply funds for equipment or at least facilitate low-cost loans for equipment purchase.

Most research contracts contain funds to support overhead—the extra administration and facilities costs associated with the research. Overhead is not profit; it reflects the fact that universities performing research incur real, extra costs. State policies on overhead vary widely. Some states allow universities to retain it while others take part or all of the overhead funds. States that fail to allow universities to retain overhead funds sufficient to cover the actual costs involved in research are behaving in an exceptionally shortsighted manner: they are providing large impediments to research at their public universities.

If states decide, as all the available evidence suggests, that strong research programs should exist at one or more of their major public universities, then some indirect support of research probably is necessary. At a minimum, this support would consist of providing facilities and some equipment for research and of allowing universities to keep overhead funds adequate to cover actual costs. Again, the evidence suggests that these actions represent a highly desirable investment for the state.

Finally, states can consider direct support of research. Most states already support some areas of research—for example, agriculture or medicine. Direct support presents a number of problems and some striking opportunities. The obvious problem is what to support and how to obtain reasonable benefits for the investment. The state has two basic choices: broad support and project support.

With broad support, the state provides funds to public universities for research without prior agreement on the projects to be performed. For example, most states already provide one form of broad support through reducing teaching loads with the expectation that faculty will pursue scholarly activities. States might provide a pool of funds for universities to allocate to research projects. The problems with broad support are that limited incentives exist for productivity and quality control is difficult. Large increases in broad support probably are unlikely and possibly are unwise.

Most states also provide project support. For example, specific areas or projects might be funded as special line items. Such funding sometimes is based more on political considerations than on the scholarly merit of the project or the investigators. Some states have proposed to operate research foundations modeled on the National Science Foundation. Awards would fund specific research proposals and would be based on merit, as determined by peer review. The state could designate part of the funds for areas of specific interest to the economy of the state. The idea of a state research foundation deserves consideration as a productive way to fund high-quality research.

In summary, states can influence greatly the level of research at public universities. Changing policies to encourage research has no cost, will have impact, and should receive high priority. States that wish to have major research programs probably will have to make significant investments in indirect support for research. Direct support is both politically and procedurally the most difficult, but merits consideration.

Most states at present support and encourage graduate and professional education. While hard evidence is difficult to find, there is a widespread belief that graduate and professional studies benefit society. The appropriate role for the states is less clear. States that use formula allocation systems for public universities tend to support graduate and professional studies by providing higher credit-hour payments for them. Since many of the programs greatly increase the potential earnings of students, there is a reasonable argument for asking students to pay part of the costs, particularly for terminal professional degrees such as law, business, and medicine.

At first examination, current state postures toward graduate and professional education probably are consistent with the needs of society. Despite the well-publicized concerns about oversupply in certain fields, these problems are largely self-correcting. When science Ph.D.s ended up driving taxi cabs, enrollment went down dramatically—not by state policy, but by the choice of students.

States legitimately might ask to what extent the state should support graduate and professional education. For doctoral education, the question really is whether or not to support research. For other graduate studies, one might ask what happens to the graduates. If a large percentage of the graduates remain in the state, the rationale for support is clearer. For example, in Texas in 1982, 90.6 percent of graduate degree recipients from public universities accepted employment in the state.

CONCLUSION

Preliminary analysis suggests that research and graduate and professional studies at public universities generate significant benefits for states and require only modest support. The evidence for large direct and indirect benefits to states from research is good. In fiscal year 1982, the federal government supported 65 percent and the states only 8 percent of the $7.3 billion of research at universities.

Since 98 percent of the research takes place at doctoral-granting universities, graduate programs are probably a necessary prerequisite for strong research. The marginal cost of graduate and professional programs, while significant, appears in keeping with the value to society of the graduates. The most significant question is not whether major public universities should have these programs, but whether the students who benefit from them should pay more of the cost.

States that decide to have or maintain major research programs at public universities have a number of effective options available. Policy review can significantly improve research opportunities at no cost. States may also wish to consider indirect or direct support of research. The review of options to enhance research by states should receive highest priority.

Appendix A

Total Research and Development Expenditures at the Top 100 Universities and Colleges
(fiscal year 1982; dollars in thousands)

National Science Foundation Rank	Public Institutions	Amount	National Science Foundation Rank	Private Institutions	Amount
3	Univ. of Wisconsin, Madison	$157,520	1	Johns Hopkins Univ.	$289,940
5	Univ. of Minnesota	146,466	2	Massachusetts Inst. of Tech.	192,462
7	Univ. of California, San Diego	138,894	4	Stanford Univ.	147,941
8	Univ. of Washington	133,115	6	Cornell Univ.	145,769
9	Univ. of Michigan	119,973	10	Columbia Univ., Main Div.	115,734
12	Univ. of Pennsylvania	112,836	11	Harvard Univ.	114,941
13	Univ. of California, Los Angeles	103,294	19	Yale Univ.	91,232
14	Univ. of California, Berkeley	102,369	22		
15	Univ. of Illinois, Urbana	95,869	26	Georgia Inst. of Tech.	71,402
16	Univ. of California, San Francisco	95,282	27	Univ. of Chicago	69,018
17	Univ. of Texas at Austin	92,069	29	Washington Univ.	68,049
18	Texas A&M Univ.	91,780	33	New York Univ.	66,139
20	Univ. of California, Davis	89,784	34	Univ. of Rochester	65,547
21	Univ. of Arizona	88,247	41	Yeshiva Univ.	52,235
23	Ohio State Univ.	82,614	42	University of Miami	51,899
24	Pennsylvania St. Univ.	82,034	43	Duke Univ.	49,655
25	Michigan St. Univ.	71,922	44	Baylor College of Med.	48,661
28	Univ. of Florida	68,370	48	Rockefeller Univ.	46,172
30	Purdue Univ.	67,299	49	Northwestern Univ.	45,810
31	Louisiana St. Univ.	66,814	51	California Inst. of Tech.	44,048

Appendix A (continued)

National Science Foundation Rank	Public Institutions	Amount	National Science Foundation Rank	Private Institutions	Amount
32	Univ. of Colorado	66,377	54	Case Western Reserve Univ.	43,129
35	Univ. of Georgia	65,161	63	Carnegie-Mellon Univ.	37,316
36	Oregon St. Univ.	56,769	64	Princeton Univ.	36,641
37	N. Carolina St. Univ. at Raleigh	55,781	74	Woods Hole Oceanographic Inst.	33,725
38	Univ. of Iowa	55,466	79	Boston Univ.	30,603
39	Iowa St. Univ. of Sci. & Tech.	55,294	80	Cuny Mt. Sinai School of Med.	29,797
40	Univ. of Connecticut	55,109	86	Vanderbilt Univ.	24,933
45	Univ. of N. Carolina at Chapel Hill	47,711	88	George Washington Univ.	23,334
46	Colorado St. Univ.	46,641	95	Emory Univ.	21,423
47	Univ. of Pittsburgh	46,548	96	Brown Univ.	21,331
50	Univ. of Nebraska, Lincoln	44,172	99	Rensselaer Polytech. Inst.	20,302
52	Univ. of Utah	43,765	100	Syracuse Univ.	19,442
53	Univ. of Hawaii, Manoa	43,439			
55	Rutgers, The St. Univ. of New Jersey	42,938			
56	Indiana Univ.	42,558			
57	Univ. of Missouri, Columbia	40,978			
58	Univ. of Texas System Cancer Ctr.	40,369			
59	Virginia Polytech. Inst. & St. Univ.	39,909			
60	Oklahoma St. Univ.	39,472			
61	Univ. of Kentucky	38,907			
62	Univ. of Alaska, Fairbanks	38,218			
65	Mississippi St. Univ.	36,582			
66	Suny at Stony Brook	36,468			
67	Univ. of Alabama, Birmingham	35,792			

68	Univ. of California, Riverside	35,539
69	Kansas St. Univ. of Agri. & Applied Sci.	34,806
70	New Mexico St. Univ.	34,650
71	Washington St. Univ.	34,257
72	Univ. of Maryland, College Park	34,251
73	Utah St. Univ.	33,822
75	Univ. of Virginia	33,661
76	Univ. of Texas Health Sci. Ctr. at Dallas	32,058
77	Univ. of California, Irvine	31,456
78	Univ. of New Mexico	30,977
81	Univ. of Oklahoma	29,785
82	Univ. of Massachusetts at Amherst	28,887
83	Univ. of Cincinnati	28,573
84	SUNY at Buffalo	27,800
85	Univ. of Arkansas, Fayetteville	26,653
87	Clemson Univ.	23,552
89	Auburn Univ.	23,256
90	Univ. of Rhode Island	23,000
91	Florida St. Univ.	22,877
92	Virginia Commonwealth Univ.	22,385
93	Wayne St. Univ.	21,542
94	Temple Univ.	21,503
97	W. Virginia Univ.	21,080
98	Univ. of Kansas	20,534

Total Public Universities—68 $3,797,819

Percentage of Expenditures
Public Institutions   63.26%

Total Private Universities—32   2,205,830

Percentage of Expenditures
Private Institutions   36.74%

3 5

Appendix B

Total Research and Development Expenditures at the Top 100 Public Universities and Colleges
(fiscal year 1982; dollars in thousands)

National Science Foundation Rank	Public Institutions	Amount	National Science Foundation Rank	Public Institutions	Amount
3	Univ. of Wisconsin, Madison	$157,520	75	Univ. of Virginia	$33,661
5	Univ. of Minnesota	146,466	76	Univ. of Texas Health Sci. Ctr. at Dallas	32,058
7	Univ. of California, San Diego	138,894	77	Univ. of California, Irvine	31,456
8	Univ. of Washington	133,115	78	Univ. of New Mexico	30,977
9	Univ. of Michigan	119,973	81	Univ. of Oklahoma	29,785
12	Univ. of Pennsylvania	112,836	82	Univ. of Massachusetts at Amherst	28,887
13	Univ. of California, Los Angeles	103,294	83	Univ. of Cincinnati	28,573
14	Univ. of California, Berkeley	102,369	84	Suny at Buffalo	27,800
15	Univ. of Illinois, Urbana	95,869	85	Univ. of Arkansas, Fayetteville	26,653
16	Univ. of California, San Francisco	95,282	87	Clemson Univ.	23,552
17	Univ. of Texas at Austin	92,069	89	Auburn Univ.	23,256
18	Texas A&M Univ.	91,780	90	Univ. of Rhode Island	23,000
20	Univ. of California, Davis	89,784	91	Florida St. Univ.	22,877
21	Univ. of Arizona	88,247	92	Virginia Commonwealth Univ.	22,385
23	Ohio St. Univ.	82,614	93	Wayne St. Univ.	21,542
24	Pennsylvania St. Univ.	82,034	94	Temple Univ.	21,503
25	Michigan St. Univ.	71,922	97	W. Virginia Univ.	21,080
28	Univ. of Florida	68,370	98	Univ. of Kansas	20,534
30	Purdue Univ.	67,299	101	University of Texas Health Sci. Ctr. at San Antonio	19,341
31	Louisiana St. Univ.	66,814	105	Univ. of Maine, Orono	18,599
32	Univ. of Colorado	66,377	106	Univ. of Vermont & St. Agri. College	18,575
35	Univ. of Georgia	65,161	107	Univ. of Texas Health Sci. Ctr. at Houston	18,281
36	Oregon St. Univ.	56,769	108	Univ. of Texas Medical Branch at Galveston	18,272
37	N. Carolina St. Univ. at Raleigh	55,781			
38	Univ. of Iowa	55,406			

#	Institution	
39	Iowa St. Univ. of Sci. & Tech.	55,294
40	Univ. of Connecticut	55,109
45	University of N. Carolina at Chapel Hill	47,711
46	Colorado St. Univ.	46,641
47	Univ. of Pittsburgh	46,548
50	Univ. of Nebraska, Lincoln	44,172
52	Univ. of Utah	43,765
53	Univ. of Hawaii, Manoa	43,439
55	Rutgers, The St. Univ. of New Jersey	42,938
56	Indiana Univ.	42,558
57	Univ. of Missouri, Columbia	40,978
58	Univ. of Texas System Cancer Ctr.	40,369
59	Virginia Polytech. Inst. & St. Univ.	39,909
60	Oklahoma St. Univ.	39,472
61	Univ. of Kentucky	38,907
62	Univ. of Alaska, Fairbanks	38,218
65	Mississippi St. Univ.	36,582
66	SUNY at Stony Brook	36,468
67	Univ. of Alabama, Birmingham	35,792
68	Univ. of California, Riverside	35,539
69	Kansas St. Univ. of Agri. & Applied Sci.	34,806
70	New Mexico St. Univ.	34,650
71	Washington St. Univ.	34,257
72	Univ. of Maryland, College Park	34,251
73	Utah St. University	33,822

#	Institution	
109	N. Dakota St. Univ.	18,101
110	Univ. of Delaware	17,875
111	Univ. of Illinois Medical Ctr. at Chicago	17,485
113	Univ. of Idaho	17,272
114	The Oregon Health Sci. Univ.	16,954
115	College of Medicine & Dentistry of New Jersey	16,123
116	Montana St. Univ.	15,333
117	Univ. of Wyoming	14,622
118	Univ. of Puerto Rico, Mayaguez	14,611
119	Inst. of Agri., Univ. of Tennessee	14,545
121	Suny Upstate Med. Ctr.	14,476
122	Univ. of Houston, Central Campus	13,932
125	Univ. of Maryland, Baly Prof. School	13,553
126	Texas Tech. Univ.	13,261
127	Univ. of S. Carolina	13,249
129	Univ. of New Hampshire	13,162
130	Univ. of California, Santa Barbara	13,102
131	Univ. of Tennessee, Knoxville	12,822
133	Univ. of Illinois, Chicago Ctr.	12,662
134	Suny Downstate Med. Ctr.	12,510
137	Arizona St. Univ.	11,511
138	Univ. of Nevada, Reno	11,441
139	Tennessee St. Univ.	11,372
142	Univ. of California, Santa Cruz	11,094
144	Univ. of Oregon, Main Campus	10,504
145	Univ. of Mississippi	9,912
146	Univ. of Massachusetts Med. School, Worcester	9,886

Total Public Institutions—100

$4,262,257

REFERENCES

(AAAS, 84) Shapley, Willis, Teich, Albert, and Pace, Jill, eds. *AAAS Report IX: Research & Development, FY 1985.* 84–1, Intersociety Working Group. (Washington: American Association for the Advancement of Science, 1984).

Chronicle of Higher Education, Fact-File Dec. 7, 1983.

Coordinating Board, Texas College and University System. *Statistical Supplement, 1982 Annual Report.* Austin, Texas, 1982.

Douglass, Gordon K. "Economic Returns on Investments in Higher Education." In Howard R. Bowen, *Investment in Learning.* San Francisco: Jossey-Bass, 1978.

(NCES, 83) Department of Education, National Center for Education Statistics, *The Condition of Education,* edited by Valena White Plisko. Washington, D.C.: Supt. of Documents, U.S. Government Printing Office, 1983.

(NSF, 84) *Academic Science/Engineering: R&D Funds Fiscal Year 1982.* Surveys of Science Resources Series, NSF 84–308. Washington: National Science Foundation, 1984.

CHAPTER 3
"STANDING ANTAGONISMS": THE RELATIONSHIP OF UNDERGRADUATE TO GRADUATE EDUCATION

SHELDON ROTHBLATT

The American land-grant or state university is, from an historical point of view, an extraordinary artifact. Not only has it proven itself remarkably responsive to a great variety of social and economic demands: in the relative absence of these, it has shown itself capable of initiating demand. In other words, the state university has not merely "reacted" to outside changes and pressures; it has anticipated or generated new demands by expanding society's knowledge base and by devising new methods and approaches to learning. These in turn have promoted internal changes in organization and structure, such as the academic department and the research institute.

Yet any thoughtful consideration of the present condition of the publicly supported university must review the extent to which a great number of disparate and sometimes opposing assignments can be successfully "balanced" (a favorite word) or accommodated. The issue is not whether a mix of professional, vocational, research, and teaching objectives can coexist within a single institution. Experience shows that they can. The real issues are the nature of that mix as measured against an historical standard, the relative weight of each form of education, and the tensions arising from antagonistic or contradictory aims and purposes. In other words, while it is possible for a single institution to accommodate multiple interests, it may not be the case that all interests can be served equally well. Furthermore, the conflict of interests may itself be the source of additional ongoing problems.

In the discussion that follows I make the point—I am hardly the first to do so—that there are profound contradictions within the structure of the state university. Using a phrase of John Stuart Mill's, one might call them "standing antagonisms." Graduate and undergraduate forms of

39

tion are not in every respect compatible. They are most compatible wherever the undergraduate major is heavily shaped by a faculty principally interested in recruiting students for graduate schools or specific careers. They are least compatible in those corners of a university's program of studies that reveal the influence of liberal or—a less satisfying but also less value-laden word—"general" education.

Liberal education has historic roots in theories of character formation, especially in relation to political roles. By extension, liberal education became in time preparation for life, to include what today we might call interpersonal communication. Graduate, that is, research and professional education (the two are not always synonymous) is more directly concerned with tasks and careers. Baldly stated, the contradictions do not appear so great; but when the question of allocating resources is taken into account, in relation to historical measures of how each form of education is best achieved, the contradictions are more apparent. Furthermore, demands on faculty time and questions of professional priorities exacerbate standing difficulties and contribute to ongoing academic tensions. These are not necessarily unfortunate, but they must be taken seriously and thoughtfully into consideration when examining the biography of the modern university.

To this sketch of issues to be considered in connection with the present state of academic life, I would add larger contradictions and dilemmas arising from two inherited complexes of values: those associated with an ethic of competition and those connected to a commitment by our culture to all the virtues, all the paradoxes, and all the problems associated with individualism, now and in the past.[1]

THE LIBERAL ARTS COLLEGE AS AN
EDUCATIONAL IDEAL

The single-campus university is commonly divided into professional schools or colleges, a general, all-purpose undergraduate college of letters and science subdivided into departments, a graduate administrative division, and a number of organized research units. Departures from this model exist; thus the University of Houston and the State University of New York at Stony Brook do not have separate colleges of letters and science. There is often an extension division for continuing education, special programs that cross college or departmental boundaries and a large number of student support services either under a separate administrative chain-of-command or subject to direct academic control. In almost all institutions of this type, members of a given faculty teach both graduates and undergraduates; but the existence of "standing antagonisms" is most pronounced within the letters and science or "collegiate" faculty. This is not accidental. It is the result of a very long history of institutional differentiation wherein the college as a separate entity was nearly swallowed whole by the university. Flies or seeds in amber, colleges nevertheless retain some of their original characteristics. They also survive as an "idea" or an ideal. In order to address the question of the compatibility of undergraduate and graduate education within a single institution, I find it necessary to restate some of the salient features of collegiate education, especially since colleges precede universities in the history of this country and continue to influence our conception of good undergraduate education. The following summary is an ideal-type construction, incorporating the principal institutional traits of the English and American college in the eighteenth and nineteenth centuries.

A college exists to provide what historically is called "liberal education." In the past, liberal education was mainly intended for elite groups occupying positions of social and political leadership and consequently acquired snob appeal. There never has been in any western country a single curricular version of liberal education, yet the classic purpose of it was almost always considered to be preparation for public not private life. Historically, therefore, content was subordinate to a conception of polity or ends: an oligarchic society, for example, requiring a different form of liberal education from a democratic one. Today liberal education or the liberal arts are often defended as learning for its own sake, but it is useful to remember that historically such education was usually considered practical and not inconsistent with preparation for careers, most notably careers in certain professions and in the state. The reason, however, was mainly because those careers were also "liberal" in character and benefited from preliminary instruction in the liberal arts. However, because preparation for public life outweighed training for specific occupations as a purpose of liberal education, specialization was undervalued. Breadth, meaning flexible-mindedness, was the preferred outcome, and in time breadth came to be spoken of as the right kind of education for life in a changing world. The liberally educated person did not have to "re-tool." Liberal subjects were supposed to illuminate the human condition from almost any point of view: historical, social, scientific, ethical, and theological. The American college, even more than its English and Scottish antecedents, was concerned with religion because of the sectarian nature of American society and because of the Great Awakening in the eighteenth century, which rendered the American Enlightenment less secular than on the European continent.

Before the middle of the nineteenth century there was little age-specific education in either the public or private sectors. There was no concept of "higher education" relative to elementary and secondary schooling, nor were there widely accepted theories about the stages of natural development. What are now distinct phases of education correlated with the life cycle were then overlapping. Pupils proceeded at their own pace, so that much instruction was tailor-made. The famous 1828 Yale Report in defense of classical education mentions "superior" education, the "higher literary institutions" and the "highest education" but not in ways signifying a correlation between specific kinds of institutions and assigned age levels of educational responsibility.[2] "Higher education," to mean postsecondary education, is, I suspect, a later German import, and is closely related to a growing national interest in a division of labor, to a conception of "national aims and goals" and to the further development of the service sector of the economy.

Typically, college students in America and Scotland (but not England) were younger than today. Liberal education was intended for youths, commonly "adolescents." Ages at entry were fourteen to sixteen. At Oxford and Cambridge students entered at or near eighteen, much as today, but even at these famous institutions there was great variation in the curriculum. The conception of a "higher education" had not yet taken hold even there, and much education was a repetition of what had been learned at school or from a domestic tutor.

Hence, especially in America and Scotland, students were not regarded as adults able to make educational, life, and career choices but as dependent persons in need of nurturing, shaping, and forming. Rules, regulations, discipline, to include corporal discipline, were required to awaken the adult in the child and produce civilized, well-behaved, and morally upright citizens. In sum, character formation was the primary purpose of liberal education from antiquity onwards.

Pedagogically, students in Britain (especially England) and America were taught in small classes or by tutors. Colleges were "total" institutions (if they were residential), and every aspect of a student's life—physical and sexual health, personal hygiene, religion, moral development, the management of finances—came under the regulation of residential teachers who stood *in loco parentis*.

The teacher was consequently a moral guide or exemplar, a role model for students, and responsible for encouraging right-mindedness, high living, and moral trustworthiness. The development of organized team sports later in the century and the growth of fraternal organizations were compatible with these earlier ideals and characteristics of liberal education, for such activities could similarly be justified in terms of socialization and character formation. In the collegiate model axiological objectives were more important than the cultivation of intellect or the encouragement of strictly academic qualities.

The purely "intellectual" ideal adopted by defenders of liberal education—one may perhaps call it the "conventional" interpretation of the meaning of a liberal education—is a late nineteenth-century addition. Mission statements in college bulletins, catalogs, and recruiting brochures normally stress cognitive more than characterological features of their programs. Critical thinking and the powers of analysis and synthesis are the rewards promised to young men and women in search of higher education. *Involvement in Learning: Realizing the Potential of American Higher Education,* a very recent report by the Study Group on the Conditions of Excellence in American Higher Education sponsored by the National Institute of Education, underscores the importance of these values in providing for maximum flexibility of conduct and thought under the rapidly changing conditions of the contemporary world. Interestingly, the report places special weight on "synthesis," suggesting that it is closer to the breadth ideal in liberal education than "analysis." [3] Indeed, the historical case could be made that this weighting is correct, that analysis is in fact a cognitive attribute particularly connected to the graduate research ethic. [4]

It does not take long to notice that the land-grant college movement was inspired by a different set of educational values and ideals. Technical not liberal education was the main concern of a nation expanding geographically and economically. Agriculture and the "mechanic arts" appeared to promoters of federal support for education to be the more pressing needs of a society that had always prided itself on practicality. Justin Smith Morrill, the congressman from Vermont most responsible for the landmark act of 1862, has been described as a major supporter of the agricultural sector. Yet historical developments are rarely uncomplicated. Morrill's public speeches, whatever judgment we choose to pass on their rhetorical strategy, often linked liberal and vocational forms of education. He spoke of the necessity to "bring liberal culture within the reach of a much larger and unprovided for number of industrial classes in every state." Whereas he believed the leading object of land-grant colleges was to offer "such branches of learning as are related to agriculture and the mechanic arts," he did not exclude "scientific or classical studies." In 1867, upon leaving the House of Representatives for the Senate, he defined land-grant colleges as "schools of science" not agricultural institutes and the instruction to be offered in them as "intellectual" not "manual." [5] It is hardly to be expected that a practical man of affairs stirred by American democratic idealism would be better able to sort out the philosophical, logical, and historical contradictions evident in his speeches than the professional academic of a century later; but here certainly, in the optimistic and vague remarks of a mid-Victorian American, were foreshadowings of battles of the books as yet to come, as well as genuine underlying belief in the value and possibility of joining together forms of education normally antagonistic and separate.

RIVAL VALUES AND INSTITUTIONS

It was appreciated in some corners of America that colleges of letters and science or however one wished to refer to the traditional and tradition-minded liberal arts component were in theory incompatible with newer vocational and professional forms of education. Law, medicine, and the church were "liberal professions" it is true, but classical and Renaissance theories of gentlemanly education had usually been vigorously anti-vocational, except for the martial arts. Originating with the Greeks, a distinction had always been made between education that was liberal and education that was servile or mechanical. The former was held to be liberating, the latter self-denying, impersonal, antihuman. From the eighteenth century onwards a special rhetoric was introduced into Anglo-American educational discourse which came in time to seriously affect the way in which liberal and vocational forms of education were regarded. The Georgian antimodernist Jonathan Swift, in his inspired parable of the spider and the bee in *The Battle of the Books*, showed later thinkers how to associate all forms of vocational education with everything vile, selfish, destructive, narrow-minded, and self-serving; and liberal education with everything humane, natural, and beautiful, or, in a memorable Swiftian image taken over much later by Matthew Arnold, possessing sweetness and light. The influence of Goethe and Plato on nineteenth-century thinking reinforced these polarities, so that the "highest" form of education— and the best—was education that was beautiful or valuable *in and for itself*. From this perspective, no other utility was required. In fact, utility was the enemy of human nature.

Such ideological divisions entered academic debate because the two forms of education were competitive for prestige, markets, influence, and resources in the late nineteenth century. The defenders of what was presumed to be a traditional collegiate education ("presumed" because liberal education had many forms) exhibited the defensiveness so evident in Swift's angry writings. Unfortunately, one of the less admirable features of arguments on behalf of liberal or humanistic education has often been either a begrudging or irritable tone or a tendency to make the ideals of humanistic education so lofty that they become unattainable and thus self-defeating.

RESEARCH

I have spoken of the competition between newer vocational forms of education, such as the agricultural or engineering sciences, and liberal education. A third factor must now be introduced, distinct in major respects from the other two, the arrival and the success of the research ideal, an importation from Germany.

The research ideal shares certain objectives with vocational education, notably specialization of function. Unlike liberal education, it is knowledge-based rather than person-oriented, so that character formation or nurturing is not a stated primary or direct purpose. It is an indirect result, however, insofar as the socialization of graduate students into the views and assumptions of the discipline or the profession inevitably affects values and behavior. The research ideal also shares values with present-day theories of liberal education, for example, the belief in knowledge for its own sake. Sociologically, the principle of the autonomy of knowledge suits the researcher for the obvious reason that the choice of a project and the pace of research, as well as its utility, are decided by the investigator. Historically, both the research ethic and liberal education acquired their peculiar emphasis on knowledge being its own reward in the nineteenth century, for liberal education certainly had always been more influenced by the Greek school of practical sophists than Plato's Academy. Whatever the precise origin of the principle of the autonomy of knowledge, it is a part of what Bruce Kimball in a forthcoming book calls "accommodation" between liberal education and research and therefore a useful means of lessening some of the inherited tensions within the university between undergraduate collegiate education and graduate education.[6]

Originality of achievement is a cardinal feature of the research function. Neither liberal nor vocational forms of education require originality as part of their educational mission. In the eighteenth century, originality was called "novelty," which conveys rather exactly how it was regarded by detractors—that is, as a value associated with fashion and consumerism, implying short-term goals, frivolity, and fads. Liberal education—being largely character-forming, based on tradition, making use of received or canonical texts and incorporating general or universal truths, concerned mainly with interpersonal communication and the arts of leadership—

looked upon originality as a threat to the existing foundations of a well-ordered society. The dominant opinion was that very young persons, not yet grown to the ages of discretion, needed a form of education that gave assurance rather than one that challenged convention and authority.

In a sense, liberal education has always been backward looking. The past was considered to be the source of great ideas and great achievements. Liberal education was also pagan, in that the gentlemanly or courtly model of behavior was secular, hedonistic, and this-worldly. In America, the liberal arts college was imbued with Christian influences and precepts, but these too had the effect of making liberal education *retardataire* since, as the melancholy Solomon taught, there was nothing new under the sun. Only research was progressive, opening up the possibility that past models may not be the only or even the best models; that history advances, and events do not necessarily repeat themselves; that societies "evolve" and cultures are "relative"; that the search for the new is more important than preservation of the old; and that the "highest" form of education is exposure to the principles and methods of discovery, for which liberal education is at best preparatory. In fact, from the perspective of the research ethic, liberal education is not "higher" education at all and therefore should be prevented from spilling over into universities and research institutes. It should be confined to institutions approximating what Europeans used to call the "upper secondary school" and now call the "post compulsory sector"—the academy, lycée, gymnasium, or sixth form.

From this point of view, the ideal solution was the separation of liberal education from research. After the Civil War, several experiments along these lines were contemplated and introduced. The founders of the University of Chicago and Johns Hopkins thought primarily in terms of advanced education, to include professional; and elsewhere, as in the case of Columbia, college and university were for a time separated, each with its own faculty. At Berkeley in the 1950s, in the golden years of master-plan enthusiasm, it was sometimes argued that the first two years of higher education could profitably be spent in what were then called "junior colleges," allowing the University of California faculty to specialize in the teaching of upper division and graduate students (suggesting a common identity between these two groups).

But I am now speaking of events that come well after the first appearance of the research ideal in the 1860s. In these years there were no graduate divisions within universities. In America, as in Europe, the research ideal either had to gain a foothold within teaching institutions that still favored liberal forms of instruction or find room for itself outside universities and colleges in technical schools, government laboratories, agricultural stations, medical schools, professional societies, museums, geodetic and ordinance surveys, where applied rather than basic research was normally required. Histories of academic professionalism record the dissatisfactions expressed by researchers in such institutions since the opportunities for independent or creative inquiry were severely limited. The most coveted positions for the creative investigator were in learned societies founded in Europe during and after the great scientific revolution of the seventeenth century. Until well into the twentieth century industrialists in Britain and America were reluctant to provide monetary support for fundamental research. There were good reasons for this: there was as yet no proven relationship between original investigation and manufacturing. However, even today relatively few firms—the exceptions are well known—provide scientists with in-house opportunities for basic research equaling that of universities. And universities themselves, while making overtures to industry, now especially in bioengineering, rely on government for primary research support.

For Europeans and Americans the university was (correctly as it turned out) the appropriate place for advanced intellectual work, but the problem of converting institutions established for other purposes to this view was formidable. Separating functions was a costly solution, but the compatibility of the several forms of education was hardly demonstrable. Differences existed in outlook between applied and basic research. In colleges, and in colleges of letters and sciences, the research ethic did not always go down well with the large numbers of liberal education teachers who were nurturing the young and inculcating the lessons of good citizenship. Nor was it necessarily acceptable to the faculty of professional schools like medicine, who, except for a few physicians in laboratories and hospitals, were clinicians rather than researchers.

From the middle of the nineteenth century onwards it was evident that only colleges or universities provided senior members with sufficient autonomy to make basic research into a career, but the trade-off was undergraduate teaching, which in many institutions was still conducted at what researchers regarded as a 'rudimentary' level. A partial solution was achieved through a growing division of labor within the education sector generally. Primary, secondary, and "higher" education separated into distinct areas. As the ages at entry rose in American colleges and universities, the upper secondary school was transformed into a college preparatory division, and this solution contained possibilities. But the critical step was the next one, the transformation of the old liberal arts curriculum with its relatively fixed syllabus and traditions of general or humane learning into one allowing for more latitude of choice and specialization. Since outside research opportunities were limited and graduate degree programs still in their infancy, the only practical alternative was to introduce the spirit of research into the undergraduate program of studies. All in all, universities were ready for Charles Eliot's famous innovation at Harvard, the course-based elective system, which in time effectively broke the back of the old liberal arts degree.

In England the solution was rather different. There specialization had been going on in the two senior universities since about 1800 with the separation of the curriculum into honors and ordinary degrees, but the decisive change was the development over the first fifty years of the nineteenth century of excellent private (in our meaning) upper secondary schools carrying the burden of basic and general instruction and acting as feeder institutions. Nevertheless, advanced research degrees did not emerge until Cambridge introduced the Ph.D. in the 1890s, mainly for the benefit of overseas students, and before then, even with more specialized undergraduate degree programs than existed in America at the time, Oxbridge dons fought bitterly over the question of whether the special kind of concentration required of students reading honors was truly "liberal" or in fact "pre-professional." More of the same subject does not mean a student is being imbued with the ideals of the true researcher.

Despite the relative antiquity of the research ideal, it did not truly come into its own until after World War II. Wars have always stimulated research, although the connection between military technology and basic research, if perhaps obvious, is not straightforward. Still, it is safe to say that present U.S. government support for big science owes much to patterns of cooperation established during two world wars, especially the last one. The expansion of state university systems, the creation of multiversities on the model of the University of California, and the spread of the research ethic to smaller liberal arts or church-related colleges are an especially pronounced feature of the history of higher eduation in the last three or four decades.

When penetrated by the research ethic, colleges in the liberal arts tradition immediately evince some of the characteristics I have noted in connection with large institutions. I have visited small private colleges where faculty complain that a change of administration or administrative policy has produced the requirement of publication as a prerequisite for promotion or advancement. Administrators respond by saying that their intentions are modest. All that is desired is some "proof" of industry, some evidence that faculty are "keeping up" in their field as revealed by the occasional article, edited book of documents, attendance at scholarly meetings, service to an academic association, perhaps local radio broadcasts. For deans, "research" can be a means for raising the standard of perceived faculty quality. For faculty it can be considered an excuse for exercising tighter budgetary control by suppressing promotions or re-allocating monies according to student demand. Some faculty, especially older ones who either did not earn Ph.Ds or were in graduate school many decades ago, may suspect that administrative pressures imply criticism that one's teaching is not up to the mark.

The adoption of research or publication criteria for advancement presents many problems for all sectors of the academic community. It creates demands at odds with student flow and other administrative considerations, presents administrators as well as faculty with questions of evaluation and assessment, and directly affects the budgets for libraries, laboratories, and leaves. Elite (and richer?) small colleges have absorbed the research ideal to a surprising degree and reward faculty accordingly.[7] Some, as at Wesleyan, house institutes or centers for visiting scholars. All of them recruit faculty from prestigious university backgrounds. Their faculty move in the same academic circles as their former professors and university-based peers, and their institutions provide sabbatical leaves for purposes of research (Swarthmore's sabbatical policy is more generous than Berkeley's). I suspect these arrangements are more satisfactory for humanities and social science faculties than for physical scientists, for the problem of establishing an adequately equipped research laboratory may be greater than the absence of a research library if the institution is located within reasonable distance of one. Furthermore, books and articles can be obtained through interlibrary loan programs, and publishers are very busy at present filming major collections of documents.

The definition of "research" is not the same for each discipline or task and is rather loosely applied to cover all forms of inquiry, including work for an undergraduate term paper. Nor is the distinction between basic and applied research always self-evident. Yet despite these considerable ambiguities and elisions, modern society is research based. It is conceded there is some useful working relationship between basic research and technology. Those who engage in research occupy prestigious positions within society and certainly within the world of higher education, globally as well as nationally. There are, of course, gradations of prestige, depending upon the *problemstellung*, the reputation of a journal or publishing house, or the level of ambition exhibited in the research design (textbooks meant for teaching in the humanities or social sciences, although they may be lucrative, do not attract as much praise as monographs or original syntheses).

The reward structure therefore favors research as a higher task requiring special gifts. Other traditional forms of creativity—imaginative writing, the plastic and performing arts—are accepted under the heading of original work; but despite the presence of dance groups, chamber orchestras, and poets-in-residence, there is a sense in which this level of creative activity lies at the margins of our universities, shading off into what the eighteenth century called the ornamental arts. In the same way mildly invidious distinctions are made between "hard social science" and "soft social science," and the development of theory is valued more highly than mere empirical work, although the two are cognitively intertwined. Historical analysis is more praised than the writing of historical narrative, although it is not always easy to disentangle these approaches. Successful researchers bring special outside recognition to their institutions: prizes, honors, grants, funding for laboratories, support for graduate student research assistants, endowments, and gifts. A culture of consumerism and advertising encourages public disclosure of these distinctions, and universities compete heavily in the open market for talent likely to enhance their reputation and support base. Graduate students follow the trail of prestige and enroll in univerities that they believe will provide them with the best life and career chances.

Research can be externally measured, assessed, rewarded. A scholarly book or article, a report of a lab discovery reaches publics thousands of miles from the researcher's home university. International meetings allow for personal contact, reinforcing the network of exchange and communication. The same cannot be said for even the most brilliant teaching of undergraduates, even if it is (as has been done) praised in a popular or semipopular national magazine. Teaching can be rewarded locally with a teaching prize. Teachers in small colleges can become Danforth teaching fellows. The Ohio Academy of History recognizes outstanding teachers nominated by individual campuses, but rarely do such distinctions result in the spirited competitive bidding characteristic of the buying of research talent, even when disagreements occur over the value of that talent. Teaching cannot possibly create the same stir.[8] Furthermore, the problem of evaluating teaching is a headache, since factors in some sense foreign to the spirit of high scholarship threaten to creep into the assessment, such as popularity.

These are greatly familiar facts of professional academic life. No one can be surprised to read them here. They are part and parcel of what David Riesman and Christopher Jencks call the "academic revolution" or "academic imperium."[9] Ever since the nineteenth century they have disturbed the proponents of liberal or humanistic education who denounced the egotism, market orientation, and external professional loyalties associated with the research ideal. It was then argued that research would detract from undergraduate teaching, endanger local support, and lead ultimately to a denaturing educational environment in which the pursuit of knowledge replaced a liberal concern for personal relations and social values. Within the twentieth-century Anglo-American higher education community many efforts have been made to set aside the arguments of moralists and detractors by claiming that knowledge leads towards humanity rather than away from it. Whitehead even claimed that specialism itself—the dreaded enemy of all nineteenth- and twentieth-century humanists—was essential for realizing human nature. "Mankind is naturally specialist," he once wrote. "One man sees a whole subject, where another can find only a few detached examples. I know that it seems contradictory to allow for specialism in a curriculum especially designed for a broad culture. . . . But I am certain that in education wherever you exclude specialism, you destroy life." [10] The fact that debates over the definition of liberal education and the place of undergraduate teaching in research universities continue, accompanied by cyclical swings between requirements, electives, and core curricula meant to recapture the spirit of liberal instruction, may well be an indication of an underlying malaise in American culture, a dissatisfaction with the quality of everyday life, the conduct of social and personal relationships, and the level of student intellectual performance. However, a less dramatic interpretation is also possible. Cyclical swings between requirements, electives, and core curricula may also be manifestations of a healthy academic restlessness.

The development of research as the contemporary university's leading function has produced structural differentiation and a further division of labor. The liberal arts teacher, standing *in loco parentis*, was expected to undertake the shaping of the student's whole character. Few modern academics can accept these awesome responsibilities. Few students are attached to a single professor who acts as a mentor throughout their university career, and few students see their teachers in settings that support a closer student-teacher exchange. Furthermore, the breakdown in consensus in modern society has given rise to plural value systems that make it awkward for individual professors to undertake nurturing with any confidence of success. The pitfalls are too obvious in any case, and the efforts likely to be misunderstood in our currently politicized universities.

So the professor's teaching is more or less confined to the subject. Loyalty to the discipline comes first. An army of specialists and paraprofessionals in counseling centers, preprofessional advising centers, health facilities, financial aid offices, and student government have stepped in to supplement the scholar and scientist's labors, as have ad hoc groups of every description. Even so, the use of these extensive and impressive resources is almost always at the student's initiative, thus illustrating once again how little remains of the notion of *in loco parentis* in the public university.[11]

THE GRADUATE STUDENT TEACHER

I have restated the common observation that the reward and incentives system favors the researcher. I have also stated that the assimilation of the idea of original work into the liberal arts curriculum and the development of the elective system—to which I now add "majors" and "minors"—are further proof of the success of the research and specialization principle within the structure of a single institution performing both undergraduate and graduate instruction. There are other structural characteristics of the modern university that appear to be the result of adopting a research function. One is the internal distribution of resources in favor of graduate teaching, so that most undergraduate instruction takes place in large lecture halls while graduate teaching typically takes place in the lab, seminar room, or tutorial. Another is the widespread use of advanced graduate students to lead undergraduate discussion sections connected to large lectures, to teach smaller, seminar courses or introductory courses like calculus and foreign languages, compensatory or remedial (the word is not liked) courses in reading and composition, and to mark essays and examinations. At Berkeley (and other campuses of the University of California) the departments usually decide how graduate teaching assistants are to be used in support of the ladder teaching faculty, and practices vary significantly, so much so that the matter is currently under review by the president's office. For many undergraduates in state universities, doubtless most of them, the TA is the only teacher they will ever personally know and can ask for letters of recommendation.

The use of graduate student teachers permits the researcher to spend more time in graduate instruction. But the use of TA's is also a result of the poor faculty-student ratios that exist in mass-education letters and sciences colleges. These fall well below what have historically been the teaching ratios in leading liberal arts colleges, private universities in America, or places like Oxford and Cambridge and British universities generally, where ratios of 1:8 or 1:9 are considered optimum. Mass education requires cost effectiveness. If the research function is to be protected, graduate students must be employed as supplemental teachers. This is commonly defended as apprentice training for entry into the college teaching profession; and indeed in a sense it is, although the argument is weakened by the fact that not every graduate student in every department is actually required to have such teaching experience before becoming independent. In a sense, historical precedent justifies the use of graduate students in teaching. One could argue that in the liberal arts colleges of the colonial and federal periods teachers were very young and performed teaching similar to the TA functions of today. At Oxbridge in the first half of the nineteenth century college tutors were only several years older than undergraduates. But today's requirement that regular faculty possess the doctoral degree (or comparable professional experience, as in law or architecture) has widened the age gap between junior professors and undergraduates, so that the use of teaching assistants cannot easily be justified as "traditional."

Not all graduate students regard their teaching functions as merely a form of apprenticeship. Some demand full membership in the guild on the grounds that they have been engaged in doctoral study for years, have an actual status close to that of assistant professors and are married with families. A number of them can claim that they have *de facto* autonomy in the classroom. They see themselves as an indispensable part of the state university teaching environment. Resenting marginal treatment, they have organized into labor unions in order to improve their financial and institutional position.

THE EFFECT OF UNDERGRADUATE TEACHING ON RESEARCH

Having given examples of the several ways in which the research function influences the kind of educational environment in existence today, I would now like to reverse the drift of my discussion and indicate the ways in which there continues to be incomplete combustion in the state university. For despite the evident success of the research ethic and the creation of what has been termed the "protograduate ecology of the undergraduate landscape,"[12] the effort to unite general and specialized teaching within a single institution has made its domination less than complete.

First of all, the very fact that we offer small discussion sections in connection with lectures, or use graduate students to teach seminars, is evidence of an ongoing concern with liberal arts ideals, of our desire to retain, however mitigated in form and substance, some suggestion of more traditional views of undergraduate teaching. There is no reason why the large lecture course cannot be an end in itself, as simply a fact of numbers, resources, mission, and academic realities, and indeed in many departments and universities it is simply that. But in large lecture courses the discussion section is often added. Reading and composition classes and foreign languages are taught in relatively small classes because of our belief that in such settings they are best taught.

Other scholars regard such efforts, which would also include tutorials, honors courses, and the substitution of written essays for course examinations, as further evidence of the influence of graduate styles and values on the undergraduate curriculum.[13] This is a fair rejoinder. The test is the content and spirit of these courses and programs, the degree to which they follow from the research interests of faculty or borrow from the tradition of person-oriented, character-shaping liberal arts instruction.

Second, there is the transfer function that is quite rightly regarded as one of the key elements in promoting upward social mobility.[14] The difficulty in maintaining the same level of program or quality among the various parties to articulation, especially in light of different political, social, and funding pressures, means that greater faculty attention must be paid to administrative and pedagogical details arising from articulation, to include what I will call "hidden remedial instruction" in the classroom (which can also arise in connection with freshman admissions of affirmative action and special admissions decisions affecting athletes).

A third consideration that arises is the pressure to reallocate resources according to what is called the "improvement" of undergraduate teaching or to encourage "experimentation." Wealth and plenty have enabled America to constantly indulge in the search for new forms of course innovation and for periodic renewal, discussed at length by Gerald Grant and David Riesman in *The Perpetual Dream* (Chicago, 1978). More common results of this dream are core curricula in the lower division, seminars for freshmen and sophomores, special colleges within colleges where classes are typically smaller, interdisciplinary courses, honors programs, and efforts to provide more tailoring in advising programs—all of which, their merits aside, strain existing faculty resources (assuming stable enrollments in the graduate program). Very likely the humanities and social sciences are most affected by these changes, for by tradition and ethos they carry the task of liberal breadth instruction, their program for majors being characteristically less structured and more flexible than in the mathematical, physical, and technical sciences, and because most faculty in these areas do not work in labs or teams where graduate apprentices keep research projects moving on a daily basis.

A fourth way in which a major undergraduate teaching mission decidedly complicates the imperatives of research is in staffing. The B.A. program relies upon classroom teaching and continuous assessment of student work to a far greater extent than do advanced degrees. Yet the pursuit of new knowledge, being slow and time-consuming, requires reduced classroom teaching assignments, sabbatical leaves, leaves without pay and other means of aiding research, as in the practice of allowing course relief for editing scholarly journals, administering research projects, or directing campus think-tanks, institutes, and clinics. It is tempting to invoke the authority of Scripture in support of the principle of released time for original intellectual work. The Old Testament commands the land be left fallow to promote regeneration, and the sages go on to say that individuals too need time for reflection, rededication, and renewal. Our present-day conception of the sabbatical leave year is rather more utilitarian than spiritual, and no doubt, when measured against its origins, thin and insubstantial.[15] Still, intellectual if not spiritual renewal is accomplished through leaves, a period of active work in which scholars and scientists are supposed to engage in lines of inquiry delayed or interrupted by teaching and administrative responsibilities.

Yet "standing antagonisms" are especially conspicuous here. Administrators facing deficits or pressed to meet budgetary savings targets are understandably concerned about the staffing of undergraduate courses; while faculty, especially in the humanities and social sciences, depend upon sabbaticals and other leaves to publish.

The specific issue is not so much the importance of leave but its frequency, faculty naturally wishing to take advantage of research or professional opportunities outside the expected cycle of leave taking, deans and provosts influenced by other priorities. When operating budgets are ample, the problem of absent faculty is not nearly so great as when they are tight, for visitors can be found to teach courses in the regular program.[16] Even in lean years, a distinguished research faculty attracts large sums of outside money, resulting in salary savings that can then be internally redistributed to meet teaching needs not otherwise supported (provided there is no state or other claim on these funds). However, if the level of savings returned to departments is less than what is perceived to be necessary for maintaining the integrity of the curriculum, the number of visitors are fewer and department resources are stretched, even to the point where from desperation courses are cancelled or low-cost lecturers and advanced graduate students are engaged to staff the program. Since administrators agree that the reward structure favors (and should favor?) the researcher and that campus reputations are based on research more than on teaching, the dilemmas are particularly troubling and the ambivalences unusually conspicuous. It is in such circumstances that one hears an echo of the ancient liberal arts assumption that undergraduates need the close, patient superintendence of wise and gentle Chirons. But of course there is also strong and encouraging support for research from campus administrators, so that what I notice is yet another instance of institutional contradiction.

A final example of how the existence of an undergraduate mission affects the research and graduate ethos of the university brings us back to tensions transmitted via the culture of research with its associated reward system. Rewards favor the researcher, but they also favor the disciplines and fields most closely identified with the idea of fundamental discovery and the development of new technologies. Faculty in the humanities, the creative arts, and the "soft" social sciences are often ambivalent about where their own educational loyalties ought to reside. They represent subjects with an historic commitment to undergraduate teaching in the liberal arts spirit. They frequently see themselves as the "bee" side of Swift's parable, and many of them realize how often their own conception of original scholarship differs from popular and governmental notions of utility or ideas of rigor represented in the exact sciences. Having inherited a special sense of responsibility towards undergraduates and therefore desirous of upholding traditions of liberal arts teaching, the humanistic faculty has also accepted a rewards system weighted towards research. The maldistribution of rewards and incentives is therefore disturbing. It is a fact of university life that the research needs of some disciplines are not as fully met as those of others. Rarely do the faculty in the humanities and social sciences automatically receive summer salaries paid out of external grants. They are short on equipment, clerical, secretarial, and research assistance. Grant support for overseas travel is less available than in the sciences. External support for research leaves is limited. Despite ongoing (if inconsistent) efforts to address these problems, many of the nonscience faculty, especially in the years before they have established a professional claim on existing resources, subsidize research out of their own pockets. Some of them, it may be suggested, have continuing difficulty accommodating the competing demands of graduate and undergraduate teaching.

PUBLIC DEMAND

Because my "charge" includes the statement that from a "states' point of view, undergraduate education is provided in response to public demand for both personal and social benefit," I would like to make a few observations about public "demand" in relation to the "supply" of services provided by the contemporary university. I do not think I have to belabor the point that in a plural society such as exists in most advanced industrial democracies there are many publics, more than the number of mansions in my father's house. Clark Kerr's multiversity is not informed by what Cardinal Newman called an "Idea" (if by no means a simple idea). Alumni, boards of trustees, parents, high-tech industries, local, state, and federal governments, legislatures, student organizations, and special-interest lobby groups are all publics with their own demands, desires, and means of mobilizing support and disapproval. The complex interlocking institutions and pressure groups constituting our modern society do not make it any easier for a university to perceive how to fit its supply to outside demand. Any student of political science or history appreciates the heuristic difficulty of analyzing the effect of such a bewildering variety of interests on the direction of research and teaching within the university. Historians of any country or period have always found the notion of "public opinion" impossible to pin down; but there is no doubt that decision-makers often act as if such a phenomenon exists. Certainly many of our universities are required to respond to more different kinds of demands than nineteenth-century predecessors, with less vocal, more easily-defined publics and relatively homogeneous student bodies. I say "many" rather than "all"—and even then perhaps not confidently—because nineteenth-century public institutions were also subject to diverse pressures and competing demands, depending upon location, clientele, and the conditions of their establishment. But it is at least safe to suggest that in those days universities were mainly concerned with undergraduate and professional instruction, and the expensive problems of maintaining a research mission had not yet truly arisen.

Not only are there many publics, with contradictory aims and demands, but no single public is consistent in its demands. An undergraduate will one day bemoan the emphasis on graduate students and research, and on the next complain that no one is available to direct a highly specialized honors thesis topic. Undergraduates will repeat clichés about large impersonal lecture courses and remain mute and unprepared in specially designed, limited enrollment discussion seminars. Politicians will admonish the multiversity for undertaking frivolous or irrelevant investigations in the name of research or question the value of "research" altogether, and at the same time ask for crash programs to meet the challenges of overseas competition. One group believes the university should use its special knowledge to promote national and international causes, and yet another believes universities are altogether too forward in these areas. Some politicians complain about ideological tendencies among students, attributing unsavory opinions to their teachers, and others demand that the university solve social problems long in the making. Parents wish their children to have a personally enriching experience at college but without being diverted from the opportunity to enter a good career, these not being viewed as identical.

INDIVIDUALISM, COMPETITION, AND EDUCATION

The greatest contradiction of all arises from a central feature of modern culture. Since the Enlightenment, we have been an individualist society, much to the disgust of Edmund Burke who talked about becoming disconnected into the "dust and powder of individuality," to be "at length dispersed to all the winds of heaven." While Europeans share this inheritance, they have mitigated some of its effect by dampening initiative through interventionist policies. The values most respected by Americans are all connected to a belief in the primacy of individual expression. Think of the words we characteristically employ in writing letters of recommendation for students or nonacademic staff. Individuals are praised for being "self-starters" or for having "initiative." We check off the box that asks whether they can work "without constant supervision." Teamwork is important, and while that appears to contradict the ethic of individualism, it is really related. Ordinarily, we would expect individuals to be self-absorbed or "selfish" in the vocabulary of utilitarian ethics, and we wonder therefore if they have developed sufficient ego control to get along with others. For the same reasons we are a nation interested in community and cooperation. Strongly held values generate opposites. We fear having gone too far in one direction.

We respect competition. It is the lever that moves our cultural universe, to freely adapt a conceit that Johannes Kepler applied to the court of the Emperor Rudolph. Nothing stretches "character" quite so much as challenge. But competition also promotes anxiety or only "relative success," which for many people is tantamount to failure. A sense of inadequacy haunts many of our youth and adults. One is somehow not quite good enough (good enough for what?). Within the educational community competition leads to conflicts over grading and the distribution of honors. Undergraduates demand that professors pay more than lip service to the ideals of liberal education. Surely education must deal with the whole person? Our response to this desperate cry is to create university support structures of every imaginable description to shore up the flagging competitor. They comprise the one conspicuous arena in the university that is *not* competitive. Only *need*, not personal worth has to be measured. This is a subject worth separate analysis. For now let me say that student support units, while they offer an astounding range of valuable services, also resemble battlefield surgery. Their object is to return the soldier to combat as quickly as possible.[17]

In western society, ever since the eighteenth century, every reformer or radical thinker, except certain categories of utopians opposed to individualism, has connected the progress of the individual to education and not merely or even essentially for occupational or vocational reasons. In fact, I would suggest that the functionalist view of education is usually anti-individualistic or at least unconcerned with what the nineteenth century called "self-cultivation." The basic fact is rather this: in a universe where individual expression is honored, the individual must be maximally equipped to function at the highest social level—some romantics would say highest "spiritual" level. This is, as I hope my remarks make clear, a qualitatively different argument from saying that socialization is the primary end of education. An individualist culture will always contain ambiguities, but it will finally have to insist, as a condition of its own survival, that as the individual must remain the best judge of his or her own interests, education is the proper means for learning how to recognize alternatives, make decisions, cope with contradictions, choose friends and acquaintances, collaborators and spouses. As long as individualism remains a central feature of American culture, so will some attenuated and even shadowy form of liberal education remain a part of the teaching offered in state universities. For although historically liberal education was rarely in the service of notions of personal autonomy, it remains today the primary form of "higher education" where the well-being of the self and the problem of self and society are central.

CONCLUSION

With characteristic and, to my mind, admirable American optimism, we have chosen to combine many different purposes and functions within a single type of institution, the public research university. In the past quarter of a century that institution has moved to the center of modern culture, where it is continually subject to media and political attention. Many of its aims are contradictory and therefore produce internal "standing antagonisms." "Is it [therefore] possible," I am asked in the charge leading to the writing of this essay, "to formulate a coherent statement of these contradictory educational purposes?" My general answer falls into the area of what certain schools of philosophy define as "quandary ethics." A "coherent statement" must inevitably recognize the structural polarities of the modern research university, which in turn incorporate most of the value contradictions of present-day American society, the result of historical pressures, decisions, and developments. No institution is ever totally free, especially educational ones. I suppose I am asking for a continuing acknowledgment of some of the fundamental limits and constraints under which we function in the public university sector.[18] This is necessary if we are to avoid "blaming" one party or another for some of the difficulties encountered in the everyday life of our universities. Furthermore, structural contradictions are not maladjustments. They are not the results of incompetence, selfishness, and ill-will. Forthright acknowledgment of the tensions in our internal life may also enable us to formulate reasonably clear responses to what are often the embarrassing questions of state officials and legislators. I am not an apologist for institutions. I do not believe that our universities are the helpless creatures of impersonal, irresistible historical forces; but I do think that choices and possible lines of action are limited, and we must be prepared to recognize those limits when contemplating curricular reform or adjustments in the relation of graduate to undergraduate education. I think we must be especially cautious when arguing that these forms of education somehow can be balanced. The word "balance" implies an equal apportionment of time, and such a division of labor may be unrealistic as well as mechanical, producing unimaginative quarrels over teaching loads, the definition of contact hours, or the allocation of course units. These matters already consume too much faculty and administrative energy.

A "coherent statement" of the relationship of undergraduate to graduate forms of instruction must also come to terms with that magnificent but complex inheritance of values and ideas called "liberal education." Not all undergraduate education offered in public institutions is even nominally "liberal." We are willing to acknowledge that fact when discussing programs in agriculture and engineering. But the vast majority of our undergraduates are not concentrating on technical subjects leading directly to careers. They are letters and science students. Are they receiving a liberal education? In some respects yes, but in others no.

Although there have been many conceptions of a liberal education in the history of western civilization, there is one unifying theme: the concern for the whole or complete person. Metaphysical, philosophical, psychological, religious, and social ideas underly the notion of "wholeness." The usual historical solution for promoting development of the whole person has been teaching that allows for both nurturing (character formation) and the enlargement of cognitive skills. "Character formation" is a terribly old-fashioned term, and it has often been a weak defense of low intellectual standards or social snobbery. Detractors used to dismiss it as mere finishing-school education. Nevertheless, character formation has always been an essential part of the historical conception of liberal education; and without it important objectives of liberal education, such as preparation for citizenship, the idea of public service, the belief in the importance of tradition, the training of political leaders, and the idea of personal development are unthinkable. It was character formation as much and probably more than the training of intellect that made liberal education synonymous with humanism.[19]

If we value "liberal" education as compared to merely "general" or "breadth" education (how much breadth, after all, does it take to be "broad"?), then we must be prepared to question current practices and policies respecting the use of graduate teaching assistants and the relationship of the vast network of student services to the academic program. Are graduate students made aware of the nurturing process in liberal education, even if, as I have mentioned, nurturing presents pitfalls in present circumstances? Are graduate assistants instructed to treat undergraduates as whole persons? The proper use of graduate students for teaching and evaluating undergraduates is a deeply serious matter, an Achilles' heel, exposing the university community to outside criticism that will not go away. But the same problems arise in connection with faculty teaching. As for student services, are they directly and positively correlated with the formative academic processes of undergraduate education? If not, can they be more effectively connected? I believe so. We must also continually reexamine the knotty problem of faculty/student ratios, an area in which we have some but unfortunately not very much latitude. Nevertheless, the question of faculty/student ratios in relation to classroom size lies at the very heart of the problem of liberal education and so cannot be avoided.

In the last five or ten years, even longer, and with an intensity I did not notice two decades ago, both public and private educational institutions have been vigorously exploring ways of improving undergraduate instruction by, in effect, reducing class size in selected programs. Core curricula, ambitious western civilization courses, freshman seminars, senior capstone courses, and team teaching are experiments currently in full flower.[20] Such programs are controversial because they divert faculty resources from other parts of an institution's educational program. They are often designed without taking into account existing systems of rewards and incentives, and resistance is thereby increased. Academic self-interest and budget are not the only grounds for hesitation; intellectual and pedagogical objections also exist. But my point is that these widespread innovations are, *inter alia*, efforts to keep alive the holistic vision embedded in the historical heart of liberal education by bringing senior or regular faculty into closer everyday association with the youngest members of our campus environment. Wherever these newer programs exist, I hypothesize, they have the desired effect of building confidence in young people who in more anonymous settings struggle to meet the demands of competition relatively unaided. Undergraduates may work harder in seminars and small classes than in lectures, especially where reading and writing assignments are heavy, but their efforts can be more closely monitored by faculty, and in my experience the level of student performance improves. Perhaps I should again emphasize that, historically, confidence-building has been an important objective of proponents of liberal education.

The new programs I am referring to are in one sense—a nonpejorative sense—"elite" experiments, not because they are designed for a privileged minority and are intended to be exclusive, but rather because they provide opportunities for the close personal interaction of teachers and taught. They allow for the development of reasoning and writing skills in ways impossible for lecture courses, even lecture courses where essays are required. I fully share my colleague Martin Trow's hope that the principle of elite liberal education in its best historical sense will survive in the face of other more profoundly utilitarian demands.[21] Liberal education is utilitarian or it would not have lasted so long, even if its present form is attenuated.

Yet in closing this discussion of the standing antagonisms between graduate and undergraduate education it is necessary to consider one of the most interesting, persuasive, and even imaginative educational integrating strategies that has emerged. Instead of continual and frustrating attempts to accommodate both graduate and liberal forms of education within a single institution or, as a more expensive alternative, creating colleges within universities to isolate and protect the liberal arts function, more attention, it is argued, should be given to finding ways of directly introducing undergraduates to research as practiced by faculty in all disciplines. The "academic revolution" has greatly improved the standard of academic achievement by extending to undergraduates the principles of method, originality, freedom of interpretation, critical rigor in analysis, the intellectual "problem," and the idea of the advance of knowledge.[22] As faculty are most comfortable in the laboratory, library, and research center, why not make greater provision for undergraduates to join them there? The obvious solution of how or what to teach undergraduates is systematic exposure to the whole notion of what is currently meant by excellence in learning.

There is much to be said for this perspective. As Riesman and Jencks have pointed out, a number of central departures in undergraduate teaching owe their inspiration to techniques developed in the graduate schools. Undergraduates who, through the medium of field work or term papers, or association with a professor's special investigations, learn something about the meaning of research at first-hand, are usually excited by the process of discovery and by the thought of sharing in the creative experience of distinguished faculty. The idea of allowing undergraduates more opportunity for understanding the direct intellectual benefits of original research is stimulating, and as the multiversity usually finds some room for nearly every impulse, doubtless it can find room for this one as well. Certainly, such a systematic innovation could go a long way towards easing the tensions aroused by some of the standing antagonisms.

At what price, however? It should not be suggested that such education, for all its great and important attractions, is in the deepest meaning of the tradition "liberal education." It is, as its supporters say it is, the logical and final triumph of the spirit of graduate over undergraduate education, a clearing out of the vestiges of old ideas and programs. Liberal education, to repeat the formula, is preparation for public affairs and, by extension, for learning how to develop a working accommodation with others in the many arenas of modern competitive culture. Such purposes are immensely assisted by the critical skills characteristic of graduate education, but critical intelligence alone is unable to effect the kind of communication, sensitivity, and understanding of human nature historically comprehended by the phrases "liberal education" and the "liberal arts."

It is time to join the phrase *liberal sciences* to the liberal arts as our medieval university forebears did in their own educational vocabulary. The values carried by the traditions of liberal education are not the exclusive possession of the arts as we narrowly define them. No subject or discipline is intrinsically liberal or servile. The curriculum is not the only answer. Liberal education is also a matter of attitude, style (in the value sense), and purpose. There is no reason why it cannot be carried on in schools of business or engineering, and I believe that such is indeed very often the case wherever faculty put person-oriented teaching above discipline-centered teaching and approach their subjects in a spirit of broad-minded applicability.[23] But this is a dangerous line of thinking, for it leads to a reconsideration of the purposes and organization of colleges of letters and science and of the relationship between professional and "autonomous" disciplines. It means that the "humanities" do not have exclusive possession of humanistic education and may, in certain situations, even be producing servile or technical results. Impossible! Finally, it means that in the world of mass education, limited resources, and rival objectives, it takes a very special commitment in order to humanize higher education when so much else of critical importance is also at stake, that commitment drawing its strength from the best examples of the past and the highest hopes for the future of the world's first nation-state democracy.

NOTES

1. I would like to thank the anonymous readers of an earlier version of this paper for their comments. I must also thank the deans and presidents who forced me to clarify my observations at the joint annual meeting of the American Council of Education and National Association of State Universities and Land-Grant Colleges held at Denver, Colorado, November 11–14, 1984. I am acutely aware of the fact that I have not answered all questions. I would especially like to thank Martin Trow of the University of California, Berkeley, for his unfailing help and kindness and Frank Newman, president, Education Commission of the States, and Joseph Katz of the State University of New York at Stony Brook for their detailed and pertinent remarks.

2. "Original Papers in Relation to a Course of Liberal Education," in the *American Journal of Science and Arts* 15 (1829): 297–351.

3. *Involvement in Learning* (October 1984), pp. 43–44.

4. A distinction similar to analysis/synthesis is made by academic historians if "narrative" is substituted for "synthesis." Narrative forms of historical writing are usually regarded as mere storytelling and not as advances in the field. Narrative historians are frequently disparaged as "popular" writers, antiquarians, journalists, or amateurs. However, official opinion is currently showing cracks.

5. Edward Danforth Eddy, Jr., *Colleges for Our Land and Time: The Land-Grant Idea in American Education* (New York, 1957), pp. 28, 31, 38.

6. Bruce A. Kimball, *Orators and Philosophers* (forthcoming, Teachers' College Press).

7. In other words, what David Riesman and Christopher Jencks noticed in 1968 is still the case today. See *The Academic Revolution* (New York, 1968), p. 492.

8. Recently efforts have been made at historical conferences to devote sessions to teaching, curriculum, teaching materials, and the design of new courses. It remains to be seen whether such panels will attract talent scouts in the former manner. Unfortunately, the experiment occurs at a time when the large annual meeting of historians has declined in importance. A lower demand for young historians seeking jobs, the higher costs of attending meetings caused by the inflation of the 1970s, the proliferation of topics, subspecialties, and special agendas, and the greater number of local, regional, and international meetings account for the fall in centrality.

9. Riesman and Jencks, p. 540.

10. A. N. Whitehead, *The Organization of Thought* (Westport, Conn., 1974), p. 20.

11. A Scottish acquaintance has pointed out to me that British academic thinking on the question of *in loco parentis* changed suddenly when tougher drug abuse laws were passed in the 1960s. Paternal superintendence appeared less attractive when faculty faced felony charges for failing to police student residence halls or houses.

12. Riesman and Jencks, p. 500.

13. Ibid., p. 513.

14. Studies have shown that the majority of community college transfers to Berkeley were in fact eligible for admission upon graduation from high school, however.

15. See Bruce A. Kimball, "The Origin of the Sabbath and Its Legacy to the Modern Sabbatical," *Journal of Higher Education* 49 (1978): 303–315.

16. While visitors cannot usually provide continuity in a given academic program or major, they are very desirable in their own right, bringing fresh faces and perspectives to the campus.

17. A passionate discussion of the adverse effects of individualism on the college idea appears in Joseph Tussman, *Experiment at Berkeley* (New York, 1969), pp. 65–67.

18. A counterargument exists. Would it not be better to deny or conceal our dilemmas on the grounds that silence in public has its uses? After all, cultural systems usually employ what anthropologists and legal scholars call "fictions" and "evasions." Truth or reality exposes root dilemmas that threaten the well-being of a culture or society. The late Erving Goffman's remarkable books provide plentiful illustrations of how potential misunderstandings and conflicts arising from the conduct of everyday life are evaded because the tensions released by open acknowledgment of them are considered unacceptable; and Clifford Geertz's justly admired essay on the Balinese cockfight (*The Interpretation of Cultures* [New York, 1973]) explains how social and cultural differences inherent in Balinese society are accommodated through play mechanisms associated with a popular institution. The cockfight is a means of concealing and forestalling more destructive antagonisms. Artists also have long been interested in these questions. Ibsen's plays, especially *The Wild Duck* and *The Master Builder*, are precisely about the comparative utility of fantasy and reality. Despite the "success" of many kinds of fictions and evasions, I obviously prefer free and open discussion of contradictions and quandaries. Fictions and evasions may be functional, but they do not permit consciously directed change.

19. "Humanities," "humanistic," and "humanism," not to mention "humanize," are always confusing terms and especially in English translations. They have strict, broad, and historical connotations. Joseph P. O'Neill, "Is a Liberal Arts Education Passe?" *American Association for Higher Education Bulletin* (November 1984), pp. 6–7, makes an interesting distinction between humanistic disciplines and the liberal arts. The purpose of the former, he states, is to provide for *private* goods such as self-development, self-fulfillment, and self-expression, the latter is preparation for *public* life. I agree wholeheartedly with his admirable statement of the liberal arts case but would reason somewhat differently about the purpose of a humanistic education. The correlation of "humanities" with a specific category of subjects dates mainly from the Italian Renaissance and can be found in courtesy authors like Baldassare Castiglione, *The Book of the Courtier* (Harmondsworth, 1967), p. 90: "I should like our courtier to be a more than average scholar, at least in those studies which we call the humanities." The speaker in this section of Castiglione's symposium goes on to mention Greek and

Latin, poetry, oratory, history, and facility in the Tuscan Italian dialect. Insofar as the Italians of the Renaissance possessed a theory of individualism, a humanistic education defined as self-expression furthered that end. In other words, the culture itself gave meaning and purpose to the curriculum. But humanism and humanistic have other historical meanings deriving from Greco-Roman conceptions of *human* nature. The classical, pre-Italian definition of a humanistic education stressed the type more than the individual, the general rather than the specific, the qualities that all people have in common rather than special traits distinguishing one person from another. Curriculum does not necessarily enter into the definition, in that few subjects are truly inherently humanistic. A subject is humanistic if it throws light on the *human* condition. The burden today rests on the teacher to demonstrate the connection. Once demonstrated, humanistic and liberal education become virtually synonymous, for a knowledge of human nature is essential for a career in public life or for living in the world as a whole person.

Incidentally, the issue of education for public life or citizenship is once again arousing interest, partly in reaction to what has been called the "new narcissism" of American culture. See Morris Janowitz, *The Reconstruction of Patriotism: Education for Civic Consciousness* (Chicago, 1984), where national service is discussed and, for a feminist perspective, the writings of Carole Pateman of the University of Sydney. A forthcoming report of the Carnegie Foundation for the Advancement of Teaching will also be relevant.

20. The most ambitious and interesting core curriculum experiment that I know (having spent some time with its designers) is at St. Joseph's College, in Rensselaer, Indiana. It is described in Zelda F. Gamson, et al, *Liberating Education* (San Francisco and London, 1984), pp. 30–40. Public institutions, however, are not in a position to make similar expensive commitments, nor does their internal organization permit the same degree of faculty cooperation.

21. See the refreshing (and optimistic?) discussion of how traditional educational values survive *because* not *despite* the structure of the multiversity in Martin Trow, "'Elite Higher Education': An Endangered Species?" *Minerva* (Autumn 1976).

22. Riesman and Jencks, p. 510.

23. Not, I hope, to be mistaken for support of the "rap session." Discipline, structure, and authority are essential to all good teaching. My appeal is rather for a working understanding of the different ways in which single undergraduates learn, so that some element of tailoring is involved. The question of staffing resources inevitably enters, but a study team headed by Edward D. Eddy, Jr., *The College Influence on Student Character* (American Council on Education: Washington, D.C., 1959), p. 74, also concluded that education for character is not wholly a question of the size of an institution. They define character as action based on principles rather than on pressure or expediency (p. 2–3). The difficulty, however, has always been agreeing on the principles.

CHAPTER 4
SELECTIVITY AND EQUITY IN THE
PUBLIC RESEARCH UNIVERSITY
ALEXANDER W. ASTIN

Like other sectors of U.S. society, American higher education is organized hierarchically, with a few elite and widely known institutions at the top, a substantial middle class, and at the bottom a large number of institutions that are little known outside of their immediate communities. While the hierarchy within the private system evolved more or less by historical accident, the development of the public hierarchies within most of our states was to some extent part of a conscious plan. The public research university, of course, occupies the top position in these public hierarchies.

This stratified arrangement of institutions within the public sector is maintained and strengthened by the process of selective admissions. Because the research unversity ordinarily enjoys the highest prestige within the state, it tends to attract a disproportionate share of the best qualified applicants. Its greater attractiveness, in turn, permits the research university to·practice selective admissions, whereby access is limited primarily to those applicants with the best secondary school grades and the highest scores on standard admissions tests. This essay explores some of the consequences of selective admissions and the pursuit of "excellence" in the public university, with particular emphasis on how these practices affect educational opportunities for minority and low-income students.

DIFFERENTIAL OPPORTUNITIES IN THE PUBLIC
SECTOR

In most states the public system of higher education is three-tiered: one or two flagship universities occupy the top rung of the prestige ladder, the state colleges and universities (many of them former teachers colleges) occupy the middle rungs, and the community colleges occupy the bottom rungs. The prototype of this model is the state of California, whose master plan formally recognizes these three levels. Most other states have emulated the California model, with minor variations. In theory, all three tiers offer comparable opportunities for lower-division undergraduate education. In actuality, however, ample evidence suggests that the opportunities afforded by these various sectors are by no means equivalent.

Quality or "excellence" in American higher education has traditionally been defined in terms of either *reputation* or *resources*. That the research universities enjoy better reputations than the four-year or two-year colleges in the public sector is demonstrated by their ability to attract the best prepared high school graduates, who presumably have a free choice among institutions yet who overwhelmingly prefer the major state universities to the state colleges and community colleges (see below). Similarly, many of the major public universities—but virtually none of the other public institutions—consistently get high rankings in reputational surveys (Solomon and Astin, 1981).

A similar picture emerges when it comes to institutional resources. Public universities, for example, spend 40 percent more per student than the state colleges, which in turn spend about 10 percent more per student than the community colleges.[1] This skewed distribution is also apparent when we look at other institutional resources like per student library expenditures, endowment, and physical plant (Astin, 1982). Further, well-prepared students are themselves considered an important institutional "resource," and, as already mentioned, the public universities enroll a disproportionate share of such students.

Longitudinal research on student development (Astin, 1975, 1977; Chickering, 1974) shows that another potentially important institutional resource is the residential experience. That is, a student's chances of persisting to baccalaureate completion, as well as other aspects of his or her intellectual and personal development, are enhanced if the student lives in a campus residence hall during the freshman year. But this resource is also distributed unequally: In 1983–1984, close to three in four of the freshmen (73.2 percent) at public universities, two-thirds of those (67.4 percent) at public four-year colleges, but only one in four of the freshmen (24.2 percent) at community colleges lived in campus residence halls. Moreover, the most selective public universities (mean SAT verbal + mathematical scores of entering freshmen $\geq$ 1100) had the highest proportion of freshmen living in residence halls: 85.9 percent, a figure comparable to the 86.9 percent for private universities (Astin, Green, Korn, and Maier, 1983).

Longitudinal studies (Astin, 1975, 1977, 1982) have also shown that freshmen entering community colleges have a poorer chance of eventually completing the bachelor's degree than do freshmen of comparable ability, motivation, and social background entering public universities. These differential outcomes are attributable only in part to the greater availability of residential facilities at the public university.

A less tangible but equally important benefit of attending a major public university is that these institutions frequently serve as conduits to positions of power and influence within state government and private industry. In short, access to a state's major public university promises career benefits not generally available to students attending other public institutions within the state.

In summary, the opportunities offered by institutions at different tiers in the nation's public systems of higher education are by no means comparable. Students who can gain admission to the major public research universities generally have access to better resources and greater career opportunities than do students who attend the four-year or community colleges.

THE CURRENT ENROLLMENT PICTURE

Since concern over educational "equity" or "equality of opportunity" is usually focused on students who are either economically or culturally disadvantaged, this discussion of enrollment patterns is confined to low-income and minority students. Table 1 shows seventeen-year trends in the enrollment of low-income college freshmen, arbitrarily defined as those from the lowest quintile of all entering freshmen, in terms of parental income. Thus, a figure of more than 20 percent represents an overenrollment of low-income students, whereas a figure of less than 20 percent represents underenrollment. Note that the public universities have consistently underenrolled low-income students and that the degree of underenrollment increased considerably between 1966 and 1973. Moreover, the degree of underenrollment was greatest in the most selective public universities, where low-income students accounted for only 8.2 percent of 1983 freshmen enrollments. As a matter of fact, the number of low-income students in these elite public universities would have to be more than doubled to achieve proportionate representation.

Table 2 shows the distribution of various racial/ethnic groups among types of institutions. The first column ("all students") provides the yardstick for determining the over- or underenrollment of each group. Of par-

Table 1
Trends in Enrollments of Low-Income Freshmen, 1966–1983, by Institutional Type
(public sector only)

Type of Public Institution	Percentage of Entering Freshmen from Lowest Quintile in Parental Income		
	1966	1973	1983
Two-year colleges	23.6	26.7	22.2
Four-year colleges	28.4	18.8	19.7
Universities	16.8	11.3	12.0
(Most selective universities) *	(NA)	(9.9)	(8.2)
All institutions (public and private)	20.0	20.0	20.0

Source: *The American Freshman* (Los Angeles: Cooperative Institutional Research Program, Higher Education Research Institute, University of California, Los Angeles).
* Mean SAT Verbal and Math of 1100 or higher (24 institutions).

Table 2
Distribution of Various Racial/Ethnic Groups, by Institutional Type
(in percentages)

Type of Institution	All Students	Whites	Blacks	Hispanics	Asians	American Indians
Private						
Two-year college	1.6	1.5	2.9	2.3	0.5	1.5
Four-year college	13.6	13.8	13.1	15.3	8.1	6.1
University	5.9	6.2	4.2	3.5	6.8	2.3
Public						
Two-year college	36.5	35.1	40.7	46.8	43.8	53.9
Four-year college	24.3	23.9	29.6	21.3	23.3	23.5
University	18.0	19.5	9.5	10.8	17.5	12.7
TOTAL	100.0	100.0	100.0	100.0	100.0	100.0

Source: Higher Education General Information Survey, fall 1982.

ticular interest here are the three groups that are historically the most severely disadvantaged in American society: blacks, hispanics, and American Indians. All three groups—but especially blacks—are severely underrepresented in the public universities. To achieve proportionate representation, the number of blacks would have to be more than doubled, the number of Hispanics would have to be increased by more than 80 percent, and the number of American Indians would have to be increased by more than 60 percent. Note that "proportionate" in this context refers solely to the distribution of these groups *within* the higher education system. Since all three of these racial/ethnic minorities are substantially underrepresented in higher education as a whole relative to their proportions in the population, the figures in table 2 actually provide a very conservative estimate of the degree of underrepresentation.

Once again, the degree of underrepresentation is greatest in the twenty-four most selective public universities. These institutions enroll 4.8 percent of all college students in the United States, but only the following percentages of minorities: blacks, 2.1; Hispanics, 2.5; and American Indians, 2.3. It is also worth noting that Asians, who are slightly underrepresented in all public universities (see table 2), are overrepresented by nearly 100 percent in the most selective public universities (these institutions enroll 9.3 percent of the Asians, compared to only 4.8 percent of all students).

If minority and low-income students are underrepresented in the public universities, then they must be overrepresented in other types of institutions. As tables 1 and 2 make clear, the representation of these groups in the public four-year colleges is roughly proportional to the representation of all students. But both minority and low-income students are overrepresented in the community colleges.

The severe underrepresentation of blacks, Hispanics, and American Indians in the nation's major public research universities was underscored in a recent report of the findings to emerge from a study of the status of minorities in higher education (Astin, 1982). Utilizing the typology of universities developed by the Carnegie Commission on Higher Education (1973), the Commission on the Higher Education of Minorities identified the "flagship" public university in each state. If more than one university in a state received the highest Carnegie classification, all such institutions were used. Most states had only one flagship university, and only one (California) had more than two.

The representation of blacks, Hispanics, and American Indians in each flagship university was determined by comparing the institution's undergraduate minority enrollment with the total minority enrollment in all colleges and universities within the state. Of the sixty-five flagship universities, fifty-six had significant underenrollments of blacks, forty-eight had significant Hispanic underenrollments, and forty-six had significant underenrollments of American Indians. Moreover, the degree of underenrollment was greatest in those states with the largest minority populations. To attain proportionate representation of the underrepresented minorities in the flagship universities in New York, Texas, California, and most of the southern states, the numbers would have to be increased by between 200 and 600 percent.

In summary, these observations show that the major public universities in most states are not as accessible to low-income and minority students as are the public four-year colleges and, more particularly, the community colleges.

INSTITUTIONAL INTERESTS AND THE PUBLIC INTEREST

Most institutions in the American higher education system have strong incentives to pursue "excellence." As has already been suggested, this effort normally takes two forms: the enhancement of *reputation* and the acquisition of *resources*, the three most important of which are money, bright students, and distinguished faculty. Resources and reputation are, of course, mutually reinforcing; that is, an institution can enhance its reputation by attracting top scholars and large research grants and, at the same time, an institution with a good reputation can attract more scholars, students, and money.

That a number of our public universities have been highly successful in enhancing their reputations is indicated by the findings from a recent National Academy of Sciences survey of the quality of graduate programs. When we compare these findings to the results of two similar surveys conducted in earlier years by the American Council on Education, we find that the reputations of graduate programs in many public universities have been on the upswing in recent years. Other studies suggest that the sheer size of many public universities has contributed to this upswing and that the formula for enhancing reputation is relatively simple: recruit as many nationally visible scholars as possible (Drew and Karpf, 1981).

The recruitment of high-achieving students is also given high priority by almost all of the major public research universities. This "resource" is valued not only because it enhances the reputation of the university, but also because faculty members tend to prefer able students, finding them easier to identify and to view as potential disciples. Thus, the drive to attract prestigious research scholars probably intensifies the quest for the best prepared students. Conversely, faculty support and enthusiasm for recruiting and teaching underprepared students becomes more difficult to generate.

But what of the public university's broader mandate? To what extent is the pursuit of institutional self-interest through resource acquisition and reputation enhancement compatible with the public university's mission of serving the public interest? While this question is obviously too complex to explore in detail, let us consider two important aspects of the university's responsibility to the public it serves: the education of undergraduates and the expansion of opportunities for minority and low-income students.

It is probably unrealistic to set precise goals with respect to the numbers or percentages of minority and low-income students that the public university should enroll. While it might be argued that the research universities are "not equipped" to educate underprepared students, most universities have explicitly acknowledged their responsibilities in this area by introducing special admissions programs, remedial and support services for underprepared students, and the like. The real issue seems to be the *numbers* of such students that the university is willing to take in. In this connection, it should be noted that several major research universities in the Midwest have a long-standing policy of open admissions. At the same time, virtually every state has acknowledged its commitment to expanding opportunities by providing all their high school graduates with access to *some* type of public institution. As the data in table 2 indicate, however, these "opportunities" tend to be confined to the community colleges and, to a lesser extent, the state colleges.

It seems clear that the public research university's interest in expanding educational opportunities to disadvantaged groups directly conflicts with its quest for "excellence" (as conventionally defined). Judging from the data in table 2, the quest for excellence has been given much higher priority. As a result, in most states *low-income and minority students do not have equal access to the best educational opportunities.*

And what of the university's obligation to provide a quality educational experience for its undergraduates? While the old research-versus-teaching issue will not be debated here, it is pertinent to observe that the drive to recruit top scholars may well conflict with the desire to strengthen undergraduate education. Most scholars are more committed to their research and to their discplines than to teaching, as is evidenced by the fact that a light teaching load is one of the "perks" often promised to scholars whom the university is trying to recruit. Indeed, the use of the term "load" in connection with teaching epitomizes a common view of teaching within the university. One never speaks of a "research load."

Table 3
Student Satisfaction with Various Aspects of the Undergraduate Experience
(1981 freshmen questioned in 1983)

	Percentage "Satisfied" or "Very Satisfied" at		
Item	Public Universities	Private Universities	All Institutions
Library facilities	90	74	77
Campus social life	77	58	67
Courses in major	80	87	81
Overall quality of instruction	72	80	76
Social science courses	68	78	67
Humanities courses	66	75	67
Science and math courses	61	69	66
Opportunities to discuss coursework and assignments outside of class with professors	63	81	74
Amount of contact with faculty and administrators	43	60	60
Overall relationship with faculty and administrators	44	60	60

Source: Cooperative Institutional Research Program, Higher Education Research Institute.

But is there any hard evidence to show that the quality of the under-graduate environment has been adversely affected by the strong research emphasis of the public university? Some clues come from a recent survey, conducted by the Higher Education Research Institute, of a nationally representative sample of undergraduates who entered college as full-time freshmen in the fall of 1981 and were followed up two years later in 1983. Among other things, survey respondents were asked to indicate their satisfaction with various aspects of the undergraduate experience and to report on their activities as undergraduates.

Table 3 compares the responses of three groups—public university students, private university students, and all students—to the satisfaction items; only those items where the public university students differed significantly from one or both of the other two groups are shown. Note that students in the public universities tended to be more satisfied with library facilities and with campus social life. But they were less satisfied than were private university students with the overall quality of instruction and with courses in the social sciences, humanities, sciences, and in their major fields. The largest discrepancies, however, related to relationships with professors: students in the public universities were significantly less satisfied with their opportunities to discuss coursework with professors outside of class, with the amount of contact they had with faculty and administrators, and with their overall relationships with faculty and administrators. These discrepancies were substantial (around 20 percentage points), regardless of whether they were being compared with private university students or with all students. (Note that the "all institutions" comparisons tend to minimize differences, since public universities are included in this category.)

These findings are confirmed by several other items from the follow-up survey. Thus, students in public universities were considerably less likely than those in private universities to participate in honors programs (19 versus 33 percent), to pursue independent research projects (14 versus 22 percent), and to be guests in the home of professors (19 versus 45 percent).

The significant point here is that the private universities, which also emphasize research and actively recruit top scholars, nonetheless manage to generate considerably more student-faculty interaction than the public universities. Neglect of undergraduates, it would seem, is not a *necessary* consequence of a heavy research emphasis. In fact, there are probably some public universities where informal contact between faculty and students is common and some private universities where such interactions are rare. A study of these exceptions to the general rule would seem to be a useful project for scholars of higher education.

Has the public university's quest for excellence in graduate education and research affected its attractiveness to prospective undergraduate students? Perhaps the best way to answer this question is to look at recent trends in the selectivity of the public universities. For this purpose, "selectivity" is defined as the mean score of entering freshmen on nationally standardized college admissions tests (SAT or ACT converted to SAT equivalents). Table 4 shows trends from 1972 to 1982. All types of institutions declined in selectivity during this period—no doubt a reflection of the widely discussed drop in the test scores of entering freshmen—although it should be noted that a substantial amount of the decline actually occurred before 1972. In any case, public universities suffered the largest declines (an average of 42 points), while private universities experienced the smallest declines (an average of only 18 points). Moreover, the decline in selectivity was sharpest at the most selective public institutions (66 points, compared with 30 points at the least selective public institutions). No such differences were found for private universities at different selectivity levels.

Table 4
Changes in Selectivity, 1972–1982

		Mean Scores of Entering Freshmen on SAT* in			
Institutional Type	N	1972	1977	1982	Change between 1972 and 1982
All institutions	1,276	964	932	931	−33
Public 4-year colleges	283	927	884	891	−36
Private universities	70	1,138	1,119	1,120	−18
Public universities:					
Total	104	1,017	983	975	−42
Most selective	22	1,143	1,097	1,077	−66
Moderately selective	36	1,029	997	986	−43
Least selective	46	948	918	918	−30

Source: Cooperative Institutional Research Program.
*ACT scores have been converted to SAT equivalents (see Astin, Christian, and Henson, 1979).

Are these differences attributable to differential growth rates? Are the public universities experiencing greater declines in selectivity because they are admitting more students? The facts suggest not. Indeed, between 1973 and 1983, the number of full-time freshmen enrolling in public universities declined slightly (by less than 1 percent), whereas the enrollments of full-time freshmen increased by 7 percent in private universities and by 19 percent in public four-year colleges (Astin, King, Light, and Richardson, 1973; Astin, Green, Korn, and Maier, 1983).

What accounts for the greater declines in selectivity at the public universities, especially the most selective public universities? Could it be that the best qualified high school graduates are increasingly attracted to private institutions because they feel they will get a better undergraduate education there? The largest public research university is often stereotyped as an institution where students are treated like "numbers in a book," and the data in table 3 seem to support this stereotype. The single-minded quest for top research talent may have diverted the public university from its mission of providing a high-quality undergraduate educational experience. Perhaps it is time to redress the balance between these two somewhat conflicting drives.

Given that most major public universities are in the business of remediating the academic deficiencies of many of their entering freshmen, the time is ripe for a renewal of a commitment to expanding educational opportunities. As long as these institutions are already involved in developmental education, they should enlarge their activities in this area, in the interest of recruiting and retaining a larger portion of the low-income and minority students in their states.

The institution's self-interest (the pursuit of traditional "excellence") would seem to be at variance with its larger obligations to provide high quality undergraduate education and to expand educational opportunity. Of course, some people might argue that the pursuit of excellence is an equally important "public obligation," but this argument ignores the finite nature of faculty and student talent. In other words, looking at American higher education from a systems perspective rather than an institutional perspective, one must recognize that the number of top scholars and highly able students is limited; there just aren't enough to go around. The institution that invests its energies in the recruitment of such faculty and student talent may gain a greater share of the talent, but its efforts do nothing to increase the size of the total pool. Thus, a public university that succeeds in attracting a top scholar or a high-achieving student away from another institution may be furthering its own self-interest, but it is not necessarily serving the public interest. As a matter of fact, it would be an interesting exercise to estimate the total amount of institutional resources committed to the recruitment of top faculty and top students. From a systems perspective, most of these resources are being wasted, since they serve only to redistribute faculty and student talent, not to improve the overall quality of the higher education system.

ATTITUDES TOWARD EDUCATION

Over the past two decades, the academic skills of entering college freshmen have declined, arousing widespread public concern and leading many experts to question the quality of education being offered in the nation's secondary schools. Such was the focus of *A Nation at Risk*, the recent report of the National Commission on Excellence in Education. As table 4 makes clear, public universities—and especially the most elite public universities—should be particularly concerned with diagnosing and remedying the causes of the decline. While many explanations for this sad state of affairs have been proposed, it stands to reason that the quality of the education provided by the lower schools depends in large part on the quality of the teachers and administrators who staff these schools.

Abundant evidence shows that undergraduates aspiring to careers in teaching tend to be poorly prepared. Indeed, among the current crop of college freshmen, those naming elementary or secondary school teaching

Table 5
Trends in Student Interest in Teaching Careers,
1966–1983

Type of Institution	Percentage of Entering Freshmen Choosing Careers in Elementary or Secondary Teaching		
	1966	1973	1983
Public two-year colleges	17.0	9.9	3.9
Public four-year colleges	38.6	21.7	7.9
Public universities	17.3	10.6	3.2
(Most selective public universities)*	(NA)	(6.9)	(2.5)
All institutions	21.7	12.7	5.1

Source: The American Freshman (Los Angeles: Cooperative Institutional Research Program, Higher Education Research Institute, University of California, Los Angeles).
* Mean SAT Verbal and Math of 1100 or higher (24 institutions).

as their probable career made poorer grades in high school than those naming virtually any other career field. Data from the National Center for Education Statistics suggest that the academic preparation of schoolteachers has always been relatively poor and that it has declined even further in recent years. Moreover, longitudinal follow-ups indicate that the graduates who actually enter teaching careers do not differ significantly in talent from the freshmen who aspire to teaching careers (Astin, 1977; Astin and Panos, 1969). A little publicized corollary of these findings is that student interest in teaching careers has declined sharply. As table 5 shows, the proportion of entering freshmen who named elementary or secondary teaching as their probable career dropped from 22 percent in 1966, to 13 percent in 1973, to only 5 percent in 1983, a 76 percent decline in the system as a whole over the last seventeen years. And the sharpest decline (82 percent) has occurred in the public universities: whereas nearly one in six freshmen entering public universities aspired to teaching careers in 1966, the figure had dropped to fewer than one in *thirty* (3.2 percent) in 1983. In the most selective public universities, the figure was only one in *forty* (2.5 percent).

Moreover, most academicians have extremely negative attitudes toward teacher education and toward research in education. Within the major public universities, schools of education are accorded very low status and may even be viewed as an embarrassment. Indeed, the faculty of the University of California at Berkeley recently tried to eliminate the Education School altogether but was overruled by the administration. This academic snobbery operates within specific disciplines as well as within institutions as a whole: in the field of psychology, for example, educational and school psychologists are looked down upon by those in other specialties.

Examples of this negative attitude abound. Just twenty-five years ago, there were more than two hundred teachers colleges in the United States; today there are practically none. Most of them have become "state universities" that devote most of their energies to emulating the flagship and other major research universities. Whether intended or not, the message is clear: institutions devoted exclusively or even primarily to the training of teachers are somehow unworthy and should be replaced by more "respectable" educational institutions.

This denigration of the art and profession of teaching takes many subtle forms. In the training of future college professors, for example, the development of research and scholarly skills is given heavy emphasis, but little or no attention is paid to the development of pedagogical skills. Academicians apparently believe that no particular training or preparation is required to produce a good teacher; anyone who has mastered the subject matter can teach well. Moreover, once hired, the new faculty member's advancement to tenure depends chiefly on his or her scholarly record; little or no weight is attached to classroom performance when personnel decisions are made.

Despite their recent declines in selectivity, the research universities are still the most successful of the public institutions in attracting well-prepared students. Thus, the fact that so few of their students aspire to teaching careers does not bode well for the future of public school teaching. Exacerbating this problem, many of the major public research universities do not permit undergraduates to major in education.

ALTERNATIVES TO TRADITIONAL ADMISSIONS PRACTICES

The major obstacle to expanding opportunities for minority and low-income students in the public research universities is the use of standardized tests and high school grade averages in the admissions process. Since American Indians, Hispanics, and blacks are at a particular disadvantage in competing for admission on the basis of such measures, their representation in the research universities will probably not increase substantially as long as these selection devices continue to be used. Alternatives such as open admissions and lotteries have been discussed extensively in the literature and will not be considered further here.

Although the *Bakke* decision prohibits the use of numerical quotas in admissions, it provides that *some* weight can be given to race. Nevertheless, many institutions are reluctant to utilize such criteria, on the grounds that to do so would constitute a kind of racism. One interesting alternative is to give students "credit" for being disadvantaged. How such a system might work was demonstrated in a recent simulation study (Astin, 1978) in which a "disadvantagement index" was utilized to analyze the applications of a national sample of more than 100,000 prospective college students. The purpose of the study was to determine what proportions of various ethnic groups would be selected for admission under varying conditions. The "disadvantagement index," which consisted of a combination of three variables (father's educational level, mother's educational level, family income), was scored so that the most disadvantaged students received the highest scores. The use of such an index assumes that affluent parents are in a better position to provide their children with the resources that promote intellectual development: space for studying, books, tutors and other special remedial assistance, and so forth. Further, an affluent family is likely to live in a community where the local high schools are relatively rigorous.

Eight different admissions models—using various combinations of test scores, grades, and disadvantagement—were used. The major findings were as follows:

1. Minorities benefit substantially from the use of a disadvantagement index, but such an index must be given substantial weight to overcome the handicap imposed by test scores and grades.

2. Tests represent a much greater admissions obstacle for minority students (blacks in particular) than grades do. Consequently, the use of a disadvantagement index benefits minority students more if it is combined with grades alone rather than with grades and test scores.

3. The handicap resulting from the use of test scores and grades becomes greater as the selection ratio increases. For example, a simple combination of test scores and grades produces an 80 percent underrepresentation of blacks when the selection ratio is one in four, but only a 65 percent underrepresentation when the selection ratio is one in two.

One especially appealing feature of this approach is that it is "color blind" and gives explicit attention to educational and economic disadvantagement. Thus, minorities who come from educated and affluent families do not benefit unfairly, and nonminority students who come from disadvantaged families are equally compensated for their disadvantagement.

Another alternative to traditional hierarchical admissions policies relates to the structure of public systems. The California model, with its three-tiered system, is not necessarily the only or even the best model. Some states (for example, Pennsylvania and Kentucky) have developed public university systems that, in effect, combine the community college model and the research university model by means of two-year branch campuses that offer the first two undergraduate years. A student attending one of these branch campuses is admitted to the university for upper-division work without having to go through the usual application and transfer paperwork. Although these systems may degenerate into an implicit hierarchy (through comparisons of the branch campus with the main campus, for example), they appear to represent some advance over more rigidly stratified systems.

CONCLUSION

In this essay I have attempted to address the issues of selectivity, diversity, and equity as they relate to the current situation confronting our major public universities. The analysis suggests the following general conclusions:

1. Most public systems of higher education are organized in hierarchical fashion, with the major research universities occupying the top position in the hierarchy. Considerable evidence suggests that the educational opportunities offered by the four-year colleges and community colleges are not comparable in quality to the opportunities offered by the public universities.

2. Blacks, Hispanics, American Indians, and low-income students are severely underrepresented among the undergraduates at most public universities, especially the "flagship" universities in each state, but overrepresented in the community colleges. This skewed distribution suggests that most states are not now providing their minority and poor students with equal educational opportunity.

3. The major public research university's obsessive pursuit of "excellence" conflicts with its efforts to expand educational opportunities. In particular, the aggressive recruitment of eminent scholars and high-achieving students makes it difficult to accommodate larger numbers of minority and low-income students, many of whom are poorly prepared academically.

4. The public university's strong emphasis on graduate education and research may have contributed to a decline in the quality and quantity of contact between faculty and students. Paradoxically, it may also have hampered the institution's ability to attract the best prepared students.

5. At many public research universities, the art of teaching and the field of education are denigrated. Over the past few decades, this negative attitude may have contributed to the decline in the quality of secondary education in the United States. Today's poorly prepared freshmen, in other words, may be the "chickens coming home to roost."

6. Opportunities to remedy some of these problems are available to most public universities. Among the possible alternatives are revised admissions practices, alterations in the public institutional structure within the state, a renewal of interest in education research, and a strengthened commitment to the preparation of public school teachers.

NOTE

1. To compensate for the greater costs of graduate and professional education, these per-student figures were calculated so that each graduate or professional student was counted as three FTE undergraduate students, and each part-time graduate or professional student was counted as .333 FET undergraduates.

REFERENCES

Astin, A. W. *Four Critical Years.* San Francisco: Jossey-Bass, 1977.
———. *Minorities in American Higher Education.* San Francisco: Jossey-Bass, 1982.
———. *Preventing Students From Dropping Out.* San Francisco: Jossey-Bass, 1975.
———. "Quantifying Disadvantagement." In A. W. Astin, B. Fuller, and K. C. Green, eds. *Admitting and Assisting Students After Bakke.* New Directions for Higher Education, No. 23. San Francisco: Jossey-Bass, 1978.
Astin, A. W. & Panos, R. J. *The Educational and Vocational Development of College Students.* Washington: American Council on Education, 1969.
Astin, A. W., Green, K. C., Korn, W., and Maier, M. J. *The American Freshman: National Norms for Fall 1983.* Los Angeles: University of California, Higher Education Research Institute, 1983.
Astin, A. W., King, M. K., Light, J. M., & Richardson, G. *The American Freshman: National Norms for Fall 1973.* Los Angeles: University of California, Higher Education Research Institute, 1973.

Carnegie Commission on Higher Education. *A Classification of Institutions of Higher Education*. Berkeley, California: Carnegie Commission on Higher Education, 1973.

Chickering, A. W. *Commuting Versus Resident Students: Overcoming Educational Inequities of Living Off Campus*. San Francisco: Jossey-Bass, 1974.

Drew, D. E., and Karpf, R. "Ranking Academic Departments: Empirical Findings and a Theoretical Perspective." *Research in Higher Education*, 14: 4 (1981) 305–319.

National Commission on Excellence in Education. *A Nation at Risk: The Imperative for Educational Reform: A Report to the Nation and the Secretary of Education*. Washington: U.S. Government Printing Office, 1983.

Solomon, L., and Astin, A. W. "Are Reputational Ratings Needed to Measure Quality?" *Change*, October 1981.

CHAPTER 5
THE PUBLIC SERVICE ROLE OF THE STATE UNIVERSITY IN A CHANGING WORLD

RONALD W. ROSKENS

Since their inception more than a century ago, state universities have incorporated public service as an essential and integral element of their missions. Some university entities, such as the cooperative extension services, have had public service as their primary emphasis. Others have engaged in such activities on a less regular and less visible basis. Whatever the form or content, however, the important point is that public service is a responsibility that permeates every segment of every institution. In this context, particularlized emphases upon specific programs, while helpful, would obscure the central point: that every individual within the university community can and must strive to integrate public service responsibilities into their work.

Through their public service commitments, state universities have forged a continuing, vital partnership with the citizens of the states that support them. The structural characteristics of this cooperative effort vary. In some states there is a single state university with one or more campuses, while others support both a land-grant institution and one or more state universities. The common denominator, however, is the institutional commitment to the principle that the campus is not limited to a group of buildings in one or another location; the university campus is, in fact, the entire state.

Public universities are, and undoubtedly will remain, in the midst of the economic and social development of their states. They provide a forum for the exploration and presentation of options, and a focal point for the development of the basic literature, ideas, data, and technology germane to these options. Accordingly, the traditional role of the university as a neutral ground where the clash of ideas is unfettered assumes significant dimensions within a state. Indeed, it may well be only at or through the university that issues of the utmost importance can receive thorough and dispassionate treatment.

In our dynamic, evolving society new trends are continuously emerging. The implications of these changes and trends for the state university warrant concerted attention. The focus of this particular examination is on that spectrum of programs that may be characterized as public service oriented. Nevertheless, any effort to conceptualize the role of a state university from that single perspective risks defining such institutions too narrowly.

Research provides the bedrock upon which universities base the preponderance of their activities. As the frontiers of knowledge become more complex, and the problems to be solved more difficult, all universities must devote more resources to both basic and applied research. At the same time, public universities must continue to design research programs geared to the needs of the citizens who sustain them. Regardless of the manner in which public service obligations are conceptualized or executed, that seminal responsibility of the land-grant institution will not change.

A correlative obligation inheres within the graduate education component of state universities. If these institutions are to assume an even greater leadership role as society approaches the year 2000, they must insure that their graduate programs are healthy. Greater flexibility must be developed in graduate—and for that matter undergraduate—educational programs. At the same time, universities must avoid any concomitant loss of academic depth. For example, critical attention must be directed at the institutional propensity to maintain strict boundaries between disciplines, and interdisciplinary approaches must be implemented to solve complex problems.

State universities provide the lodestar from which concerned citizens structure and direct the social consciousness that will illumine their actions as citizens. The common denominator for university programs must be an intense awareness of the symbiotic relationship between the community and the university. Too often, postsecondary institutions seem unaware—or choose to ignore—the correlation between social enrichment and support for higher education. Public universities are rightly aware of their responsibilities to their students and faculties. They are, unfortunately, less vigilant in the area of service to those citizens who want simply to enhance their lives. Yet these same citizens are the ones to whom public universities turn for the tax dollars required to sustain and enhance university programs. Given the need to forge direct and continuing bonds with these individuals, public service efforts should, accordingly, become a high priority.

THE UNIVERSITY AS A PUBLIC ENTERPRISE

Fortunately, land-grant institutions have developed a lasting partnership with society. They represent the realization of a uniquely American concept first expressed by those New England colonists who observed in 1642 that "one of the things . . . we longed for, and looked after, was to advance learning and perpetuate it to posterity." The colonists' hope sustained their own educational institutions and became reality for the entire nation some two centuries later with passage of the Morrill Act. This landmark legislation directed the states to establish and endow "at least one college where the leading object shall be, without excluding other scientific and classical studies, and including military tactics, to teach such branches of learning as are related to agriculture and mechanical arts, in order to promote the liberal and practical education of industrial classes in the several pursuits and professions of life."

Any exploration of the role of the public service component of post-secondary education must acknowledge that neither the colonists' concept nor the Morrill Act's mandate to the states and their land-grant universities has changed. However, the methods, the breadth of responsibilities, and direction may have been altered—in some cases drastically. Much of this has been dictated by certain pervasive social, economic, and cultural trends in the United States and the world. Further changes are undoubtedly forthcoming. While the precise implications of those trends that will influence higher education in the near future have not yet been clearly defined, it is imperative that those associated with state universities come quickly to terms with them. This responsibility is particularly acute in the realm of public service, which provides the most direct and continuous source of university interaction with our evolving society.

Any attempt to enumerate the dynamics of the future is inherently speculative. Nevertheless, the following list, while not exhaustive, is both representative and instructive.

1. *America is becoming a service oriented economy, but there will be continuing emphasis on basic production. Communications is and will continue to be the most important emerging industry under a broad service umbrella.*

The telecommunications revolution has become a reality for higher education and for the off-campus clientele that the state university serves. Basic telecommunications components are becoming commonplace on campuses, and are increasingly finding their way into people's homes. This is altering society's approach to even the most basic and common forms of communication and carries substantial implications for post-secondary education.

Telecommunications and related technologies will be employed increasingly as a delivery system to satisfy a desire for education at times and locations convenient to the university's clientele. As important as these new tools are, however, it is doubtful that they can drive the educational enterprise. Rather, available technologies must be placed at the service of institutions for postsecondary education and adapted to their basic requirements and mission. Moreover, regardless of the manner in which technology is utilized, it will be essential for institutions to preserve the direct citizen contacts that have been the core of public service efforts. Accordingly, institutions must, even as they integrate technology into their programs, devise creative ways to maintain personal relationships with students and clients.

2. *Significant demographic changes will include an increasing percentage of older citizens and a concomitant decrease in the percentage of younger people. There will be some increase in total population. Mobility will continue at a rate slightly lower than during the last decade.*

The gradual aging and increasing movement of citizens will require greater commitment to adult education. This will, of course, have a pervasive impact upon state universities. Each component of the university will need to address the new challenges posed by the diverse needs of an older population and clientele. This will be particularly true in university public service programs.

Recent cutbacks in funding, particularly at the federal level, have sharply reduced the range of social services provided by public agencies. State universities cannot, and *should* not, be expected to fill these gaps. Nevertheless, university public service efforts can provide invaluable supplementary assistance. Accordingly, public institutions should be cognizant of the unique needs of older Americans and both develop new service efforts and modify current ones to assist this population.

3. *There will be greater interest in the arts as people seek to improve the quality of life.*

One of the most important, yet least discussed, areas within which public universities have made substantial service contributions is the arts. Public universities have a long and distinguished record of support for the arts. Recent surveys indicate that 93 percent of those polled said availability of the arts is important to the quality of life in their community,

86 percent want arts events available everywhere, and more than 60 percent regularly attend arts events. Among those with no arts facility nearby, the majority said they would attend events if any were available. Moreover, those surveyed indicated that theirs was an active support, with the majority also favoring increased government funding of the arts.

In many areas of the nation, the state university has been historically, and remains today, the only agency capable of presenting arts programs. The parameters of university resources are as diverse as the arts themselves, subsuming personnel and facilities, the presentation of performances and exhibitions, and the provision of technical support required for local productions. These efforts are appropriate and should be expanded. As tax-supported institutions, state universities have a responsibility to the state and its communities to bring the arts and artists to the people. State universities must, therefore, place a higher priority on the arts and seek actively to increase public and private support. This emphasis is of critical importance, for in a very real sense it is at these institutions that the preservation, expansion, and private enhancement in the arts will occur.

4. *More leisure time will be available to most Americans. They will want to make constructive use of it.*

Individuals from all walks of life have more time for leisure activities. As a result, people expect and will actively seek more education and information not directly associated with their careers. Americans want to improve their quality of life intellectually, physically, and psychologically. Individuals, both in and out of the work force, are intensely interested in diet, nutrition, exercise, and other activities that promote wellness. Older citizens who found too little time for the humanities while working are now eager to enmesh themselves in the arts, history, philosophy, and political science. There will be more emphasis on consumer education, and almost all citizens will at some point seek assistance in understanding the wide array of options available as they make decisions about personal finances.

5. *Americans will become increasingly aware of and influenced by the fact that they live in an emerging world community. Growth of international trade and transportation will continue.*

Ours is an increasingly interactive world, and technological evolution has effectively condensed the globe. State universities have been and remain the primary technical assistance and research resource within this nation. Accordingly, it is necessary and appopriate that these universities actively address the international implications of their missions of education, research, and service.

International emphases have, in fact, been an integral and significant dimension within programs dedicated to each of the three traditional roles of the state university. This record needs to be examined and future efforts expanded. In this regard, it is important to note that one of the principal impediments to international efforts is rapidly being eroded: where there was once indifference or even hostility, citizens are now aware of the interactive and synergistic nature of international linkages. Public understanding of the importance of international efforts will, in turn, generate not simply support where previously none was forthcoming, but new pressures to initiate or expand such efforts.

6. *Concerns about the environment will continue, if not accelerate.*

The harsh realities imposed by decades of indifference and misuse have forced an awareness of the damage that our intensely industrial society has wrought upon our environment. What were once regarded as the limited concerns of naturalists and outdoorsmen have now become the essential agenda for a nation besieged by pollution, acid rain, and the depletion of vital natural resouces.

University research and service programs are central to the solution of problems stemming from a shrinking land base and diminishing supplies of traditional natural resources. The public will look to the state university to place increasing research emphasis on handling industrial waste and pollution of air and water. Traffic problems and noise pollution, affecting both agricultural and industrial workers, will demand more attention. And the continued viability and vitality of American agriculture between now and the end of the century will depend to a great extent on state university development and application of effective management techniques for our land and water resources. Research and service efforts in this area are more than a fad; they are the essential keys to national survival.

In addition, as the ratio of space to people decreases, relationships among people become more crucial. The increasing complexity of life has heightened people's concern about the quality of society. Because of the many areas of unique expertise represented within its faculty and staff, the state university has both an opportunity and a responsibility to address social and physical environmental concerns in urban and cultural areas. This expertise can be drawn upon to study, to teach, and to provide direct service to citizens who want to improve their environment.

7. *The cost and availability of energy will affect the national and world economy in the year 2000 even more than it does today.*

Universities, through intensive research efforts, have striven to develop more efficient methods of energy utilization in the face of the diminishing supplies of natural fuels. In the long run, however, crash efforts to increase productivity of petroleum and other fuels will not permanently solve the problem of finite resources. As costs increase, perhaps to one and one-half times the present level by the year 2000, state universities will be searching for new resources and for more efficient uses of current energy products. Such efficiencies must be realized, for example, in irrigation, fertilizer, field operations, and food processing. At the same time, there is a concomitant need to examine uses of energy in the home, business, transportation, industry, and government, and subsequently to increase efficiency of use at the consumer level. Service functions in the realm of energy conservation and fuel development and utilization will assume many forms, all of them vital. In addition, state universities have a responsibility to provide and interpret options for energy regulations and government policy, and to suggest legislation dealing with alternative energy development.

IMPLICATIONS FOR THE STATE UNIVERSITY

Public universities have continued to grow because they are close to the people and responsive to their needs. They have become focal points in all of the states because of their unique blend of instruction, research, social, and cultural programs. Citizens of all of the states derive considerable satisfaction from the presence and accomplishments of their state universities. This support is by no means confined to alumni. It is important to understand that countless individuals who have not attended these institutions count them as their own.

Public university research efforts represent only an essential first step in the process by which we seek a better world. The relationship between research and service is symbiotic and synergistic. As important as new research discoveries will be, they can become widely effective *only* if the university is in a position to offer assistance in the application of new technologies and methods at the consumer level.

It is, however, not enough to state simply that state universities must continue or enhance their research and service efforts. Nor will an ability to discern and respond to new challenges and trends suffice. Rather, public universities must conceptualize their responsibilities both in terms of the particular requirements of their traditional obligations and the evolving dynamics of the entire postsecondary enterprise.

In doing so institutions should not be content simply to conduct a survey or develop a plan for future service roles and responsibilities, no matter how comprehensive or visionary. Continuous reevaluation and rededication will be required to insure that outreach programs remain or become available to all citizens. Increasingly, the campus of the state university *must* be the entire state. All citizens deserve equal attention from the university in areas as diverse as the arts, cultural enrichment, recreation, technical assistance, and direct patient care. Nor will it be a sufficient precondition to merely identify and respond to the various trends identified. Serious internal management questions remain for state universities that seek to address the needs of a dynamic society.

Obviously, any broadening and strengthening of public service offerings may unavoidably strain already overextended resources. Substantial policy questions are a necessary corollary. Who will allocate resources for teaching, research, and public service programs? What kinds of guidelines should be devised to dispense them fairly? To what extent should citizens—taxpayers—support public service activities? To what extent should the user pay for services? The answers to these and other major questions are, at best, elusive. Funding is *not* likely to increase substantially, if at all. And, while enrollment changes will provide opportunities to redirect programs and efforts, these and related policy decisions will require strong leadership from administrators and governing boards.

One very specific challenge to the state university, which may of necessity take precedence over all others, will be to devise better ways to explain diverse yet complementary missions to more of the people who pay the bill. The presence of this responsibility has been long understood, and progress has been made in meeting it. Nevertheless, describing what a university is about is still not what those associated with the state university do best, and enhanced research and service efforts, often perceived to be at odds with the more narrow public perception of "education," will inevitably compound this already serious difficulty.

Citizens often take research at the state university for granted and assume that research funds will be available. Persons with special interests generally know what public service programs have to offer them, but they may not appreciate the breadth of the contribution that state universities are able and willing to make. Those to whom the future of our state universities has been entrusted must explain that the boundaries of the campus are not the real boundaries of these institutions. They must stress continuously that university activities inevitably benefit the state, the region, the nation, and the world and that educators have a responsibility to be forceful members of a global society. If they achieve this objective, the logical next steps toward full integration of the state university into the marrow of the nation that supports it will become easier. And the ultimate attainment of a free and supportive society that responds to the needs of its citizens will approach reality, rather than remaining a seductive, yet ever elusive dream.

CHAPTER 6
THE FUTURE
OF THE STATE UNIVERSITIES:
CONTINUING EDUCATION AND
RESEARCH IN AN ERA
OF SCIENCE-BASED INDUSTRIES

BARBARA W. NEWELL

I believe that the remaining two decades [in this century] will see a revolution based on high technology. I think the leadership will emerge from those countries which have the strongest science and technology base, which are able and willing to make major capital investments, and which have a level of education of the public and the work force worthy of the new technologies that will emerge. The economic viability of the University System in the next two decades will depend on how well we perform in all these areas.

Frank Press, 1982

The importance of knowledge is a striking characteristic of our post-industrial society. Never before has the country's economic well-being depended so crucially on having a high proportion of educated workers, on the continuing emergence of new discoveries and insights, and on the rapid and effective dissemination of information.

Ernest A. Lynton

HISTORICAL RELATIONSHIP OF UNIVERSITIES
WITH BUSINESS AND INDUSTRY

Intensifying the effects of a shift in technology has been the change in American foreign trade and competition. We have had little incentive to look abroad, and little competition from abroad. But the decade of the seventies has seen a gradual shift in balance. Today America is a part of the international markets and in stiff competition. Many of our foreign competitors have strong government support for industrial research and innovation. As American industry better positions itself to compete, there is a reexamination of the interaction of the university with industry and government.

America's land-grant colleges turn naturally to the successful model of agricultural extension. The Morrill and Hatch acts together brought into being colleges that were not only designed to teach the scientific and classical studies, but also created branches of learning that were related to agriculture and mechanical arts so as to promote the liberal and practical education of the industrial classes. When the Morrill Act was passed the field of agriculture was not yet a science. Agriculture required new knowledge, both to establish the scientific basis of study and to answer a growing number of questions from farmers and farm societies. In the absence of curriculum, accepted methods of teaching and texts, this knowledge could be supplied only through research and experimentation.

Further, much work needed to be done to improve farming techniques and technology. The Hatch Act and its supplements provided federal support for such research functions within the university and established experiment stations. These programs brought problems from the field to the academy to be included in the university research agenda. As solutions to these problems were found they were incorporated into the curriculum so as to prepare the next generation, as well as to be disseminated through the agricultural experiment stations to the farmers. Through the agricultural model the needs of the industry were addressed; basic research was funded, and the results incorporated into the teaching curriculum. To the American taxpayer the productivity of American agriculture has been testimony to the success of this model.

Another model of successful partnership occurred during World War II, when in the name of national defense, business, government, and industry bonded in an unprecedented manner. Patriotism provided the incentive, federal dollars the lubricant. New weaponry, new medical aids and techniques, and ultimately the atomic bomb were results of this collaboration. The success of the academy in a broad range of support activities rendered during the war led the government to view postwar university research as fundamental to the country's well-being, and large-scale federal funding was forthcoming for basic research. This support was spurred on when the Russian space program stunned the United States. The country's leadership vowed to beat the Russians to the moon. Again, the federal government directed funds into universities and encouraged the successful cooperation of the universities and industries.

We reached the moon, but over time there was increasing emphasis on short-term versus long-term gain. The time between discovery and application of knowledge has been estimated at about twenty years. This lead time needed for scientific research does not correspond to the terms of elected government officials, nor fit comfortably with a corporate leadership that wishes to affect annual profit statements. This push for immediate pay off, a change in defense strategy, plus inflation reduced markedly basic research funding in the late seventies.

Today, the cycle turns. The race in the knowledge-based industries has made all units of government—cities, states, and federal—examine issues of research and technology. Government has asked how education could join with American business to create new products and to bolster the economy. The issue is how to do this most effectively. New research modes and diffusion mechanisms must be invested if we are to meet the challenge. We can borrow from some of our own past experiences, but the fit is not perfect. The agricultural model is handicapped because of the differences between the agricultural sector and today's industrial sector. In agriculture there are few proprietary interests and brand names. By and large, the market is competitive and the entrepreneurs are too small to engage in proprietary research. By contrast, the businesses that approach the universities are now speaking of proprietary secrets and patented products. Does a new partnership with industry compromise the basic university mission of generating and disseminating knowledge for the general welfare?

Politically, there is another difference. When America's agricultural extension programs were first created, the farmers were America's majority, and the agricultural colleges were developed with the full support of the body politic. In contrast, the proposal of industrial/university partnership is coming at a period of tax revolts and retrenchment of government programs. Recent federal cutbacks mean education needs new funding sources, just as industry has become more aware of its need for sophisticated research and training. Even though the need for a cooperative arrangement is evident, the political incentive for development of a cooperative model is not considered as critical as the war effort nor as popular as the agricultural effort to the political community.

These political and economic circumstances dictate that the new partnership has to be based on interdependence of business and educational institutions rather than federal funding. A central issue in this new interdependence will be determining how to create a partnership between an industry looking for profitable applications of innovative ideas and the university research community, whose basic charge is to explore knowledge for knowledge's sake. University and industry leaders have begun to explore these differences in values and institutional "culture." Accommodations are being reached, most frequently on an ad hoc basis.

The general guidelines drawn for universities by Chancellor Danforth of Washington University (ACE Conference, October 1983, Toronto) are extremely useful. His points are paraphrased and elaborated below.

1. Universities are not businesses. Profit is not their goal. Knowledge is their business. The creation and dissemination of knowledge must remain central to their value system.

2. In the United States the university has been the home for basic research, and the universities have served the U.S. well. There are few alternative institutions to provide the basic research function. If the U.S. does not keep basic research healthy it will, in effect, be eating its seed corn.

3. Faculty must be free to choose their own research problems. This does not guarantee funding, but freedom of inquiry is essential, not only to maintain the free market place of ideas in the academy, but also so that researchers may follow an idea as they see fit. Much of scientific advance has been the produce of the serendipitous.

Freedom to publish graduate work is basic to the free exchange of ideas, and as a tenet is fundamental to a university in an open society. Open access also pays from the viewpoint of advancing knowledge. New techniques—just the knowledge something can be done—are often of assistance to other researchers.

5. University faculty reward systems should reflect their job values and not underscore research for personal gain.

6. Faculty are there to serve the university. Faculty allocation of their time should reflect this responsibility.

7. Universities should establish support for faculty in their dealings with business. An example would be in the areas of conflict of interest.

8. Each university must work through the question of what its business and investment relationship should be with faculty members. In this area, there is a wide diversity of practice. We can learn from each other over time.

9. The bottom line is that the business and university communities must know themselves before they enter into contracts, and they must stay true to their own sectors if such partnerships are to gain the strengths of their complementarity.

The area of faculty rewards may be particularly troublesome. Faculty members whose work is on the cutting edge of research can excite the next generation, and it is this person who is most apt to find the academy rewarding. Yet, as faculty members interact with industry, they will inevitably compare their institution's reward system with that of industry. If there are significant discrepancies, talented faculty members may defect. Estimates of the faculty defections to industry in the past two years have run as high as 25 percent in some universities (Gibson, 1984). There are accommodations that can be made, such as shared appointments, and that support academic researchers and build research partnerships. But the main problem is the level of faculty salaries. Faculty salaries must be kept competitive if we expect the American research apparatus to remain healthy and free. Universities must have a reward system that attracts the brightest minds. No partnership can be effective if the academic team if uninspired, underfunded, and overworked.

Faculty who participate in projects with industry not only may lack rewards for their action—they may actually fall behind their peers in the department who devote their time to the traditional activities. Reward systems and judicious use of paraprofessionals need to be reexamined to make sure the most productive interaction between business and higher education takes place.

In sum, universities must have a reward system that continues to attract the brightest minds and reinforces external activities related to industry. There will always be a limitation on the number of first-class researchers and unlimited demands on their time. Sophisticated technology, industrial seminars, employment of graduate students—a number of devices may be used to spread these talents. But, fundamentally, the choice of how to spend one's time must remain with the faculty member.

With these tenets as general guidelines to maximize the effectiveness of the interaction between business and university, it may be helpful to take a systems approach and identify barriers to interaction, devise ways to make the systems compatible, and provide incentives for both faculty members and the private sector to overcome the barriers that exist. This systems model has been the approach used by Florida and so is used as a case study. While the focus is on Florida, it must be recognized that much of what is described is a variation or duplication of other programs elsewhere in the country.

FLORIDA: APPLICATION OF THE AGRICULTURAL MODEL

Florida is a fragile sandspit pointed toward the Caribbean and Latin America. This geographic position has made it the gateway to Latin America. Sun, sand, and phosphorous are the natural resources. Distances are vast. It is farther from Pensacola to Key West than from Pensacola to Chicago. A favorite description of Florida is a state of southern hospitality, the western frontier, and eastern money markets. This dynamism means the state has just surpassed Ohio in population, and all projections see Florida by the decade of the nineties as the third or fourth largest state in the nation. Florida will have people. The issue facing the state is whether it will have the industrial base to provide a comfortable standard of living for its people while assuring that the industry developed is complementary to the state's fragile environment.

Recently, new clean industry has been successfully recruited, particularly in the strip that runs from Tampa on the west coast to Cape Kennedy and Boca Raton on the east. As high technology began to move into the state, the Florida Engineering Society and the Board of Regents conducted independent studies on the relationship of engineering education to the rising expectations of this developing industry. Both studies agreed on the need to improve the overall quality of the engineering program by increasing faculty salaries, improving faculty-student ratios, adding to the scientific and technical equipment, improving facilities, and increasing the total number of engineers to be graduated. From this broad community consensus the Board of Regents devised a five-year legislative program. The program is in its third year, and all requests have been fully funded.

The state's emphasis on engineering education has attracted private funding, particularly in the equipment area. However, the most innovative of the Florida approaches to private giving is the plan for eminent scholars. By act of the Florida Legislature, if a donor contributes $600,000 toward a faculty chair, the state of Florida will match its contribution with $400,000 for the establishment of an endowment for a faculty chair. Schools of engineering, with their new visibility and strength, have been particularly attractive for this program. The establishment of this strong base in engineering is critical for the rest of the state's outreach program to business, because only a strong core will assure the academic strengths necessary to be supportive to industry.

The Florida Engineering Education Delivery System (FEEDS) has helped address the first and most urgent request from the private sector— to provide for continuing education for engineers. Florida firms need the opportunity of graduate engineering education courses as a device to help recruit and sustain engineers. Such programs are also necessary to upgrade skills. The very size of the state of Florida and the dimensions of this project are such that a plan was written to combine all of the engineering academic resources as a single pool to be drawn upon by any employer in the state. FEEDS is made up of the four graduate engineering colleges that are now cooperatively offering master's degree programs in electrical, mechanical, civil, and industrial engineering. Although electronic blackboards and computer-assisted instruction are a part of the program, the heart of the FEEDS system is taught by full-time faculty, videotaped, and sent to a number of industrial and university sites throughout the state. Mentors are on site. This delivery system makes the faculty and deans responsible for the quality of the system and assures industry that their employees are receiving a sound education at the locations and times that are convenient.

Each of the colleges participating in FEEDS has agreed to transfer credit from courses offered by other institutions so that students can draw upon the strengths of several institutions. Since each student is assigned a faculty advisor in his or her master's program, the students are assured that their courses will meet the degree requirements. The operation of FEEDS is supervised by representatives from the industries using FEEDS and by representatives from the universities participating in FEEDS. This policy board provides a continuous forum at which industry and the universities can jointly discuss the problems of providing a better educational product through new technologies and new approaches. Although four master's programs are in place, the state university system expects to expand these offerings to include specialities in the basic sciences. Parallel efforts are underway to expand Business Administration course offerings to the business community.

Other outreach mechanisms are in place. State technology application centers were established around the state in 1977 when NASA wished to make more readily available to American industry the technology that has evolved from the space program. In cooperation with the state university system, this NASA information base has been indexed and made computer accessible. Three to four hundred other indices have been added to the NASA base. Individuals wishing to track a given problem may do so at six different sites in the state.

A plan has been drafted to add to the NASA data base a listing of university faculty and research interests so the industrial community may have computer access to the state university system research community. This index will be organized by a series of key-word subject areas so that faculty and members can be identified in a number of subject areas as well as by location. In addition, the index will be expanded to include a state-wide list of entrepreneurs also organized by subject area, to facilitate contacts between researchers and enterpreneurs. The Small Business Innovation Research (SBIR) categories will be used to allow Florida to determine which faculty members and enterpreneurs might be good partners for developing joint proposals for submission to the SBIR. Given Florida's past performance in developing SBIR proposals, this structure may allow Florida to take more advantage of this funding source in the future.

A number of proposals are underway to assist in the marketing of faculty ideas. One proposal would establish faculty review committees at all state institutions and invite individual faculty members to submit proposals. These committees will work with the Small Business Development Centers (SBDC) and the State Technology Application Center (STAC) to give these new proposals the support they need for success. This approach is an attempt to reduce the risk involved in beginning a new industry by giving the inventor and entrepreneur the managerial and technical support they need to succeed.

Basic to this proposal is the network of Small Business Development centers across the state of Florida aimed at trying to give technical assistance to small business. These centers have proved helpful to a broad range of companies, primarily in the services sector, in the past. Frequently the pattern in high technology industry is that of a scientist with a bright idea who develops a good product but begins to falter when it is necessary to put in place an accounting and personnel system, and to develop marketing strategy or other service. Florida hopes to closely link supports in technical development with the Small Business Development centers, placing particular emphasis on the needs of high technology companies, in order to alleviate this mortality problem.

As a part of the program to develop new industry, research parks are being developed on four campuses. The system anticipates having an incubator building on each of the sites before 1986. The extent to which faculty expertise, computer support, and other services will be available has been outlined with general guidelines at each park. In two cases the research park development has been organized in partnership with business enterpreneurs who specialize in park development. In two other cases the universities themselves are taking on the responsibility for park development.

Whether it is in the research park, individual seminars, or through faculty listing, the undercurrent of all of Florida's activities has been to try to get researchers from the university community and industry to become acquainted and to work with each other. The personal factor is critical to a productive mix. It is from this mix that the system is gradually developing cooperative research projects, shared equipment, and shared and joint appointments.

Florida is in the process of developing expertise in technical assistance for international trade. High technology is apt to have an international horizon, and Florida is a natural center for trade to Latin America, Africa, and the Caribbean. The technical problems of international trade, cultural differences, and language barriers are all concerns that can be addressed by the university. We have expanded the Small Business Development centers so that businesses needing assistance may find appropriate expertise.

Over the course of the last year and a half, a survey of small business executives and technical training experts was conducted. The objective of these inquiries was to determine the extent to which unmet technical training needs constitute a significant practical impediment to exporting by small- and medium-sized businesses. To a surprising degree consensus emerged among both business executives and the technical training community that training needs often rank as high as financial needs and the unfamiliarity with business clientele as an obstacle to exporting by small businesses. But, while a variety of public and private organizations have sought to assist small businesses in obtaining export and preexport financing, to develop overseas leads and to understand the business community, a sustained and coordinated effort has been undertaken to address technical training needs.

The fundamental export problem is that for most companies, development of reliable overseas markets presupposes the ability to ensure proper installation, maintenance, and repair of the exported product. For small business executives with limited contacts and experience in the target market, this inability to guarantee ultimate quality control over their own products acts as a barrier to sustained international operations, especially when compared to the safe and familiar alternative of relying on domestic sales. Unless the business in question has already made a permanent commitment to full-scale overseas operations, it is unlikely to have the resources to develop an in-house training program tailored to each target market. Furthermore, while the business might be able to afford contracted training services, it has no means for identifying and assembling experts familiar with the business, language, cultural, and social aspects of the target market, and with the technical needs associated with its product lines, fixed within a period of time. As a result of this technical training gap, many companies occasionally dabble in foreign markets when domestic sales justify the perceived risk, but never make the long-term commitment to exporting.

On the other side of the technical training gap, few individual academic institutions and corporate training organizations employ the full range of training experts needed to serve a specific small company's needs. Most training organizations do not have fully developed outreach programs to identify potential small business clients, and in any event cannot assemble training teams at one time and in one place among themselves.

The states of Georgia and Florida are attempting to provide this support by creating the World Technology Center, which will fill the technical training gap by: (1) creating an outreach program to identify small- and medium-sized businesses for which technical training needs constitute a significant impediment to initial or expanded export sales; (2) creating a network of technical training resources in Georgia and Florida, including experts on every available foreign market and technical field; (3) pulling together from this network training teams tailored to an individual company's (or group of companies') target market, product line, and scope of projected overseas activities; (4) designing specialized one-stop training packages, including some generally applicable in-house training on basic aspects of exporting; and (5) providing additional one-stop help by making available information on technical assistance, trade leads, and other programs and services offered by federal and state governments and private-sector economic development organizations. With the initiation of WTC, Florida's industries will no longer have to depend on a single university for training. Again, if this approach is successful, nonexport businesses in Florida will be offered similar training programs.

Not just the university community is affected by the growth of the knowledge industry. The reexamination of vocational education will also be required. As trainers of vocational education teachers, the university community needs to be a full partner in this reexamination. Although Florida as a state has been highly supportive of vocational education, the university community has not taken the initative to bring together those doing the planning and training of the voc-tech teachers with those working in the science of new technologies. This gap needs filling.

Each piece of this mosaic of general programs for development must be coordinated. The aim is to bring into full coordination the continuing education program of FEEDS, the State Technology Application centers, the Small Business Development centers, the World Technology Center, and vocational and international supports so that as a company moves into a community there can be one contact for the business entrepreneur to gain the kind of university assistance that may be necessary.

Like many states, in addition to broad strategies for development, Florida is trying to focus on the specific needs of some new industries. The state is in the process of taking a census of existing talents and efforts so it may consider field by field how to be supportive of desired industrial development. In one field we may need more research advocates, in another technicians. Venture capital may be required or basic research supported. Resources are limited. The efforts should be concentrated as needed.

In summary, the question has been asked: "What responsibility should state research universities assume in continuing education in the professional and highly technical occupations, and for extension of research results to private industry?" The role of the university presented here is for a much more active partnership with industry than we have seen in the past. Universities must reach out. Pragmatism has been America's ideology. We must learn again to wed effectively the dreamers and the knowledge makers with knowledge brokers and practitioners. The stakes are America's future.

RERERENCES

Agenda: Recommendations for national action in higher education. The 96th Congress: A joint statement of the National Association of State Universities and Land-Grant Colleges and American Association of State Colleges and Universities.

Ashby, Sir Eric. *Technology and the academics: An essay on universities and the scientific revolution.* London: MacMillan and Company, 1959.

Dakenwald, Gordon, et al., eds. *Reaching Hard to Reach Adults: New Directions for Continuing Education,* No. 8. San Francisco: Jossey-Bass, Inc., 1980.

Dubin, S. S. *Professional Obsolescence.* Lexington, Mass.: Lexington Books, June, 1970.

————. Facts '79. Washington, D.C.: NASULGC, 1979.

————. Quest for excellence: The Master Plan of the State University System of Florida, 1983.

Gibson, G. Thomas. Research for Sale, *Venture* (March 1984), pp. 80–86.

Johnson, Elmima C., and Tornatzky, Louis G. Academia and industrial innovation. In G. Gold, *Education New Directions for Experiential Learning: Business and Higher Education—Towards New Alliances, 15.* San Francisco: Jossey-Bass, September 1981, pp. 47–63.

Lynton, Ernest A. A Crisis of Purpose: Reexamining the Role of the University, *Change* (October 1983), pp. 18–53.

————. High Education's Role in Fostering Employee Education, *Educational Record* (Fall 1983), pp. 18–23.

————. Improving Cooperation Between Colleges and Corporations, *Educational Record* (Fall 1982), pp. 20–25.

————. The Missing Connection Between Business and the Universities. To be published by the ACE, draft of July 1983.

————. The Economic Impact of Higher Education, *Journal of Higher Education,* Vol. 54, No. 6 (Nov./Dec., 1983), pp. 693–708.

Melchiori, Gerlinda. Relations Between Higher Education and Industry. University Industry Partnerships: Incentives and Barriers. In *Higher Education in Europe,* Franz Eberhard, et al., eds., Vol. 8, No. 4 (Oct-Dec., 1983), pp. 5–16.

Minshall, C. W. Development of High Technology Industries in New York State. Undated Final Summary Report prepared for the New York State Science and Technology Foundation by Battelle Columbus Industries.

Paulson, Steven R., et al. Industry-university Research in Florida: Incentives, Barriers, and Prospects. A Final Report: Submitted to the Florida Institute for

Local Government and the Office of the Governor under STAR Research Grant, Sept. 30, 1983.

Phillips, Ione. *The Added Dimension: State and Land-grant Universities Serving State and Local Government.* Washington, D.C.: NASULGC, Undated.

Rainsford, George N. *Congress and Higher Eduation in the Nineteenth Century.* Knoxville: University of Tennessee, 1972.

Tornatzky, Louis G. et al. Fostering the Use of Advanced Manufacturing Technology. Undated draft.

Tornatzky, Louis G. The Process of Technological Innovation: Reviewing the Literature. Productivity Improvement Research Section, Division of Industrial Science and Technological Innovation. National Science Foundation, May 1983.

————. Targeting the Process of Innovation: An Agenda for U.S. Technological Leadership and Industrial Competitiveness. Recommendations of U.S. House of Representatives, First Edition, May 1984.

————. Technology, Innovation, and Regional Economic Development. Background paper. Census of State Government Initiatives for High-Technology Industrial Development. Congress of the U.S., Office of Technology Assessment, Washington, D.C., May 1983.

————. University-Industry Research Relationships: Myths, Realities, and Potentials. Fourteenth Annual Report of the National Science Board, Oct. 1982.

CHAPTER 7
STATE UNIVERSITIES AND INTERNATIONAL PUBLIC SERVICE: A CHANGING WORLD, A CHANGING UNIVERSITY

C. PETER MAGRATH
JAMES T. BORGESTAD

In the modern world, even the strongest and most independent nations cannot live in isolation.

George P. Schultz, Beijing, 1982

What Secretary of State Schultz observed about the modern world is equally true of the modern university. As the global community shrinks and countries become more intertwined economically, politically, and for security, there is an increased demand for international awareness, cooperation, and competence. Meeting such demands is a fundamental responsibility of any nation's educational system. In the United States, a major part of that responsibility has been assumed by our state universities and land-grant colleges, institutions that have long recognized the costs of ideological as well as educational isolationism.

When the Morrill Act was passed in 1862, international competence—much less international service—was hardly considered to be a pressing priority. The United States was a world apart, geographically, culturally, and philosophically, from the rest of the world. Manifest was its destiny; isolationist was its policy. Both were assured if not by a public consensus, then at least by thousands of miles of ocean.

With the advent of the twentieth century, the distance between America and the rest of the world began to fade, at first slightly, then dramatically, and finally inexorably and forever. A country that had disdained "foreign entanglements" could not escape involvement in two world wars. A people whose economic fortunes required new markets could not assume a fetal position in foreign relations. A nation that incited a technological and communication revolution could not close its ears and borders to the rest of the world.

New challenges for the nation meant new responsibilities for its public universities. The gates of state campuses had to be opened wider; the diversity of scientists and scholars and teachers and technicians had to be increased. As a consequence, an expanded interpretation of the land-grant mandate emerged, one fully consistent with Senator Justin Morrill's call for "practical and liberal" as well as agricultural and technical education. The results were impressive and far-reaching. As America evolved into a world power, its state research universities developed world-renowned schools of science and education, business and economics, medicine and health, law and the liberal arts, and, of course, agriculture and technology. The end product, according to many observers, was the creation of "the most comprehensive system of scientific, technical, and practical higher education the world has ever known."

The application of this rich base of experience and knowledge to international issues, however, came relatively late in our history. Not until 1949 did the U.S. government turn its attention to the indigenous problems of needy countries. The Marshall Plan had been launched, and, in his famous Point Four initiative, President Truman suggested that what worked so well in Europe might well work in the so-called developing world. Responding to the president's recommendation, a number of NASULGC institutions embarked upon a bold new course: they created programs of international public service, applying their educational and research talents to the problems of other countries.

Over the next third of a century, the concept of international service matured. At first, it was interpreted largely in terms of agricultural development, an emphasis that many public universities continue to stress. The primary goal of agricultural development was different from those of early foreign assistance programs; the objective was not to feed the people, but to teach the people to feed themselves. This required sending agriculturalists abroad, conducting on-site research, creating extension networks and training foreign nationals both in the host country and in the United States. Ultimately, the task was defined in terms of "institution-building," or developing agricultural institutions that would serve a country long after a visiting team of American specialists had returned home.

Despite the success of such programs—and agricultural development programs continue to be successful—it soon became evident that the problems of Third World countries required more than agricultural know-how in a narrow sense. At a minimum, two additional activities had to be strengthened. First, greater attention had to be paid to promoting the essential "tools" of international service. That is, foreign languages had to be expanded, international studies' programs broadened, interinstitutional linkages created, area specialists attracted, and government-funded ventures increased. Second, both these tools and the overall professional base inherent in the NASULGC schools had to be applied to wider varieties of development problems, including technological, environmental, economic, and health-related issues that might be unique to a particular country or region.

A RATIONALE FOR INTERNATIONAL INVOLVEMENT

Taking on wide-ranging international responsibilities required considerable soul-searching, for the resources of public universities were simultaneously being stretched by expanding enrollments, increased demands for research, and new expectations for outreach programs. If foreign activities were to be added, they had to be justified to the satisfaction of the internal academic community as well as to state and federal officials and funding agencies.

Fortunately, a strong case could be made in support of international public service. That case has been argued many times, but it bears repeating, because the rationale is even more compelling today than it was yesterday. Simply stated, international service programs represent sound domestic and foreign policy. More specifically, they reflect the following shared objectives.

TO SERVE HUMANITARIAN NEEDS

Historically, compassion for the less fortunate—at home and abroad—has been a defining characteristic of the American people. Such proven initiatives as the Marshall Plan, the Peace Corps, the Agency for International Development, or for that matter, foreign assistance programs in general, were largely created out of a sense of humanitarianism. That same sense of altruism persists today. Even in a modern age of cynicism, a compassionate chord is struck when we hear that half of the people in the world go to bed hungry every evening, that one in eight world inhabitants is afflicted by some form of malnutrition, or that twenty-one people die of starvation every minute of the day and night.

As the richest nation in the world, the United States enjoys the means and wherewithall to alleviate part of this widespread suffering. One of those instrumentalities is international public service through which American expertise is extended to the needy, the underdeveloped, and often the poorest of the poor nations.

TO PROMOTE INTERNATIONAL STABILITY

There is a Mexican saying, "A full belly, a happy heart. An empty stomach, be careful." Every day, there are 150,000 additional reasons to be careful as half of all newborns in some countries join an estimated 950 million persons who are already suffering from severe malnutrition. A planet that contains a billion hungry people is a planet ripe for instability.

The explosiveness of the situation is all too familar. In recent years, it flared up in famine-stricken Africa and war-torn Southeast Asia. Currently, it can be seen closer to home in Central and South America. The collision of unchecked birth rates and limited food resources gives rise to unrest and tension, to revolution and civil war. By itself, rapid development will not prevent such flare-ups because development means change and, by definition, change can be destabilizing. Still to the extent that the benefits of agricultural advances are broadly shared across socioeconomic lines, the volatility of many global hotspots can be defused. In this sense, international development represents an inexpensive investment to ward off what a United Nation's commission recently called "the largest single crisis for world, social, economic, and political stability over the next twenty years: worldwide famine."

TO FURTHER THE UNITED STATES' AGRICULTURAL PRODUCTIVITY

State universities and land-grant colleges have contributed enormously to making the United States the predominant agricultural power in the world. Yet even the overall leader cannot afford to be complacent; we too have room and opportunities for improvements. Average yields, for example, in wheat, barley, rice, and other basic grains are higher in some Third World nations than in the United States. Moreover, we lag behind a number of countries in irrigation, fermentation, and land conservation methods. To ignore the successes of our neighbors makes little sense; to refuse to learn from them makes even less sense.

In fact, science recognizes no national boundaries, and the lessons learned by researchers abroad have applications for agriculture at home. Accordingly, scientists from the United States and foreign countries have long collaborated on common problems. The range of joint projects is as diverse as agriculture itself, from fungi to fire ants, from ladybugs to livestock, from pesticides to potatoes. What these and countless other cooperative efforts promote is an expansion of overall agricultural knowledge and capacity, benefiting farmers and agricultural sectors across the nation as well as the world.

TO STRENGTHEN AMERICAN UNIVERSITIES AND COLLEGES

The motivation behind international programs can also be traced to the enlightened self-interests of state universities and land-grant colleges. In other words, quite aside from addressing foreign needs, international involvements assist NASULGC institutions in serving their traditional clientele: students, scholars, and the broader American society.

In teaching, for example, there is a clear obligation to prepare students for the world in which they will live. At a minimum, this means attracting or developing a faculty whose members are not only familiar with the global dimensions of particular subjects, but who can incorporate them in their classroom activities. It also means internationalizing the core curriculum, establishing foreign language requirements or expanding area studies. A faculty whose background includes foreign experience is better equipped to assume these responsibilities than one that has never ventured outside the American cultural cocoon.

Similarly, international service activities promote the potential research contributions of faculty members. The scholar who works abroad is able to develop linkages with foreign investigators and research centers, thereby insuring a communication network that will persist long after his or her travels are completed. The importance of scholarly linkages to our nation's research base should not be underestimated, for as Dr. Sven Groennings pointed out in a March 1984 address, "Not long ago two-thirds of the world's science was in America, but now two-thirds is abroad."

The third traditional responsibility of state research universities—providing outreach services—is also directly advanced by institutional involvements in international programs. Faculty members with foreign experience are increasingly sought by federal policymakers, state agencies, and private corporations on issues ranging from foreign aid to world trade centers to international business practices. These officials recognize that the line between foreign and domestic issues has been blurred, if not obliterated, in many areas. They turn to international specialists not to retrace the line, but to draw the larger global picture, a picture that has tremendous consequences for policymakers in both the public and private sectors.

TO ADVANCE UNITED STATES' ECONOMIC INTERESTS

Foreign trade has become the locomotive that pulls America's economic train. Fueled by ever increasing imports and exports, the length of the train continues to grow.

1. Since 1960, the total value of U.S. foreign trade has jumped from 10 to 25 percent of our Gross National Product.
2. Twenty percent of our industrial output is for export.
3. The jobs of one in six American production workers are directly dependent upon foreign trade.
4. 40 percent of our farmland produces for export.
5. More than a third of America's corporate profits are generated by international activities.
6. Our commercial banks have $130 billion in loans to developing and Eastern Bloc countries, with 1,500 U.S. banks being involved in loans to Latin America alone.

In other words, our nation's economic destiny is tied to the economies of our trading partners and to their ability and willingness to engage in international commerce. To the extent that a country is developed, it has the capacity to produce goods for self-consumption and sale as well as to generate revenues for purchasing imports. By hastening development, international service programs promote potential consumers of American goods. In turn, by promoting international competence through foreign languages, international business studies, and intercultural awareness, state universities and land-grant colleges insure a more competitive position for American corporations in the world marketplace.

TO FURTHER UNITED STATES' SECURITY AND
FOREIGN POLICY OBJECTIVES

Modern nations have long outgrown the era in which military preparedness alone can meet their national defense and foreign policy requirements. Instead, a country's security as well as its role in the global community is dependent upon its ability to foster understanding and cooperation with peoples. This requires the training of interculturally competent leaders, diplomats, foreign service officers, businessmen, and professionals. As a practical consequence, American security is tied just as closely to the graduates of state universities and land-grant colleges as it is to those of West Point, Annapolis, or the Air Force Academy.

The furthering of national security and foreign policy interests is largely a product of three NASULGC activities, each of which falls within a broad definition of international service. First, through educational and research programs in the foreign languages, area studies, international relations, and related fields, universities develop a trained pool of graduates who can serve the sophisticated manpower needs of our defense and foreign policy communities. The demands of those communities have outstripped supply over recent decades. Moreover, as Admiral Bobby Inman, the former deputy head of the National Security Agency and the CIA, has stated, the need for sophisticated foreign specialists "is going to be much greater in the next fifteen years than it has been in the last fifteen."

A second vehicle for promoting foreign policy interests takes the form of academic exchanges. The premise here is basic: there is no substitute for face-to-face interaction as a means of building trust, understanding, and cooperation. Exchange programs do precisely that. Some of the programs are based upon agricultural partnerships as, for example, the 1,100 cooperative relationships that fifty-eight NASULGC members developed with foreign institutions during a recent twenty-year period. Other exchange activities are broader in scope, as illustrated by the Fulbright Program, an initiative that has provided study abroad opportunities to 45,000 American students and scholars and 85,000 foreigners over its thirty-eight-year history. Still other exchange ventures are regionally targeted, as exemplified by the Kissinger Commission recommendation, which proposed 10,000 scholarships for students from Latin America and the Caribbean. Whatever their scope, academic exchanges have proven to be invaluable tools of modern diplomacy, sending thousands of Americans abroad and attracting an even larger number of foreign visitors to our shores, including some thirty-three eventual foreign leaders and heads of state.

Third, state research universities promote ties between America and foreign countries by educating thousands of international students on campuses across the United States. Since World War II, more than two million students from other nations have enrolled in American universities and colleges, with 350,000 currently enrolled. A majority of those who seek graduate and professional training—some 40 percent—attend NASULGC institutions. Not only do these sudents receive training that will benefit themselves and their native countries, but they also receive an education on America, its traditions, and its peoples. In return, these students represent an indirect export of up to $2 billion and, more importantly, a rich resource for promoting understanding by American students of foreign cultures, views, and peoples.

LINGERING QUESTIONS FOR INTERNATIONAL PROGRAMS

All of these reasons and considerations explain why our state universities and land-grant colleges have sponsored international public service programs for over thirty-five years. It is a history rich in aspirations and actions, in altruism and achievements. It is also a history that raises questions of "what might and might not have been."

It is, for instance, difficult to estimate what events would have transpired had NASULGC schools *not* assumed various international responsibilities. How many more starving people, for example, would the world have known had the U.S. agronomist and Nobel Peace Prize winner, Norman Borlaug, *not* undertaken the "Green Revolution" to improve grain yields in underdeveloped countries? Would agricultural development in the Phillipines, Colombia, Morocco, and other Third World nations have advanced as quickly had some 3,000 American agricultural faculty *not* served abroad in the 1960s and 1970s? Would the People's Republic of China have moved in five short years from purchasing $44,000 in onion seeds to being one of our largest trading partners if America's universities had *not* promoted collaborative research projects, cultural and academic exchanges, and institutional and trade linkages? Would Egypt have terminated its alliance with the U.S.S.R. in favor of one with the U.S. had Anwar Sadat *not* been impressed by the America he witnessed early in his career as a member of an American exchange program?

On the other hand, there are just as many questions as to what the world would be like today had state research universities been able to *expand* their international involvements years ago. Would Nicaragua, for example, have turned leftward if the efforts of NASULGC schools to build strong agricultural institutions been continued rather than terminated due to a phasing out of federal support? Would Angola and Ethiopia be as close to the U.S.S.R. today if our nation had matched the 24,000 study abroad opportunities that the Soviets annually extend to Africans instead of offering only 1,800 opportunities to study in American universities? Would America have to spend $876 million a day on promoting its security interests around the world if support for foreign studies programs had been maintained rather than slashed by 36 percent in Asian studies, 44 percent in Near Eastern programs, 49 percent in African affairs, and 60 percent in Latin American studies between 1965 and 1975? Would the United States be more competitive in Third World relations if its support for communication, cultural, and academic exchange programs were not one-fourth of what the Soviets spend? There is, of course, no way to answer these questions. Missed opportunities seldom provide clear answers; they do, however, shed some light on the fundamental problem that has long plagued international service ventures. The problem is one of financing, or more precisely, who should fund international service activities. During recent years, the debate among the three traditional supporters of these programs—the federal government, state governments, and universities—has taken on a Pontius Pilate aura, with each party washing its hands and disclaiming ultimate responsibility.

On the one side are state officials who point out that international activities fall under the category of foreign affairs and, as such, are the primary obligation of the federal government. On the other side are federal policymakers who argue that international programs are educational in nature and, as such, fall under the traditional purview of state governments. In between are many university administrators who, in the absence of available resources, look upon international service programs as candidates for retrenchment rather than expansion.

The responsibilities are, in fact, shared by all three parties, because international programs serve common national, state, and university interests. The time has come to move away from arguments over who is responsible and return to the original premises upon which international activities were founded. As Professor Lambert has put it, "We must either actively promote our participation in the growing world intellectual culture or we will become increasingly irrelevant to it." The world can't afford to wait—even for America!

CHAPTER 8
THE PROFESSORIATE
BURTON R. CLARK

The academic profession is an odd occupation. It is intrinsically many professions, since it trains for medicine, law, and other advanced occupations and therefore possesses practitioners certified in those fields. It is also intrinsically many disciplines, since the spectrum of fields based primarily in the academy stretches from anthropology and astronomy to Western civilization and zoology in the alphabet of academic interests, ranging across all the many specialties of the natural sciences, social sciences, humanities, and even many of the arts. Variety is its name, a profession structured as a conglomerate of interests in which purposes and tasks are evermore divided around new subjects, new clienteles, and new linkages to other occupations. And opaqueness is its style: who can fathom an econometrician when he or she is in full stride, let alone a high-energy physicist or a molecular biologist?

This uncommon profession was once relatively simple: in its medieval form of some six to eight centuries ago it was organized around a few fields of study and a small clientele. But the growth in knowledge that began to accelerate markedly in the nineteenth century and the growth in student numbers that has been the hallmark of the twentieth have together led to the large institutions and huge national systems that support and require a complex professoriate. Nowhere among the nations of the world has this complexity become greater than in the United States. And nowhere among universities and colleges has the division of the profession into a host of large and small autonomous specialties become greater than in the American state university.

In the face of growing complexity and increasing division, the state of this profession should concern public officials, university administrators, and professors alike. What is the shape and general health of this occupation in its American setting, a swollen profession whose members serve not only as the central workforce of the academic enterprises but also as the main carriers of the values of science and higher learning? How is the profession positioned in the increasingly bureaucratic university? What divides it and what holds it together? What determines its strengths, and its weaknesses?

Five topics will serve to point to primary elements in the modern situation of the profession, thereby orienting discussion around the basic rather than the trivial, the enduring problems rather than those found in the morning headlines: (1) higher education is structured around a dual commitment of its mainline professionals to disciplines and institutions; (2) there is a basic division between professional school faculty and liberal arts professors; (3) there is an intrinsic clash between professional self-government and institutional control; (4) the profession's strongest competence is its productivity in research; and (5) the profession's weakest area of performance—in its public university locations—is in undergraduate teaching.

The discussion that follows will progressively move toward the modern American public university. Its strengths and weaknesses vary somewhat from those of the American private university and are generally different from those found in the traditional university of other countries. As we sow, so will we reap: the American public university has put together a unique mixture of commitments to research, professional education, general education, and community service; to advanced students and beginning ones; to elite and mass functions. We should expect the professoriate to be thereby shaped, exhibiting major strains and contradictions.

However briefly, I want also to identify some lines of reform. In this most complex of all occupations, there are no clear issues to be solved with the wave of simple answers. But as we highlight the profession's structural foundations, we can suggest certain broad directions of effort along which reform might move in decades to come.

DUAL COMMITMENT[1]

Academics have a host of memberships that bring them under various influences. We may picture them analytically as caught up in various matrices,[2] with memberships running on different axes that shape their work, call upon their loyalties, and apportion their authority. The matrices of affiliation are legend. Numerous academics have a meaningful home within a specific subspecialty of their own discipline while at the same time they belong to the discipline as a whole. Many belong simultaneously to a discipline and a multidisciplinary unit, be the latter a problem-centered unit such as environmental studies, an area studies program such as African Studies, a multidisciplinary professional school such as Education, or an undergraduate residential college, the form historically modeled by Oxford and Cambridge. Academics belong simultaneously to their own discipline and to the more inclusive holding company that we call the academic profession. Such dual assignments naturally stretch commitments. The assignments become a set of multiple affiliations, with an academic readily picking up four or five or more of them. They clearly are sources of tension and conflict: in the language of sociology, there is a role enlargement or role elaboration in which the individual moves in a seamless blend from one posture, one set of demands and expectations, to another. But these multiple memberships are also a fundamental source of integration—*the* way by which the system "naturally" combats the fragmentation of specialization. Absolute isolation is reduced; individuals are caught up in two or more perspectives; interpersonal and symbolic bridges, numbering in the many thousands, help link the many autonomy seeking parts.

Central among the many matrices is the most common fact of academic work anywhere in the world: the academic belongs simultaneously to a field of study (for which we may use the metaphor of "discipline") and to a university or college (which we may call simply "the enterprise"). Looking at an entire national system, we may speak of a fundamental two-way stretch. The organized foundation of the system in Nigeria or Sweden, Brazil or Japan, Indonesia or the United States, is inherently dualistic. Two primary modes of organization crisscross one another. Each specializes: the one by subject matter, the other by geographic location. Each is comprehensive: the one knitting together particular specialists across the system, and even internationally, the other collecting in one place some members of different specialties. In the language of matrix analysis, the disciplines are the specialist groups. The enterprises are the project or problem groups, albeit with the specialists typically on lifelong or indefinite, rather than temporary, assignment from the disciplines to a given enterprise.

If we start from the bottom of the higher education system, then, and ask only a few simple questions about the natural affinities of the main work force, we encounter a permanent master matrix as the foundation of the system and the academic profession, an arrangement in which the primary memberships of individuals and groups of workers go off in two quite different directions. Thus, a national system of higher education must be approached as simultaneously a set of disciplines and a set of enterprises. At the organizational heart of higher education is this criss-crossing arrangement that turns large systems such as the American one into thousands of linked intersects occupied by autonomy seeking groups of thinkers who uphold specific types of thought. These "departmental" intersects are where the work of teaching and research gets done. Within them, the productive powers of disciplines and enterprises converge.

Two directions of thought immediately follow. We shall become more insightful about the academic profession and higher education generally when we learn about how disciplines shape enterprises and how enterprises shape disciplines, and then study the effects of those interactions upon teaching and research, upon professional education and liberal education, and upon competence, equity, choice, and all the other primary values that we want to effect. Quite simply, what is it like to be a biologist in a small, poorly funded private liberal arts college? A chemist in a public community college? Do such academics drift out of the academic profession or are new roles elaborated that hold them within their disciplines and their profession, even if their institutional locations should push them toward the periphery of academic identification and influence?

Second, the coming together of disciplinary and institutional ties in the many departments, schools, and research centers that constitute the factory floor of the university gives those units uncommon primacy, turning the university into an inordinately bottom-heavy organization. The disciplines have been ascending in strength in the leading systems of higher education for a century and a half, even since the research imperative became the main driving force of the early nineteenth-century German university. Disciplinary strength is represented locally as departmental strength. The disciplines are units of affiliation for academics that have their own peculiar nature. "They are not organized to carry out the will of legitimate superiors. They are going concerns with problems and procedures that have taken form through generations of effort and have emerged into highly conscious goal-oriented actitivies."[3] Notably, they subordinate institutional values to disciplinary ones. They thereby make the modern professoriate an efficient instrument of science and scholarship.[4] What they do to such institutional concerns as undergraduate teaching is another matter, to which we shall return.

THE SCHISM BETWEEN PROFESSIONAL SCHOOLS AND THE LIBERAL ARTS

Buried among the many lines of academic affiliation within the university is the divide between professional schools and liberal arts departments that threatens to turn into a serious schism. Our common image of "the professor" is someone in the letters and science part of the university, be it Mr. Chips chatting up undergraduates, the Great Professor offering his pearls of wisdom to hundreds of students in a large lecture hall, or the lone scientist isolating himself among test tubes in the laboratory. In all such idealized types, the professor has been someone who devotes a lifetime to the creation or distribution of knowledge for its own sake. But that image has always left out a good share of the faculty of the modern university,[5] a share that now grows steadily larger, namely, those directly involved in specific professional training. For American research universities, 60 percent of the professoriate is now a good estimate of the numerical presence of professional school faculty.[6] And as every senior university administrator knows, the budgets are impressive: medical school outlays alone can readily reach one-quarter of total university expenditures, and medical school and university hospital budgets together may exceed that of the rest of the university campus. Such powerful campus segments often have to have true "professionals" more than they have to have "academics." For example, anesthesiologists are indispensable to the workings of the university hospital, but they commonly lack research interests and are deficient in producing the publications by which academics normally judge one another for appointment and promotion.[7] And the "professionals" increasingly have to be paid more than the "academics," in order for the university to compete for their services in the context of well-paying professions, often in the full view of everyone in the form of separate salary schedules, e.g., for engineering and business as well as medicine and law. The differentiation of professional interests and concerns produces new roles and career lines for large segments of the modern professoriate that are a far cry from the posture of the history or classics professor "back there" in a letters and science department. The schism grows.

How is that divide bridged? Can the differentiated parts still be linked? Research universities evolve partial solutions. Many faculty members in the professional schools are drawn from the traditional disciplines and act as carriers of "L and S" norms, as in the basic science part of the medical school. Many of their more practice-minded colleagues in the more clinical part gradually assimilate those norms, particularly centered around the value of research and scholarly production. A gradient of formal roles in the professional schools develops, rather than a sharp line between pure research and pure practice. Then too, professional schools develop dual appointment systems in which nontenure-track appointments can be made in addition to the tenure tracks. There is a recognition that both types of "academics" are necessary, even if one develops a normative order in which tenure has no meaning. Universities may also decide to live and let live, notably by locating key personnel decisions within the professional school itself rather than insisting that they come up to the all-campus level where they will be handled by senate and administrative committees dominated by letters and science professors. Meanwhile, back in the L and S departments, all is not academically pristine. Physicists, chemists, mathematicians, economists, psychologists, and others do outside consulting and otherwise work on practical problems of the day, thereby socializing themselves to the values and rewards of the applied and the more narrowly professional. And cleavage is generally reduced by the mutual ignorance of those who are nominally in the same organization but work in quite different disciplinary cultures. But the potential for increased conflict between two major parts of the professoriate exists. A major schism that would divide the university into two parts is an issue to be watched.

THE CLASH BETWEEN PROFESSIONAL SELF-GOVERNMENT AND INSTITUTIONAL CONTROL

Considerable self-government is the hallmark of any major profession. An "academic," here and abroad, has long had his or her own special assortment of ideas and habits that spelled considerable self-government: defining doctrines such as "community of scholars" and "freedom of research and teaching"; engrained practices such as one-person-one-vote decision making in department meetings and peer review in research councils. But as professions take up location within bureauracies, bottom-up forms clash with top-down precepts of organized hierarchy. The academic profession has been no exception: it is evermore encapsulated in large administrative vessels that bring lay as well as bureaucratic controls. The issue becomes: how does academic self-government remain reasonably strong and effective in the context of opposing forms of control?

American universities have evolved their own answers throughout the twentieth century. Everywhere we find extensive use of collegial controls at the department level. On matters of who will teach, and what they will teach, and who does what research, the local faculty clusters have primacy, with much individual choice, especially in research. Then, the department head regularly serves as a mediator, first among equals in the collegial group and simultaneously the lowest line officer of higher management. There is a department-to-center line of representation in which collegial and bureaucratic controls mix with and shade off into one another. In this mix, as pointed out earlier, the departments typically have uncommon autonomy, more than in large organizations in other domains. There is a natural federalism in which departments and professional schools, empowered by their disciplines and fields, negotiate with the central administration. As Graeme C. Moodie and Rowland Eustace noted in the English university, "there is an important sense in which the 'higher' bodies seek validation from the 'lower.' Whatever the precise boundaries of departmental autonomy, its existence makes of every university a 'federal' structure rather than a strongly centralized system."[8] This inherent federalism gives strong states rights to the many subject-centered clusters of the faculty.

There remains the special role of all-campus faculty bodies, preeminently the academic senate. Senates have changed from all-in to elected representatives, but they remain fundamental instruments of faculty influence. As universities grow larger and more complex, the senates extend their web of committees. Individual faculty members serve on a number of these committees, standing and ad hoc, often more than they would like. And out of the midst of the senators there develops a major oligarchy of faculty members who devote much time, even full-time, to campus affairs. Thus, at the top of the campus collegial lines there are faculty-administrators whose daily activities put them in close touch with regular administrative staff and whose responsibilities push them toward all-campus views.

In short, in the major universities, faculty members administer a great deal: in their department-centered roles; in campus committees that decide such key matters as promotion to tenure; in senate participation, for some; and in campus oligarchy, for a few.

What happens if these traditional lines of faculty influence weaken significantly? There are two major long-run alternatives for the profession by way of enhancing influence. One is civil service, the use of personnel categories of government to ensure job protection and to enlarge the authority of different faculty ranks and disciplines. For example, nationalized systems of higher education abroad use common civil service grades and universal rules across institutions. Job protection can then be extremely strong and much desired: recent decades have seen dispossessed lower strata in European systems lobby their way into the civil service, with virtually instant tenure. The result is massive rigidity in mobility within the profession. The second alternative is unionization, unified or segmented, industrial or craft. Nonmilitant unions can and do co-exist with senates and other traditional forms, particularly to concentrate on bread-and-butter economic issues. But if weakened traditional forms leave faculty feeling quite powerless, then the vacuum of influence can be filled by militant unions that take over representation. Such unionism then brings the third-party involvement of professional unionists, the additional bureaucratic rules of labor-management contracts, and the institutionalization of adversary relations.

The traditional forms of professional self-government clearly make for something that looks like "organized anarchy" as they interweave with the bureaucratic forms of hierarchical administration and the controls that trustees can exercise under their basic responsibilities. Like democracy in government, traditional academic self-government does not look very good until you weigh the alternatives. The alternatives are "harder": more legalistic, more formal in character, more impersonal. In the many institutional settings where faculty never had much power, e.g., community colleges and state colleges that have a normal-school genetic imprint, the alternatives readily capture the imagination. In the research universities, the contest is still open and can be affected one way or the other by actions of administrators and officials: e.g., attacks on tenure are a clear way of inducing more academics to favor one or the other, or both, of the alternatives of guaranteed government employment and collective union protection.

COMPETENCE IN RESEARCH

The German solution to the problem of scholarly creativity in the nineteenth century became the American solution in the twentieth—put research and teaching together inside the university, rather than separating them in different institutions, and make the role of the professor a seamless blend of the two. The American extension of this solution involved a two-tier structure: namely, to keep the old college that had been *the* American form for over two centuries before "the university" landed on these shores, and to put a graduate school (and most professional schools) on top of it, thereby providing a special home for research and advanced training, beyond the first major degree, that was also largely beyond the reach of those already in power who wanted to devote the institution entirely to undergraduates. There evolved a departmental structure in the new universities in which the coverage of courses stretched from the freshman year to structured sequences that led to the dissertation and the doctoral degree itself. The university professoriate in the letters and sciences was now to handle these levels together.

This American combination has been an expensive business, with the high costs of research and advanced training added to the old costs of teaching, across the huge professoriate of the many universities and reaching increasingly in the last half of the twentieth century into four- and five-year colleges, public and private. The result has been an enormous amount of scholarly publication, much of it appearing trivial and excessive. But the long-term payoffs have been tremendous. Near the end of the twentieth century, the American research univerisites are the class of the world, with large cadres of specialists in one subfield after another charging ahead in research and scholarship at a pace that others cannot match. The benefits from pure and applied research, in terms of sheer productivity in new ideas, techniques, and applications, more than outweigh the costs of the huge subsidies that allow professors to be in the classroom as little as four to six hours a week and to devote a third, a half, or more of their time to research. Notably, science has become a key component of the legitimacy of the American higher education. The national government cannot do without it; state governors now maintain popularity on a platform of high technology; the population wants better medicine. It is the university that fills such wants, training for science and doing much of it.

The research productivity of the professoriate has been markedly aided by special conditions of American higher education. Since the last half of the nineteenth century, the system has been a large one, just on grounds of general population size. Large size became huge size when the country moved into mass higher education well in advance of other countries, toward a workforce that now tallies something like 800,000. This huge system is then composed of an unbelievable number of units (unbelievable in crossnational comparison) with some 1,500 private as well as 1,500 public institutions. Further, public control is radically federal, centered in fifty states. Such distinctively American conditions led early on to a high degree of institutional competition among the research and would-be research universities that has entailed a heady chase after talent. Even under the depressed conditions of economic turndowns, job mobility remains relatively high among American academics, with leading lights able to write their own ticket. For all of its crudeness, there is a competitive dynamic that stimulates the professoriate as well as the universities.

Relative institutional rank is on everyone's mind; prestige is the critical resource, since it brings money and additional talent; high status becomes the great motivator for institutions and professors alike. And in this struggle, professors often join hands with administrators and trustees (and the football team!) in a unity of institutional pride and effort. It is "us" against "them," sometimes friendly but always serious.

This institutional competition that becomes in some places a mad chase, a headlong dash, clearly puts a major strain on the old collegial ideals of a community of scholars. But most scholars stay in place for most of their careers, even in research universities, especially after tenure, and they develop the bonds of local commitment. There also remains a certain unity centered in respect for competence and achievement. In short, on the research side, the professoriate comes off rather well.

THE WEAKNESS IN UNDERGRADUATE TEACHING

But the effects of the American system on undergraduate teaching have been a different matter, especially in the state universities and particularly upon the students' first two years. Rare is the material or symbolic reward that does not push or pull the professor toward research and graduate students. The dual nature of the American university is a great ambition that strains organization: to put together the graduate and professional schools with a four-year undergraduate realm that is to provide a liberal or general education. Something has had to give, and that something is the undergraduate program. Someone has to come up on the short-end, and that someone is the freshman-sophomore student. Since the turn of the century, and especially in the post–1945 decades, the task of teaching those students at that level has drifted toward the margin of reward and interest. Why else would major universities, including the private ones, year in and year out send away brilliant young teachers rather than give them tenure? As Sheldon Rothblatt points out so well in his paper on undergraduate education, such professional behavior on the part of academics results not from personal willfulness but from the structural features of American universities.

The research function may well be more deeply hostile to undergraduate education than we have yet allowed ourselves to grasp. Following Rothblatt's argument: research looks to the future, liberal education to the past. Research can be externally measured, assessed, rewarded; undergraduate teaching cannot be. Research stresses originality of achievement; general education imparts eternal truths. And, most telling, "from the perspective of the research ethic, liberal education is not 'higher' education at all and therefore should be prevented from spilling over into universities and research institutes. It should be confined to institutions approximating what Europeans used to call the 'upper secondary school' and now call the 'post compulsory sector'—the academy, lycée, gymnasium, or sixth form."[9]

This fundamental strain—now an old story—cannot be eliminated. But it can be nibbled at, with marginal adjustments by faculty and administrators that over time lessen the natural weakness of the undergraduate realm. Models are available to us that offer partial lessons. The best private colleges instruct us in the care and feeding of "liberal education," with the great luxury of an able faculty that has nothing else to do other than to work in an undergraduate program. The best private universities are even more relevant: they make the objective, or the perceived objective, of a high quality undergraduate life into a competitive advantage, one by one against each other and particularly against public university competitors, to overcome in the latter case the competitive disadvantage of high cost.

We know by now the main dimensions for improving undergraduate work in public universities. One is substructuring, the gradual incremental, trial-and-error development of units of membership for faculty and students that break the large campus into more personal and more tangible parts, *in addition to* the departmental structure: e.g., honors programs, special subcolleges, special sets of seminars for freshmen and sophomores. The other is symbolic definition, the strengthening of the identity and image of "the college" within the university, including that of the subcolleges and subunits that structure it on other than disciplinary lines. *The* great competitive advantage of the Ivy League universities, of course, is that they were colleges before they were universities and the college components have endured well, not the least because alumni support has made the college the sentimental and symbolic "heart" of the organization. For example, at Yale, Yale College remains vibrant. Inside the college, the twelve residential subcolleges are key units for students and for a fair number of faculty members, especially faculty in the humanities departments. While state universities work ever harder on their overall images—the symbolic representations by which they are known by the world—they could well work for stronger definitions of "the college" and its parts.

None of this comes to pass, we know by now, unless faculty and administrators are willing to differentiate rewards for the professoriate. The political joke has it that certain politicians are so dumb they cannot walk down the street and chew gum at the same time. Modern American public universities seem genetically "dumb" in that they cannot keep two thoughts in mind at the same time: that there has to be a reward structure for undergraduate teaching as well as a reward structure for research— even at the risk of a dual-faculty division. Some small gains have been made by way of stiffening the teaching criterion in promotion decisions, but imagination, administrative leadership, and faculty professional common sense could substantially enlarge those gains. The weak undergraduate performance of the professoriate in the public research university is an Achilles heel, a vulnerability that should not be allowed to endure. It may cost us all dearly.

NOTES

1. This section draws upon more extended discussion in Burton R. Clark, *The Higher Education System: Academic Organization in Cross-National Perspective* (Berkeley, Los Angeles, London: University of California Press, 1983), Chapter 2, "Work"; and Burton R. Clark, "The Organizational Conception," in *Perspectives on Higher Education: Eight Disciplinary and Comparative Views*, ed. Burton R. Clark (Berkeley, Los Angeles, London: University of California Press, 1984), pp. 106–128.

2. On the concept of matrix in organizational thought, see L. R. Sayles, "Matrix Organization: The Structure with a Future," *Organizational Dynamics* (Autumn 1976):2–17; and Henry Mintzberg, *The Structuring of Organizations* (Englewood Cliffs, N.J.: Prentice-Hall, 1979), pp. 168–175.

3. Norton E. Long, "Power and Administration," *Public Administration Review* 9 (1949):257–264. Quotation, 262.

4. R. Steven Turner, "The Growth of Professorial Research in Prussia, 1818 to 1848: Causes and Context." In *Historical Studies in the Physical Sciences*, ed. Russell McCormmach (Philadelphia: University of Pennsylvania Press, 1971), 3:137–182; especially 159.

5. It also overlooked the simple fact that from its very beginning the Western university has been primarily, especially on the European continent, a set of professional schools. Alan B. Cobban observed: "The medieval universities were largely vocational schools. They trained students in the mastery of areas of knowledge that could be utilized in one of the secular professions of law, medicine, or teaching or in the service of the Church. . . . The normal student ambition was to gain lucrative employment within the safety of the established order." The more things change. . . ! Alan B. Cobban, *The Medieval Universities: Their Development and Organization* (London: Methuen and Co., 1975), p. 165.

6. Sydney Ann Halpern, "Professional Schools in the American University: The Evolving Dilemma of Research and Practice," in *The Academic Profession: An International Perspective*, edited by Burton R. Clark. Comparative Higher

Education Research Group, Graduate School of Education, UCLA. Unpublished manuscript.

7. Halpern, "Professional Schools," p. 7.

8. Graeme C. Moodie and Rowland Eustace, *Power and Authority in British Universities* (Montreal: McGill-Queen's University Press, 1974), p. 61.

9. See chapter 3 in this book, Sheldon Rothblatt, " 'Standing Antagonisms:' The Relationship of Undergraduate to Graduate Education," p. 46.

CHAPTER 9
THE FUTURE TEACHING, RESEARCH, AND PUBLIC SERVICE MISSION OF THE HISTORICALLY BLACK PUBLIC UNIVERSITY

IVORY V. NELSON

The next sixteen years will bring many changes. These changes will affect the historically black public universities with teaching, research, and extension missions in ways unlike that of majority institutions which have similar missions. Thus, it is my intent to provide a discussion framework within which these institutions might begin to plan and direct their futures.

Looking ahead is tricky and risky business. Whatever happens is substantially affected by what the institutions and individuals responsible for those institutions decide to do. However, speculation about the future can be a useful activity. It can provide the stimulus for the various institutional constituencies to make decisions about such things as the faculty, buildings, competition, heritage, student body, labor market, funding, technology, policies, and leadership. These decisions should define and answer the questions: What public policies should be financed and supported to insure the viability of the historically black public colleges? What new internal institutional policies should these colleges and universities promote and develop? To what extent can these colleges and universities realistically plan for the future? What contingency planning should these institutions undertake? What can they do best in their research, teaching, and extension programs? What are the advantages and disadvantages of these institutions as they compare themselves to their competition, clientele, and such? What is threatened that is worth preserving, and what is new and worth developing for this particular set of institutions?

During the next sixteen years, it has already been predicted that there will be general demographic depression for higher education. However, minority youth will increase in numbers and comprise nearly 30 percent of all youth by the year 2000. Thus, the need and place for historically black public colleges in this milieu is quite apparent if one considers the projected increase in minority enrollment as the only factor. But if one considers the total needs of higher education, then higher education must also provide:

1. Places to accommodate by the year 2010 approximately the same number of students as were enrolled in 1978. It will not make sense to substantially reduce capacity only to have to recreate it again in the near future.

2. Institutions representing at least the degree of diversity we have today. The United States is an intricate mosaic of races, ethnic groups, religions, occupational pursuits, styles of life, and is becoming ever more so, at least in occupational pursuits and styles of life. Institutions, *like the historically black public land-grant universities*, that pay attention to these diversities will be at least equally needed in the future as in the past.

3. Capabilities for greater equality of opportunity.

4. Capacities for providing more services to the surrounding community.[1]

THE CULTURAL CONTEXT

The historically black public colleges and universities have been the academic meeting places for the disadvantaged of this nation. These colleges and universities reflect the social, political, economic, and cultural milieu in which they exist, and as such, this set of unique institutions has an important and irreplaceable role in fostering educational development in this country. Certainly the history of these institutions is an example of what hope and commitment can accomplish as they have demonstrated the know-how to identify latent talent; the willingness to use their expertise to develop that talent; the commitment to persevere in working with latent talent; and the understanding to know where that talent can best be used to insure maximum impact for development.

Examination of population characteristics indicates that not only are these universities relevant to the American system of higher education but also they have the potential to provide a vehicle for possible solution to global problems. In 1957, there were 2.5 billion people on earth. By 1984, the number had grown to about 4.8 billion with prospects of doubling again in less than forty years.[2] In China, the world's most populous nation, forty-five babies are born every minute.[3]

Since World War II, the political boundaries of the earth have been drastically altered. New nations such as Algeria, Burundi, Cameroon, the Central African Republic, Chad, the Congo, Cyprus, Dahomey, Gabon, the Ivory Coast, Jamaica, Kuwait, the Malagasy Republic, Mali, Mauritania, Niger, Nigeria, Rwanda, Senegal, Sierra Leone, Somalia, Tanzania, Togo, Trinidad and Tobago, Uganda, Upper Volta, Western Samoa, and Zaire have been created or granted independence.

Today, the world's 165 independent nations are tightly interlocked. What happens in the farthest corner of the world now touches everyone instantly. Through technology we share a common classroom, and the world has become a threatening and unsafe place. If the historically black public universities are not utilized and involved in providing experiences that make students see beyond themselves and better understand the interdependent nature of our world, then America will have squandered one of its greatest resources.

During the last ten years, American productivity increased by about 23 percent. In 1980, the United States' share of world manufacturing was 17 percent. During the 1960s, America had a baby boom, but it is projected that by 1990 the school age population will have declined 14 percent from its peak in 1970. By the year 2000, it is predicted that only 34 percent of all Americans will be under twenty-five, while about 28 percent will be fifty and over. The comparable percentages in 1981 were about 41 and 26, respectively.[4]

The demographics are clear and only need interpretation in institutionally specific terms. The historically black public universities are a link with this new reality, and they must be included in the "master plan" for higher education in this country, whether that planning retrenches existing programs or develops new programs and services for a changing population.

SPECIAL NEEDS OF STUDENTS

The youth population among black and Hispanic Americans remains large and is increasing. In 1980, slightly less than one-third of all white Americans were nineteen years of age and under, but 43 percent of all Hispanics and 40 percent of all blacks fell into this category.[5] These changes could have profound significance for historically black public universities as the enrollment levels for college-bound youth are predicted to decline.

In 1981, 71 percent of all black and 75 percent of all Hispanic households had children under eighteen years of age. Contrast this to only 52 percent of all white families that had children under eighteen years.[6] It is apparent that the education of minorities in the year 2000 will be inter-locked with the economic vitality and security of the nation. Opportunity still remains unequal and movement within the social order suggests that this will still be the case in the year 2000. The failure to educate every young person to his or her full potential threatens the nation's social and economic health, an event that need not occur if the historically black public colleges are developed to their full potential to address this seg-ment of our society. It must be stated here, however, that while in prin-ciple there may be a willingness for this to occur, there are loyalities rooted in past history and apprehensions about future changes in institu-tional roles. The primary objective proposed here is the attainment of numerical ratios of ethnic distribution consistent with the purpose of ex-panding opportunity and resources for all citizens, but focused on spe-cific clientele.

This idea is further complicated because of widely differing concepts of what should be the status of historically black public institutions within their state systems. While there is general agreement that these institu-tions should serve all ethnic groups and become a part of the mainstream of public higher education, there is also strong support for their continu-ing role as a major resource for blacks. Questions that must be answered are: What is meant by "the elimination of all vestiges of dualism" through state planning? To what degree must these institutions lose their identity as black colleges and universities? Federal agencies do not seem to have a common stance on this matter, and civil rights leaders hold widely vary-ing positions.

Irrespective of the positions of present leaders and agencies, tomor-row's youth will be born, and will live, in an era of unprecedented tech-nological advance and global interdependence. The resultant complexity and gravity of tomorrow's problems associated with minorities and blacks pose special challenges and add new dimensions to the fulfillment of stu-dent needs at the historically black public university with teaching, re-search, and extension obligations. The whole concept and approach to the fulfillment of student needs as a benefit both for the individual and society will be questioned.

Granting the importance of all the influences that enter into the ques-tioning of the special needs of students at the historically black public universities, if in the end these institutions provide an in-depth knowl-edge of the major values in Western democracy and equip these students with the intellectual tools for informed thought and criticism, then they have fulfilled their total mission by preparing well-rounded citizens who will perpetuate and serve a free society.

EMERGING DEVELOPMENTS

The next two decades do not appear to be a period in which colleges and universities, especially the historically black public universities, can afford to adhere and cling to present approaches and in the process think that the American society will adopt an educational attitude to provide all the needed funding. It will be necessary during this period to provide a model of higher education that can be redirected toward a new direction of capital-intensive technological strategies. Given this direction and the conservative attitude of the populace in the nation and especially the conservative attitude that exists in the states where these colleges and universities are located, how might these universities and colleges approach this change?

One approach might be to define a new function for the historically black public colleges and universities. That is, these institutions could best prepare themselves for the future by engaging in the following practices:

1. Coordinating the process of anticipating societal needs for knowledge;
2. Developing in these institutions the capacity for training appropriate, significant levels of quality human resources;
3. Assessing the ability of these institutional research mechanisms to generate knowledge relevant to societal needs; and
4. Organizing the dissemination of vital knowledge to citizens so that it is fully utilized.

What is needed by the historically black public universities to explore this potential new direction? First, a series of studies could be undertaken to determine what it is costing these universities for not coordinating their present efforts. Second, a clear delineation of the central scope, role, and focus of these universities could serve as evidence for public and private support. Third, the historically black public universities need to assess and improve the production of knowledge and the distribution mechanisms. The quality and competitiveness of existing programs must be documented and their cost effectiveness must be shown.

If the historically black public universities follow this direction and carefully build and document this approach, the very trends that threaten the well-being of these institutions will become arguments for the priority of their maintenance and existence.

POLITICS AND GOVERNANCE

The historically black public universities, in their quest to fulfill the functions of teaching, research, and public service, must become keenly aware of the financial pressure that the citizenry will exert. The "antitax" movements and the antiregulatory arguments will take a pervasive "reduce government support" stance. Public response to the emerging resource crisis will continue to be directed toward programs for crash priority. These programs will tend to be oriented toward high technological sophistication rather than toward conservative measures involving life-style changes. Competition among federal and state priorities will become extremely intense, to the relative detriment of long-range needs and issues.

The historically black public universities must recognize that the demand for accountability and evidence of competence will force conservative decision making and the proliferation of paperwork, requiring computers to document performance. These demands will impede the ability of these institutions to respond to change. Academic freedom and tenure will be seen as luxuries by the taxpayers.

These universities must establish governance structures that will rely heavily on modern management techniques, including planning and evaluation. They must release themselves from the traditional disciplinary organizational schemes that have prevailed in the past.

In pursuit of their mission the historically black public universities must recognize that an emergence of the economic and military status of the United States is reappearing. National defense has already emerged as a top priority area, and business, industry, and government will compare the performance of these colleges and universities to that of all their counterparts.

EDUCATION OF THE INDIVIDUAL

As we look at the global and life-style changes that the future may hold for the individual, we can imagine quite a new set of conditions and educational needs that a person will require to live in the twenty-first century. Thus, the historically black public universities need to think about the nature of the individual's education in different terms. Generally, universities have focused for most of the twentieth century on the development of subject matter and have organized their research and teaching in academic disciplines. This has been one of the reasons for the expansion of knowledge. We have generally expanded the disciplines by dividing and creating new courses to accommodate the expanded knowledge in each discipline.

Advanced technology and vast improvements in the quality of life will create both jobs and the need for a greater number of persons with college degrees. However, higher education during the next decades will no longer be an automatic vehicle guaranteeing upward mobility. In fact, an undergraduate education will probably no longer lead inevitably to a preferred job in the future. While 20 percent of the jobs will be classified technical/professional, there will be 2.5 qualified college graduates competing for every such job opening.

It should be the role of the historically black public universities to focus their thinking, in the twenty-first century, on learning and the student, instead of subject matter and the teacher. The universities should talk about "lifetime learning" from the standpoint of needing to continue one's education and they should update information and new professional techniques. If this is done then these institutions might force the educational enterprise to think differently about the different kinds of education needed for different people. This might require different standards for judging the relative importance of one need versus another. It might require specialized educational programs to meet certain educational needs. We do a little of this now, but in general we think of one B.S. degree about the same as any other B.S. degree. The curriculums in most universities meet about the same academic and accreditation standards. It would appear that we do this because we think the subject matter and the professor teaching the courses are required. The historically black public universities must raise and answer the question "Is this need the same for each student?"

It thus seems evident that with the pluralism and individualization of our society and the projected changes in educational needs, the historically black public universities must change and become more flexible and responsive to meet the needs of the future.

RESEARCH: AN ESSENTIAL PART OF EDUCATION

In the historically black public universities research has received less than desirable emphasis. This is because very few funds have been available for research, and research has been seen to be in competition with teaching. This view, however, should not be continued. Research in these universities must be given an integral role. It must be supported in spirit as well as financially if the historically black public universities are to achieve what they should and deserve. Howard R. Bowen has expressed it:

Not only are the three functions of teaching, research, and public service carried on jointly; they are often mutually supported. Teaching may be enriched if it occurs in the environment of discovery, intellectual excitement, and contact with the real world and its problems. Similarly research and public service may be enhanced when they are combined with teaching. This does not imply that every community college or liberal arts college should become a great research center. Nor does it deny that universities can overdo research and public service to the neglect of instruction. It implies only that the spirit of inquiry and public service enriches academic enterprise and lends coherence and unity to the American System of higher education.[7]

If possible, the historically black public universities must include research as part of the educational process, and research should not be carried out by research staff and faculty without direct involvement of students.

The historically black public universities must adopt the principle that knowledge must constantly be renewed, and it is the search for new knowledge that is called research. Teaching must be viewed as a process that leads to learning to ask questions that will produce a knowledge base. These universities must understand that the greatness of America has been its unwillingness to accept prevailing beliefs. Discoveries were made because individuals were willing to question, to experiment, and to reach independent conclusions. This is the essence of teaching as it is also of research. The historically black public universities can do no less in the following decades.

If the problems of tomorrow are to be solved, it will be necessary for the historically black public universities to train persons to solve them. This occurs only by letting students participate in research as part of their education. One learns to be a scholar by practicing scholarship.

If the historically black public universities are concerned with the quality of their research and instruction, and the true educational public service they should provide, they must be keenly aware of the quality and scope of research carried on by their faculties. These universities must foster an atmosphere that will allow faculty to remain abreast of new developments. They must allow faculty to pursue research in their fields of interest and utilize this research in the teaching and training of students.

CONSTITUENT ELEMENTS OF QUALITY ACADEMIC PROGRAMS

The historically black public universities must identify and articulate precisely a set of standards to demonstrate that high quality is intrinsic to all their academic programs. This set of standards should embrace the following considerations:

ADMISSION

The criteria for admission in the historically black public universities should be based exclusively on educational considerations established on the basis of a publicly stated policy. Only students having the potential to complete their programs with the help of all the institutional resources should be admitted.

TEACHING

The historically black public universities should emphasize creating, maintaining, and evaluating their instructional programs purely on the basis of sound educational principles rather than on gimmicks. They should offer programs only in areas in which sufficient resources are available. Faculty members teaching in each discipline must be trained in the discipline, and must keep up-to-date. The same standards of excellence must govern off-campus and nontraditional programs.

SUPPORT SERVICES

The historically black public universities must provide support services comparable in numbers and nature with their respective academic programs. Compensatory services and sound competent academic advising should be available to all students lacking the ability to complete institutional requirements.

CERTIFICATION

The historically black public universities should clearly articulate the meaning or significance of their institution's degrees, and they must award these degrees strictly on the basis of academic merit.

EVALUATION

The historically black public universities must insist on the principle that academic program evaluation will be fair, just, reasonable, and appropriate. The principles of academic honesty must be strongly embraced and enforced.

PUBLIC SERVICE

In considering the historically black public universities' investment for the next sixteen years, there are two major questions involving their public service commitments: What should be the mixes of professional and technological programs that are needed the most and how can they be financed? To what extent will these universities be involved directly and formally in providing in-service, continuing education?

To answer these questions, the historically black public universities must fully understand that legislators and state budget makers have very little sympathy for the claim, "The public demands this or that." Consequently, they must realize their mission to offer and provide off-campus credit and noncredit courses and various forms of technical assistance is not being greeted enthusiastically. They must realistically answer the question, Does this offering amount to institutional lifesaving? Given the declining number of eighteen- to twenty-four-year olds is all the talk and to-do about outreach and public service simply the creation of a new market to make up for the declining one?

Despite the problems inherent in these questions, the historically black public universities can justify and fulfill their public service commitment. First, to the extent these universities have difficulty in knowing and identifying their primary constituencies, outreach can be a very effective bridge. No university with its many faculties working on production-line problems, public education, international problems, and the like, can remain an ivory tower bastion. It is reasonable to assume that the quality of teaching will be enlivened by participation in problem solution. Points that the historically black public universities may use as a basis for a strong outreach program may include the following:

1. The historically black public universities have had an impact on American agriculture through the interconnection of research, teaching,

and extension through demonstration, special instruction, and advice on specific application.

2. As people change careers and as more and more women enter and reenter the job market, retraining will be needed.

3. As people attempt to remain competent and current in their vocations, education will have to be continuous rather than once and for all.

4. The problems of public agencies and private business make it inevitable that job-specific experts be retrained.

The historically black public universities must demonstrate to the public and business communities the advantages of utilizing their resources. They should develop formal contractual agreements that incorporate the following principles:

1. Since academic freedom is the stalwart of the academic community, professors delivering this contracted service are protected in following any line of inquiry that develops.

2. Since technical assistance is the university's primary function and means of support, and because the university does not operate for a profit, the costs of technical assistance should be competitive with private vendors.

3. Since the faculty does not leave when the service is over, both they and their institution are dependent on and responsible for the long-term good will of their constituency.

Whether our economy becomes technological and postindustrial or reindustrialized or both, the historically black public colleges and universities must be involved in this major socioeconomic agenda through continuing education.

BASIC AXIOMS FOR THE FUTURE

Politically, the historically black public universities have to be realistic about the future. First, these universities must put their intellectual assumptions in clear, sharp focus. They must articulate clearly the kind of colleges and universities they will become. They must stimulate the public with definitive arguments over ideals and ideas.

Second, the historically black public universities must push everybody harder, beginning with themselves, in academic endeavors and decision making. They must concentrate on higher standards of study, teaching, research, conduct, discussion, argument, public information, and governance. They must assume the responsibility in the decades ahead to understand, interpret, and defend those who must make the difficult choices affecting quality in program and personnel. If the historically black public university is to survive, it must endure, sponsor and support the "hard nose" who gets the work done. The days of the loved administrator are over. Something must and shall be done. The universities' best services will lie in defending the doing even though they may dislike the doer.

Third, the historically black public university must not engage in deception by trying to pull the wool over the public's eyes. They must begin to find solutions to the problems they most encounter. They must provide initiative, leadership, instruction, and research. In this pluralistic society, these universities must strive for excellence in all their endeavors.

Fourth, the leaders of the historically black public universities must never stop taking chances. They must continue to advocate their universities as portals of access for the downtrodden, deprived, denied, and the disadvantaged. They must understand that all true success and creativity involves risk and high risk in this cultural milieu. These universities must provide the right atmosphere within which innovation might flourish to tackle the problems associated with this risk.

Fifth, the historically black public universities must never stop dreaming. Without dreams their past accomplishments would never have been realized. Continuous dreaming will ensure that their future accomplishments will not cease.

Sixth, the historically black public universities must not allow their accomplishments to go unnoticed. They must brag truthfully and without shame. They need not apologize for any of their pursuits.

Seventh, the historically black public universities should help all students move with a high degree of confidence from college to the workplace. Looking to the year 2000, a four-year college education will not be sufficient. The future graduates will change jobs several times. New skills will be required; new citizenship obligations will be confronted. Of necessity, education will be lifelong.

Eighth, the historically black public universities should not carry on their functions in teaching, research, and public service in isolation. They must align themselves with the high schools and junior high schools. The quality of their educational enterprise will be shaped in a large measure by the quality of these connections.

Finally, the existence of historically black public universities is dependent on public commitment. They must find ways to garner support from citizens, state agencies, legislatures, and the federal government.

CONCLUSION

If the historically black public universities are to remain viable, cope with change, and predict and determine their future role in the realm of higher education, rather than having it determined by others, they must establish and maintain a vigorous planning and achievement capability tied to a long-range outlook. According to Gerald O'Neill in his book *A Hopeful View of the Human Future*, "The long term health of the *historically black public universities* will be shown more clearly by the time scale of the programs they undertake. The willingness to commit to ventures of many years duration will be the hallmark of a *university* confident of its future. . . ."[8]

To determine programs for the next ten and fifteen years, and to have the confidence to commit themselves to their future achievements, the historically black public universities will need to establish excellent futures research capability. This research capability must pinpoint future boundaries of operation with confidence and imaginative leadership that will generate a commitment to achieve those goals.

The historically black public universities cannot adopt the byword of "flexibility" of present-day planners and administrators on long-range planning; flexibility is often translated to mean "the absence of a decision." They must understand and recognize that the lack of a decision is a decision, and in most cases, it is a very bad decision. The historically black public universities must develop the confidence that they can accurately and properly look into the future. They must put forth bold plans for coping with what they think will be future needs. They must not be afraid to commit and implement their developed plans. They cannot use uncertainty as an excuse or a reason for nonaction. They must use the advice of John Naisbitt in his book *Megatrends*, "We must make uncertainty our friend, it is one of the few certainties we have."[9]

NOTES

1. "Final Report of the Carnegie Council on Policy Studies in Higher Education," *Three Thousand Futures: The Next Twenty Years for Higher Education* (San Francisco: Jossey-Bass Publishers, 1980), pp. 89–90.

2. United Nations, Department of International Economic and Social Affairs, *Demographic Year Book*: 1981, 33rd issue (New York: United Nations, 1983).

3. Population Reference Bureau, Washington, D.C. March 1983. Unpublished data.

4. Bureau of the Census, *Statistical Abstract of the United States*, p. 27.

5. U.S. Department of Commerce, Bureau of the Census, *Current Population Reports*, Series P–20, No. 374 (U.S. Government Printing Office, Washington, D.C.), p. 20.

6. U.S. Department of Commerce, Bureau of the Census, *Current Population Reports*, Series P–20, No. 371 (U.S. Government Printing Office, Washington, D.C.), pp. 131–734.

7. Howard R. Bowen. *Investment in Learning* (San Francisco: Jossey-Bass, 1977), p. 507.

8. Gerard K. O'Neill, *2081: A Hopeful View of the Human Future* (New York: Simon & Schuster), 1982.

9. John Naisbitt, *Megatrends* (New York: Warner Books, Inc.), p. 252.

CHAPTER 10
THE FUTURE ROLE OF THE URBAN
UNIVERSITY IN TEACHING,
RESEARCH, AND PUBLIC SERVICE

HENRY R. WINKLER

While an urban university's commitment to educating students from the area in which it is located assumes the conventional interaction and interdependence among teaching, research, and public service, its mission of providing "resources responsive to the needs and priorities" of that area requires a particular interaction between the university and community itself. As the city changes, so does the urban university.

And, throughout the next two decades, the city will change. Ethnic and cultural amalgams will be altered by a variety of social forces. New values and perspectives will be assimilated into the whole. New concerns and new challenges will arise, testing the existing municipal systems and structures. Ever-advancing technology will continue to affect the way our society gathers and shares information and to create an increasing demand for a well-educated and well-trained work force. A constituent of, and accommodator to, these changes will be the urban university, imparting specific skills within the context of a broad education, embracing the urban environment as a laboratory while searching for solutions to municipal concerns, generating new knowledge and new technologies, and acting as a catalyst for cultural and economic revitalization.

Because education is the means by which society keeps pace with change and the city is at the center of that change, the urban university has become an institution of significant social, cultural, and economic importance. In the decades ahead, it stands to assume an even greater role as the pace of change accelerates. The urban university, however, must be prepared for, and able to respond to, change if it is to meet the challenges and seize the opportunities that will be presented.

143

Demographic projections, therefore, serve as important indicators of the forces that may shape the future of teaching, research, and public service at an urban institution. The most dramatic and most widely acknowledged of those changes is the decline in the number of high school graduates, a trend that is expected to continue well into the 1990s. In less than six years, those under the age of twenty will, for the first time in our history, account for less than 30 percent of the population. For urban universities, the most obvious consequence of that trend is declining enrollments and the concomitant fiscal constraints, but the most critical issues will not revolve around enrollments but the manner in which the urban university adapts to the change; the factors, forces, and interests weighed in the decision-making process; the determinations of academic strengths and weaknesses, of the role and scope of public service; the balance that is sought between internal and external interests; and, ultimately, the confirmation or redefinition of the basic mission. If the many interests can be balanced judiciously and the basic commitments preserved, the urban university will enter the twenty-first century as a more prominent, more effective institution.

Declining enrollments, however, will not have the same impact on every geographical region. While universities in the Sun Belt are expected to show a modest increase in the number of undergraduate students, the result of continuing migration to the South and West and a disproportionately higher birth rate, universities in the Frost Belt will show a general decline in undergraduate enrollments. By 1990, approximately 50 percent of our total population will reside in the Sun Belt. With the discrepancies in population will come discrepancies in political influence. Distinct regional differences could affect the development of a comprehensive program of federal support as Congress might prove reluctant to appropriate funds that seemed to favor some regions over others. In the absence of federal support, the individual states could assume a greater role in the funding and regulation of urban universities. In general, state funding formulas have tended not to make distinctions for the special needs of urban universities but the importance of these institutions is becoming increasingly apparent to many public officials.

In addition, there is evidence to suggest that, without the proper preparation, the enrollment declines could be more pronounced than the raw figures might suggest. By 1990, for example, minorities will represent approximately 20 to 25 percent of the total population, while their proportion among students in elementary and secondary schools will be even greater. In states such as California, Hawaii, Texas, South Carolina, Mississippi, and Louisiana, minorities account for more than 40 percent of the students enrolled in elementary and secondary schools. For urban universities, the result of that trend could be a decreasing percentage of high school graduates opting for a college education. For instance, only about 28 percent of the blacks between the ages of eighteen and twenty-four enter college, while the rate is even lower among Hispanics of the same age group, somewhere between 5 and 15 percent. To stabilize enrollments as much as possible, urban universities will have to attract and retain an increasing percentage of these students.

Other factors that could influence enrollments at urban universities include a decreasing proportion of young adults in the work force, which could create more opportunities for high school graduates to find employment without a college education, and a growing number of children raised in single-parent families, who, studies suggest, tend to have more learning problems and are, therefore, less likely to attend college than their counterparts from two-parent families. In addition, the urban environment and, therefore, the urban university will be affected by increasing immigration, the further stratification of society, the continued movement away from an economy based on production toward one based on service, deteriorating transportation systems and infrastructures, and other familiar urban concerns. Each of these concerns presents an opportunity but no single model or formula will serve the differing and diverse needs of urban universities throughout the country. Even the needs of a single minority group will vary from city to city and region to region. Cubans in Florida and Chicanos in California, both Hispanic, will have different needs and values. A program designed to address the needs of one will not be applicable to the other. Urban universities will have to prepare for the general demographic trends and scan their local environment for the more specific changes. Curricula will have to be adjusted, perhaps to provide more remedial programs, while a system of support services, sensitive to changing concerns and values of various minority groups, will have to be strengthened. In many areas, public service will have to be expanded if cities are to cope with the change. Each institution will need an urban policy and an implementation strategy to preserve its basic commitments.

To fulfill their urban commitments and protect their own interests, urban universities will have to expand their relationships with the inner-city schools. A variety of models for increased cooperation between urban schools and urban universities are available. The University of Cincinnati's Urban Initiatives Program, for instance, is a comprehensive, statewide effort supported by the Ohio legislature. The program, developed in conjunction with Central State University and Cuyahoga Community College, is designed to eliminate language deficiencies throughout the state through the creation of a new curriculum for learning language, the training of teachers in that new curriculum, and the interaction of the universities with many public schools and community groups.

Another model is provided by the partnership established by the University of Wisconsin and the Milwaukee public school system. In addition to redesigning the curriculum of a local school to reflect the needs of employers and the strengths of the university, the partnership has developed articulation standards to facilitate admission to the university, prepared a brochure to advise high school students on the appropriate courses to take to prepare for the university, created a transition program that brings high school students with a proficiency in math and science to the campus for seven weeks of courses taught primarily by university professors, developed a series of conferences on the evaluation of student writing for teachers throughout the state, and produced a directory of faculty and staff members willing to share their expertise with the local schools.

Unfortunately, in some urban universities, there is a lack of urban focus where it would be clearly useful, most obviously in many Colleges of Education, some of which offer no courses in urban education or in the special problems of the inner-city schools and teachers. Often, past recruitment practices ignored the need for faculty with expertise and interest in city school systems, and cooperative projects with city schools were conspicuous in their paucity. If urban universities are to attract a greater percentage of minority students and reduce the need for remedial courses, such expertise and interest will have to be developed.

To provide productive assistance to the community during a time of fiscal constraint, urban universities will have to examine their public service offerings to decide if funding for all can be justified in the light of competing budget demands of teaching and research. Public service, a nebulous term at best, can be used to define any activity of the university that enhances the quality of life within a metropolitan area. A definition developed by the University of Massachusetts separates the category into three subgroups:

1. Advice, information, and technical assistance to business, government, neighborhood groups, and individuals on problems that the university has competence to assist in solving;

2. Research toward the solution of public policy problems, whether by individual or groups of faculty members or by the formal institutes and centers of the university;

3. Conferences, institutes, seminars, workshops, short courses, and other nondegree-oriented upgrading and training for government officials, social service personnel, various professional people, business executives, and so on.

Five basic models for providing public service have been identified by Arnold Grobman and Janet Sanders. Under the academic model faculty within a traditional academic unit have primary responsibility for providing public services. The extension or continuing education model incorporates a division of continuing education or the equivalent to provide courses for nontraditional students through a variety of delivery systems on and off campus. The service unit model employs a series of service units within the university but outside the typical academic structure, while the center model provides a center, typically outside the academic structure, to offer various services and applied research pertinent to the urban community. The last, a brokerage model, brings representatives of the urban area together with those of the university to identify and address problems of mutual concern.

From among these many models and services, urban universities will have to decide which are most effective within, and appropriate to, their particular area. In the instructional area, distinctions will have to be made between public service activities that offer expertise and those that are merely sanctioned by the university, between those that render instruction and those that cloak political activism in altruistic terms. Because the urban mission is best served by appropriate instruction, it is imperative that public service per se should remain subsidiary to instruction broadly defined and should occur as a function thereof. In other areas, distinctions will have to be made between those services that complement and support city programs and those that replicate metropolitan services or the functions of social service agencies. New partnerships will have to be infused with a realistic assessment of the proper functions of a university.

Urban universities *should* assist local governments in attempting to resolve urban problems and issues faced by the metropolitan area. They *should* provide advice to cities. They *should* provide continuing education for personnel in local government. They *should* use, not exploit, cities for intern and experimental purposes when needed. They *should not* be, however, in the business of providing or delivering services directly to the public save those related to the provision of higher education within the context of the particular institution's teaching and research goals.

The shaping of public policy by educating the city's future professionals should remain central to the mission of the urban university. It should be further enhanced by the development of interdisciplinary and intercollege degree programs, such as planning-law programs, certificates in historic preservation, and engineering-business options. Because urban problems, by their nature, require an interdisciplinary approach, academic planning should actively encourage the development of such courses of instruction whenever possible.

Urban-related research could be made more effective through greater coordination that would help reduce the potential for a wasteful duplication of effort. Such research often suffers from the insularity engendered by collegial and departmental organization. Each institution needs, therefore, a voluntary clearinghouse for urban-related research. The emphasis must lie equally on "voluntary" and "clearinghouse": no one should be required to register his or her investigations, and no one should be invested with the power to approve or disapprove a given project unless traditional standards concerning the use of human subjects and equitable access to facilities are violated. However, faculty members should be encouraged to file project descriptions with a clearinghouse whose mission would be simply to place people with mutual interests in touch with each other. Such a clearinghouse might facilitate the dissolution of present barriers to cooperation by resolving or transcending long-standing problems.

Though urban-related research will remain dependent on outside funding, the urban university will have to decide if it should provide the facilities for and grant implicit sanction to what are essentially independent consulting organizations, such as the various institutes of governmental research. Although the directors of these institutes may argue that these units provide a "university presence" at city hall, the benefits of this visibility are doubtful at best. There is, however, a need for more long-term research on urban problems, often made prohibitive by intermittent external funding. But, if complex urban problems are to be solved or ameliorated to any degree, urban scholars will have to enjoy the freedom of their academic counterparts in the physical sciences to pursue questions that will not necessarily have immediate applicability but may well result in some significant progress.

By prudently managing decline, avoiding a duplication of effort, and other such measures, urban universities will be able to protect many aspects of their urban mission. In many cases, however, skillful management of dwindling resources may not be sufficient to protect vital services. The urban university's ability to make a continuing contribution to the city will depend on increased external support.

An early model for such support was provided by the Ford Foundation which, from 1959 to 1974, granted over $36 million to a handful of universities to direct their resources toward the solution of urban problems. The results of that experiment were disappointing but insights into the complexity of the situation were gained. In assessing the effect of the program, Harold Howe II of the Ford Foundation asserted that the most successful efforts were those based "on a clear-headed assessment of the strengths of the university and an intelligent view of what an institution that specializes in education and research can contribute to a set of problems traditionally outside its purview." Programs that attempted to "attack directly the ills of central city populations or the myriad challenges facing city governments did not do as well." To encourage a concerted effort in addressing urban problems, Howe estimated that approximately $500,000 a year for a minimum of five years would be required to "produce useful output in even a moderate-size urban institution." Despite its shortcomings, the Ford Foundation experiment did lead to the inclusion of Title I, which provides support for some community services and for continuing education, as a part of the Higher Education Act of 1965.

A model for federal support was offered by the Urban Grant University Act, authorized under Title XI of the 1980 amendments to the Higher Education Act of 1965. Based on the land-grant concept of the late 1800s, the Urban Grant University Act was designed to bring the urban universities' "underutilized reservoir of skills, talents, and knowledge" to bear on the "multitude of problems that face the Nation's urban centers" in the same way the Morrill Act had focused the educational efforts of the land-grant colleges on solving the pressing agricultural concerns of the day. The architects of the Urban Grant University Act, as well as those testifying on its behalf, realized, however, that the problems of the modern urban environment were infinitely more complicated than those of the rural world of the nineteenth century. But the concept of urban grants remains an untested one as funds approved under the act have never been appropriated.

While federal support, such as that envisioned under the Urban Grant University Act, would help urban universities preserve or enhance their commitment to the community, it would not, by any means, alleviate other crucial funding problems. Foremost among those is the need to retool and refurbish university laboratories. A study conducted by the National Science Foundation shows that one-fourth of the research equipment in the major research institutions is considered obsolete. Without a major source of funding, critical research will be hampered and the retention of prominent researchers will become increasingly difficult. As much as $40 billion may be required to maintain research facilities and upgrade equipment throughout the country. While some federal support may be forthcoming, urban universities, like others, will still have to bear a large percentage of those costs.

The costs of new technologies, including innovations in telecommunications that could bring enormous change to the urban university, represent another major budgetary concern. Though such technologies will, in the long run, broaden the access to the urban university by providing more instructional opportunities to a larger segment of the population, the construction of the "electronic university" will be a costly enterprise. Urban universities will have to be the educational innovators in developing those technologies to improve and expand delivery systems while making sure those delivery systems further the urban mission. The quality and applicability of the courses offered will have to be protected in the race to be "first" or to capitalize on the new technology. The technology cannot be viewed as an end in itself, as is so often the case, but a means by which the services of the university can be extended to larger audiences.

While these fiscal concerns are shared by all universities, they are felt most deeply by urban institutions. In difficult financial times, the urban university cannot, like others, simply concentrate its resources and eliminate programs deemed outside the academic mission. Because of the interaction and interdependence of teaching, research, and public service, reductions in one area cannot be made without considering the impact they could have in other areas. Like that of the more traditional land-grant institutions, the mission of the urban university extends beyond the campus; cutbacks in services, therefore, will have an impact on community as well as on the university. In addition, the urban university is committed to educating denizens of the city, many of whom are poor or disadvantaged, which obligates the university to keep tuition affordable while providing a number of special support services. Instead of falling back on a simple formula of covering all new expenses with increases in tuition, the urban university must balance increased expenses with cost savings, reallocation of resources, maintenance of a lean administration, prudent financial management, and by attracting more external support. Furthermore, urban universities are committed to offering a wide range of academic programs to serve many diverse constituencies; they cannot consolidate programs in such a way as to abrogate their commitment to one of those constituencies. The exceptional range and depth of the commitments at an urban university require an exceptional level of support.

The realistic expansion and improvement of partnerships with business and industry, partnerships that recognize the capabilities and limitations of each institution, would allow urban universities to diversify their support and thereby decrease their dependence on state and federal funding as well as provide access to advanced technologies. Corporate financial support of higher education has increased at an average annual rate of 11 percent for the last thirty years, from approximately $40 million to more than $1 billion, and is expected to continue to increase. While corporate money represents only 1.3 percent of college and university budgets, it offers income equivalent to a $14 billion endowment. A recent report issued by the Business-Higher Education Forum states "the need for expanded corporate aid to higher education today is more critical than at any other time since World War II." For the urban university, the need is particularly acute.

The commitment to the urban environment should be unquestionable. The needs of our urban areas are too great and the human and intellectual resources of the urban university too plentiful not to be offered in service. But a caution from J. Martin Klotsche, one that has been frequently overlooked, should not be forgotten:

> The urban university must not . . . become so committed to the affairs of the city that the purposes for which it exists will be compromised. There is always the danger that a university can become too immersed in the problems of its community. It would indeed be fatal to its historical mission were problem solving and local politics to become its primary goals. Implied in the term "urban university" is a quality of cosmopolitanism and sophistication that makes it a part of the city while it remains apart from it.

Urban universities that are able to manage the inevitable reductions while remaining accessible to urban students, to maintain a balance among the variety of commitments, to preserve educational breadth, to devise strategies for strengthening faculty morale, and to continue responsive to the changing needs of the community, will emerge in the next century as prominent institutions.

The urban university of the twenty-first century will be stronger for the trials it has endured, richer for the greater number of minority students it has attracted, and more productive for the growing number of citizens it will be able to reach through new educational offerings and new technologies. The urban university of the twenty-first century may be changed markedly by the events of the next two decades, but the mission it maintains will be a familiar one. It will seek to educate, not merely train, to add to the store of human knowledge, to stimulate scholarly research and creative expression, to contribute to economic vitality, to develop human capital, to break the intergenerational chain of poverty, to create a less stratified society, to advance the Jeffersonian ideal of an informed and educated citizenry; indeed, to further the most basic aims of democracy.

In advancing these ideals over past decades, the urban university has become a vital institution. By confronting the challenges of the coming decades with the full force of its intellectual and creative energy, it will, by the twenty-first century, stand ready to make even greater contributions.

SUMMARY

The mission of the urban university leads to an interaction and inter-dependence among teaching, research, and public service and between the university and the community itself. That interaction and interdependence will be hastened in the next two decades as shifts occur in the nation's population.

A decline in the number of high school students, compounded by more specific trends, will present both problems and opportunities for urban universities. To preserve their mission and stabilize their enrollments, urban universities will have to expand their relationships with inner-city schools. They will have to decide from several models and numerous activities which public services are most appropriate to their individual environments. Decisions will have to be made between public service activities that offer expertise and those that are merely sanctioned by the university, between those that render instruction and those that cloak political activism in altruistic terms.

Urban universities should assist local government, provide advice to city officials, offer continuing education to personnel in local government, and embrace the urban laboratory, but they should not offer services that compete with those of the city or become so enmeshed in the affairs of the community that they sacrifice their academic perspective.

Commitments to the community will be difficult to maintain in the face of declining enrollments and the need to retool laboratories and keep pace with advanced technology. Increased support from the federal government under programs such as the Urban Grant University Act and greater support from the business community will help urban universities continue to fulfill their mission.

Urban universities that are able to manage enrollment declines and maintain a balance among their many commitments will emerge as prominent institutions in the twenty-first century.

REFERENCES

American Council on Education. "Concern Grows About Business, Higher Ed Health." *Higher Education and National Affairs*, May, 1984.
"Fourth of Equipment for Research Found Obsolete, Unused." *Chronicle of Higher Education*, May 16, 1984.

Crossan, Patricia H. *Public Service in Higher Education: Practices and Priorities.* Washington, D.C.: Association for the Study of Higher Education, 1983.

Grobman, Arnold B. "The Missions of Urban Institutions." *Liberal Education* 66, Summer, 1980.

Grobman, Arnold B., and Sanders, Janet S. "Interactions Between Public Urban Universities and Their Cities." *A Report of the Division of Urban Affairs.* Washington, D.C.: National Association of State Universities and Land-Grant Colleges, 1984.

Hanson, Royce, ed. *Rethinking Urban Policy: Urban Development in an Advanced Economy.* Washington, D.C.: National Academy Press, 1983.

Hodgkinson, Harold L. "Guess Who's Coming to College: Your Students in 1990." *A Research Report from the State-National Information Network.* Washington, D.C.: National Institute of Independent Colleges and Universities, 1983.

Klotsche, Martin J. *The Urban University.* New York: Harper and Row, 1966.

National Research Council. *Critical Issues for National Urban Policy: A Reconnaissance and Agenda for Further Study.* Washington, D.C.: National Academy Press, 1982.

Urban Grant University Act of 1977. Washington, D.C.: U.S. Government Printing Office, 1979.

Watkins, Beverly T. "Joint Project with University Aims at Revitalizing High School." *Chronicle of Higher Education,* May 16, 1984.

Whitehead, A. N. *The Aims of Education and Other Essays.* New York: The MacMillan Company, 1929.

CHAPTER 11
WHO BENEFITS? WHO PAYS?:
A CONSIDERATION OF THE
DISTRIBUTION OF UNIVERSITY
SCIENCE/ENGINEERING RESEARCH
COSTS AMONG ITS SPONSORS

SAMUEL F. CONTI

One question, "What do you believe to be the ideal mix of government/ industry/university support of research?", was only answered by a few and then reluctantly.[1]

In recent years, arguments have been presented and data collected on the purposes and benefits of scientific research and the costs and methods of funding that research. Federal agencies and the U.S. Congress have published, sponsored, or elicited testimony on the continuing pivotal role of basic research in maintaining the nation's welfare in the areas of defense, health, and social issues.[2] Similar studies, both publicly and privately sponsored, have pointed to the vital role that targeted research must have in maintaining national industrial competitiveness and general economic growth and development.[3] Considerations of the cost of research in the face of these growing needs and its implications for the structure of research support in the United States have also appeared.[4] These two bodies of literature have remained largely independent, however: one concerning the need for and the benefits derived from research, and the other examining the costs, the funding, and the division of research among various producers of research. This situation, coupled with the tendency to argue either the costs or the benefits of research to one particular constituency—be it society in general, the federal government, or industry—has created a fragmented picture of both the values and the costs of research and of the resulting division of responsibility for its support. The picture is not clarified substantially when the focus is narrowed to consider the contributions, costs, and the division of funding responsibility for research conducted by only one sector of America's research producers—

universities.[5] Further, the unique role and position of the state university within the current research climate and funding structure has gone largely unnoticed or unconsidered.

If we are to clarify the importance of the public research universities in the nation's research enterprise, and if we are to present a persuasive argument for the funding of research at these universities by their interested constituencies, then we must do so by remedying the situation exemplified by the current literature. We must develop a unified framework that encompasses not merely a presentation of the benefits of university research, but one that provides a mechanism by which to consider an equitable distribution of responsibility for the funding of that research among its several direct beneficiaries. The model for such a framework exists in the cost-benefit study of graduate education conducted for the Council of Graduate Schools (CGS) in 1972.[6] The general methodology of this model, rather than the detailed cost analysis and cost allocation process it provides, can be enormously useful in considering both the specific benefits and the beneficiaries of various elements of the university research enterprise. It provides, even on the most basic level of analysis, an interesting paradigm for the allocation of research benefits among constituencies, one with important implications for the funding and support of sponsored research at public universities.

THE COST-BENEFIT MODEL

The primary intent of the CGS cost-benefit model is to enumerate both the end products and the constituent costs of all aspects of graduate education, including university research, and to suggest a method that would aid in determining the intrauniversity distribution of those costs between the instructional and the research components of graduate education at the department or program level. For our purpose it is necessary both to expand and to modify this model. We will expand it in two ways: by more detailed analysis of the two primary outputs of university research identified in the earlier literature (new knowledge and educated men and women) and by the inclusion of what might be termed secondary outputs, outputs whose existence is only now being recognized through more thoughtful consideration of the full impact of university research on society and on the nation's economy. We will modify the earlier model, then, by focusing not on these outputs or end results of university research but rather by focusing on the nature of the benefits produced by

Table 1
Beneficiaries of University Research

Abbreviation Key	
G/F—Federal government	P—Private sector
G/S—State government	NP—Nonprofit sector
G/L—Local government	S—Society

Primary Output	Benefit	Beneficiary
Personnel		
Researchers (45.8% total/49.5% new)	Production of new knowledge, techniques, and processes	
% to government		
Federal (8%/7.6%)		G/F
State (1.9%/2.6%)		G/S
Local		G/L
% to industry		
Profit sector (29.8%/30.7%)		P
Nonprofit sector (6.1%/8.6%)		NP
Academic Faculty (53.4% total/49.6% new)	Continuation of the system of higher education and research	
% privates (32.2%)		P
% publics (67.8%)		G/S
New Knowledge (Percentages of total university research support)		
Basic (70.1%)	Advancement of knowledge	S
Federal (69%)		S
State		
Local (21.4%)		S
Institutional		
Industry (3.5%)		P/S
Targeted (29.9%)	Problem-specific	
Federal (60.5%)		G/F
State		G/S
Local (26%)		G/L
Institutional		
Industry (5%)		P

Table 1 (continued)

Secondary Output	Benefit	Beneficiary
The Research Climate	Economic development: attraction of new business	G/L
	Encouragement of new research	G/S
		G/F
Increased Payroll and Research-Related Expenses	Economic development	G/L
		G/S
Creation of a Pool of Specialized Research Talent ("standby value")	Available expertise	G/L
		G/S
		G/F
		P
Intrainstitutional Outputs:		
Research assistants	Research assistance	G/S
Teaching assistants	Teaching assistance	G/S
Enhancement of faculty/student recruitment	Improvement in quality	G/S
Enhancement of the quality of graduate and undergraduate teaching	Improvement in quality	S

those results (see table 1). Additionally, we will consider the implications that the distribution of these benefits among various elements of society has for the relative allocation of responsibility for the funding of research costs (see table 1). This is a question specifically not addressed by the earlier study or by its companion commentary volume,[7] but whose importance was clearly recognized.[8] It remains a vital question as the central role of research in our nation's future becomes clearer to all levels of a society that has increasingly benefited from the discoveries of research and has become increasingly dependent on their continuation. It is not our purpose to undertake extensive economic analyses in order to develop an actual allocation model, but rather to suggest issues relevant to such a model based on consideration of both the current status of and current trends in university research funding, particularly at public institutions.

BENEFIT: THE PRODUCTION OF NEW SCIENTISTS AND ENGINEERS

Determining the ultimate benefits and beneficiaries of sponsored research conducted by universities first requires a reconsideration of the outputs or end results of that research. The earlier cost-benefit analyses of graduate education as a whole clearly recognize the extent to which the research and instructional components of graduate education interact. Through their development of a model that offers a method of analyzing the degree of interdependence, they demonstrate that the two components cannot be considered independently, and they correctly delineate the dual outputs of research conducted in a university setting: new knowledge *and* educated men and women.[9] The research enterprise exists in an academic institution not merely for the production of new knowledge, new techniques, and new processes, but, equally important, it exists to educate the next generation of men and women in the methods of scholarly and scientific inquiry. It is not only the outcome of research that is of interest, but the research process itself that becomes a subject of study and instruction. Because of this dual purpose of research conducted in a university setting, a major benefit results in the form of educated teachers and researchers as a direct consequence of the university's research program and not solely—perhaps not even primarily—as an outcome of the institution's instructional program. Because the process of academic research embodies as an integral part of its mission this teaching component, this inherently self-conscious analysis of its methods, any discussion of an equitable allocation of academic research costs must include a consideration of the constituencies ultimately benefiting from the production of research personnel, as well as from the production of new knowledge.

There is no question that academia remains the primary employer of the teachers and researchers educated in the doctoral-level scientific and technical programs of the nation's research universities.[10] Slightly more than half (53.4 percent) of the currently employed scientists and engineers who hold the doctorate are employed by academic institutions, from elementary school through the university, with a majority (51.2 percent) employed by four-year colleges, universities, or medical schools. However, the trend in the employment of doctoral scientists and engineers who graduated in the period 1975 to 1980 shows a shift in this concentration. Although 49.6 percent of these recent Ph.D. graduates continue to be employed in academic institutions, increasing numbers are going to other sectors: 30.7 percent into business or industry where the overall concentration of Ph.D. scientists and engineers is 29.8 percent, 8.6 percent into hospitals and other nonprofit organizations where the overall concentration is 6.1 percent, and 2.6 percent into state or local governments where the overall concentration is 1.9 percent.

In addition to this general trend away from academic employment for recently graduated doctoral-level scientists and engineers, graduates holding degrees in certain fields continue to show greater overall employment in nonacademic sectors. This is true for graduates in the fields of chemistry (where 56.3 percent of all currently employed doctoral scientists and engineers are employed in industry, compared to 34.2 percent in academic institutions), engineering (where the percentages are 53.7 percent and 33.9 percent), and computer science (where the percentages are 49.7 percent and 40.9 percent). Again, this trend is even more pronounced when we consider which sector employs the majority of recent Ph.D. recipients in these fields: 68.1 percent of recent doctoral chemists are employed in industry, 60.5 percent of recent doctoral engineers, and 51.1 percent of recent doctoral computer scientists. Physics and astronomy has become the only scientific field in which academia maintains the highest overall employment of Ph.D. recipients (49.1 percent of the doctoral physicists and astronomers), whereas among recent graduates industry has become the primary employer (42.8 percent). Overall, the employment of doctoral scientists and engineers by industry rose at an annual rate of 8 percent between 1973 and 1981, whereas the annual rate of increase of these graduates in other sectors was only 5.7 percent.[11]

Although the education of doctoral scientists and engineers in the United States has been shared by public and private institutions, it has neither historically nor recently been equally divided between the two sectors. Public institutions represent 61 percent of the nation's top one hundred institutions when ranked in order by the number of doctorates granted in the sciences and engineering between 1920 and 1974, and these institutions produced 58 percent of the total number of graduates during that period.[12] Recent enrollment figures show that public doctorate granting institutions are enrolling twice as many graduate students in science and engineering fields as are private institutions. They also lead in the number of students who concentrate in the areas of primary concern to business and industry as reflected by the employment patterns of recent graduates: chemistry, engineering, and computer science.[13]

As these statistics illustrate, industry is directly benefiting from the production of doctoral-level scientists and engineers, and it must continue to do so if the nation is to maintain and enhance its competitive position in the world economy. Most company representatives questioned in the National Science Board's recent survey of participants in university-industry relationships said that access to manpower, and particularly to graduate students who are potential employees, is the most important factor motivating their interest in establishing joint university-industry research programs.[14] The importance industry places on graduates educated through the university research process and its understanding of the integral relationship between graduate education and research is further reflected in the establishment by the Council for Chemical Research of a central research fund whose monies will be distributed to university departments according to a formula based on the number of Ph.D. scientists each produces.[15] Historically, public universities have produced a majority of Ph.D. scientists and engineers. They continue to do so. In view of these facts, does industry's support of university research reflect the degree to which it benefits from the researchers educated by those institutions, and particularly by public institutions? Does the federal government's support of the research process at public universities adequately reflect the role of these institutions in producing educators and researchers in areas of vital importance to the nation's future?

BENEFIT: THE PRODUCTION OF KNOWLEDGE

In order to consider the beneficiaries of the new knowledge created by university research, it is increasingly necessary to distinguish between the direct beneficiaries of the end *results* of that research and the beneficiaries of the *process* of research. The beneficiaries of the results of research are those groups that benefit from the end products of the research process: the insights, techniques, processes, and discoveries of research. Those benefiting from the process of research are those who benefit from the fact that research is being conducted, from both the intellectual and economic processes of research, regardless of specific outcomes. This distinction has not been clearly stated nor its implications fully considered, yet it does have important implications for devising a balanced allocation of responsibility for the funding of university research.

Historically, the emphasis has been on differentiating the beneficiaries of the outcomes or end results of research, and this has been done by pointing to the differences in mission and intent between basic and targeted research. While the immediate beneficiaries of targeted research are, by definition, readily apparent because of the problem-specific nature of this research, the question of who are the beneficiaries of fundamental research is more complex. Society or the nation in general is usually considered the prime beneficiary of this type of research. But in recent years two factors make it necessary both to question this supposition and to explore its implications for funding responsibility in the context of basic research conducted by the nation's universities.

The first of these factors is the central importance of the university research endeavor to the conduct of basic research in the nation. University research interests and expertise have been and continue to be centered in this area of research, with 66 percent of all university research funds being received for the support and conduct of basic research.[16] In addition, universities not only focus their research activities in this area of scientific activity, but in so doing, have become the nation's most significant performer of this vitally important sector of research. Universities and colleges received 48.9 percent of all funds expended for basic research in 1982, far ahead of the percentages received by the next closest performers, business and industry (17.7 percent) and the federal government (15.3 percent).[17] If the nation is the primary beneficiary of the outcomes of this research, then the nation, through the federal government and its agencies as the institutions established with primary responsibility for the national good, should be the primary source of support for basic research conducted by the major performers of that research, the nation's universities.

The other important factor in a consideration of the beneficiaries of basic research conducted in universities is the importance of basic research to industry. One qualitative and three quantitative measures can be considered reflective of the importance that industry itself, through its collective statements or actions, places on the production or use of basic research in its own endeavors.

In the National Science Board's study of university-industry relationships, researchers found that the second of fifteen reasons given for industry participation in joint research interactions was "to obtain a window on science and technology."[18] The meaning of this phrase and the aspect of university research that it is meant to reflect become clearer when other survey findings are considered as well. That it does not intend to imply a primary interest in those research activities with high potential for immediate translation into new products or processes is clear from the inclusion of the item appearing next on the list of motivating factors: "To solve a problem or get specific information unavailable elsewhere."[19] The window to which industry wants access is the one providing the view of the new concepts, ideas, or approaches discovered or developed in university research. Industry does not look to and rely on the university for technological innovation but for the breakthroughs of basic research carried out in its laboratories. This point was underscored most recently by Roland W. Schmitt, senior vice president for Corporate Research and Development at General Electric and chairman of the National Science Board, in his keynote speech to the National Conference on the Advancement of Research when he said, ". . . the most important step that government can take to strengthen U.S. innovation is to ensure and to strengthen the health of our university research system—in both the performance of basic research, and the training of research manpower."[20]

Quantitative evidence of the importance of basic research to industry can be found in three measures: the level of industry's internal funding of this area of research, the level of reliance on university research evident in publications originating in industry, and the level of university-industry cooperative research.

In 1982 industry expended $1.615 billion in support of basic research.[21] Data for the previous year show that three industries—chemical products, electrical equipment, and machinery—accounted for 44 percent of total industry expenditures on basic research (see table 2).[22] The chemical products industry alone spent 10 percent of its total research and development funds on basic research activities,[23] a significant percentage considering that only 12 percent of the entire nation's estimated research and development expenditures in 1982 supported basic research. Even the federal government, the most important source of funding for this area of research activity, dedicated only 17 percent of its research and development resources to basic research.[24]

The method of citation analysis, which studies citation patterns found in the research literature, also provides a way of measuring the extent and direction of influence of the research published by industrial and university scientists. In a study of articles published in leading scientific research journals between 1978 and 1980, citation ratios were calculated to reflect the degree to which the industrial and academic sectors cite the work of the other in their published research. In this study, a citation ratio of 1.00 meant that the cited sector (academia or industry) received a share of all citations made in the literature of a given field equal to the share of publications it contributed to the field; the higher the ratio, the higher the citation rate. The overall university-to-industry citation ratio was .37 whereas the ratio for industry-to-university citation was .52. The ratio of industry's citing of prior university research was even higher in specific fields: earth and space sciences (.80), mathematics (.77), clinical medicine (.76), biology (.61), and chemistry (.60).[25]

In the field of cooperative research, two measures are indicative of the value industry places on the approaches and orientation as well as on the processes and results of university research. One of these is the number of

Table 2
Basic Research in Industry, 1981

Industry	Total R&D (millions)	Percent of total R&D company-funded	Total basic research (millions)	Percent of total R&D spent on basic research	Percent of company-funded R&D spent on basic research	Percent of companies doing basic research
Chemicals	$ 5,325[a]	92.8	$544[b]	10.2%	9.3%	77.6%[c]
Petroleum refining	$ 1,917[b]	92.7	$137[b]	7.2%	7.5%	38.9%[c]
Electrical equipment	$10,466[a]	62.1	$288[b]	2.8%	3.6%	5.5%[c]
Aircraft/ missiles	$11,702[a]	27.4	$135[b]	1.6%	2.2%	18.9%[c]
Machinery	$ 6,800[a]	89.1	$127[b]	1.9%	2.1%	5.3%[c]
Professional/ scientific instruments	$ 3,685[b]	82.7%	–	–	–	5.2%[c]
Motor vehicles	$ 4,929[a]	87.2%	–	–	.5%	11.9%[c]
Nonmanufacturing	$ 2,060[b]	58.2%	–	–	–	4.9%[c]

[a] *Source: Research and Development in Industry, 1981. Detailed Statistical Tables* (Washington, D.C., National Science Foundation, 1983), tables B–28 and B–29, pp. 34–35.
[b] *Source*: Shapely, Willis H., Albert H. Teich, and Jill P. Weinberg, *AAAS Report VIII: Research and Development, FY 1984; Budget Analysis Colloquium Proceedings*, a report prepared for the executive officer and the AAAS Committee on Science, Engineering, and Public Policy (Washington, D.C., American Association for the Advancement of Science, 1983), table 3–12, p. 149.
[c] *Source: Research and Development in Industry, 1981*, table B–33, p. 38.

articles coauthored by industry and university scientists. In the period from 1973 to 1980, this number increased 29 percent, even though the absolute number of all articles authored by industrial scientists dropped 14 percent. In addition, industrial researchers published jointly with academic scientists more often than with either government or other industrial scientists.[26] The second indication of industry's interest in cooperative research with universities lies in the number of university-industry relationships now in existence. Although the precise number of these relationships is unknown, some indication of their extent can be found in the recent National Science Board study. This survey identified 39 universities and 66 industrial companies engaged in 475 research interactions of all types, including cooperative research grants and centers, industrial parks, equipment donations, partnerships, contracts, seminars, internships, and the endowment of faculty chairs.[27]

Obviously, industry has demonstrated that it considers as vital elements in technological development and innovation the approaches and methods as well as the discoveries and solutions that are the results of basic scientific inquiry, most of which is undertaken by the nation's universities. Industry must therefore be considered an important, though often indirect, beneficiary of the results of university research.

BENEFIT: THE PROCESS OF RESEARCH

Although historically attention has been focused on the beneficiaries of the results of university research, the nature and extent of the benefits resulting from what we have termed the secondary outputs of research, or what could be considered the benefits of the research process, have been only marginally considered. These have been mentioned and discussed largely in other contexts—in cost-benefit discussions of graduate education, for example, and in discussions of the economic impact of universities and of university-industry relations—yet their position in a cost-benefit model of university research and their implications for university research funding have not been explored. These secondary outputs include the following elements:

1. The creation of a pool of specialized talent within an institution whose expertise can be called on by various constituencies to address specific problems as they arise; Bowen and Servelle have referred to this potential as the "standby value" of university researchers;[28]

2. The creation of a "research climate" that not only fosters the undertaking of further research within the institution, but extends to the creation of an intellectual climate of importance in attracting research-dependent businesses and industries;[29]

3. Increased payroll and other related expenditures resulting from research activities, expenditures whose effect on the local and state economies is enhanced by the multiplier effect;[30]

4. Intrainstitutional benefits, among which could be included the creation of a pool of teaching and research assistants, the enhancement of the quality of undergraduate and graduate teaching, and the enhancement of student and faculty recruitment and retention.[31]

The inclusion of consideration of the effects of these secondary outputs of research greatly affects the degree to which state and local governments can be seen to be beneficiaries of the research conducted at universities; yet such consideration has been largely absent from any analyses of the beneficiaries of research.

COST: THE CURRENT DISTRIBUTION OF
UNIVERSITY RESEARCH SUPPORT

Considering now the current pattern of university research support, it becomes clear that a more equitable division of responsibility for the support of that research, one that more closely reflects the balance of research benefits, is necessary. The nature and balance of the beneficiaries are not fully evident in the current structure of the allocation of costs of university research. Of the estimated $4.56 billion received by universities and colleges in 1982 in support of basic research activities, $3.15 billion (69 percent) came from federal sources and $275 million (6 percent) came from nonprofit organizations, percentages that seem reasonable since these institutions represent the nebulous beneficiary, society.[32] Of the remaining 25 percent of the funds, however, 21.4 percent came from universities and colleges themselves (including state and local government funds), with only 3.5 percent from industry. It is, however, not only the fact that industry contributed so small a percentage to an enterprise from which it can potentially and does actually gain so much which is problematic. More important is the fact that the amount industry expended in 1982 in support of basic research in universities is only 10 percent of the total amount it spent in support of this activity by all performers.[33] For the funding of targeted research conducted in universities, the relative levels of support from each source remain the same: 60.5 percent of the total funds came from the federal government, 26 percent from universities and colleges, 9 percent from other nonprofit organizations, and 5 percent from industry.[34] In addition, many state universities contribute additional funds to research through the fact that they do not recover from external funding sources the cost of that portion of faculty salaries represented by the time dedicated to sponsored research activities. It seems clear that industry benefits from the results of university research as well as from utilization of doctoral scientists and engineers to a greater degree than it currently contributes to the support of university research.

The lack of equitable balance in the funding of university research becomes even more pronounced when we consider the sources of funding for that portion of research undertaken by the nation's public universities.[35] Although these universities numbered seventy of the country's top one hundred institutions when ranked by the total amount of funds received for research and development in 1981, they received only 64.4 percent of the total amount of research and development funds. The distribution of contributions from the several sources of support was even more revealing: only 57.9 percent of all federal funds given to support research and development at universities and colleges went to public institutions, and these funds represented only 60.7 percent of the total amount given by all sources in support of research at public institutions. However, federal funding represented 80 percent of the monies expended by private institutions on research and development. Conversely, public institutions spent from their own institutional funds 18.7 percent of the total they expended on research, while the comparable figure for private institutions was only 7 percent. Eighty-two percent of all institutional funds expended in support of research and development was spent by public institutions.

IMPLICATIONS FOR THE FUTURE FUNDING OF UNIVERSITY SCIENCE/ENGINEERING RESEARCH

Even this cursory view of the current balance of the costs and benefits of university research seems to point to the need to reconsider the present pattern of that support and to attempt a redistribution of responsibility for research support by looking more closely and more analytically at the primary beneficiaries and their current levels of responsibility in that effort.

Because basic research is of vital importance in the process of product development as evidenced by industry's own internal expenditures on this type of research, there exists, at the minimum, a potential direct application of university research for which industry should accept a portion of responsibility. The degree of self-interest and responsibility becomes even clearer when the benefit that accrues to business and industry in the form of personnel educated in the research process by the nation's universities, and especially by its public universities, is included. The mechanisms for this support—including the development of research parks, the extension of cooperative research ventures, the donation of sophisticated research instrumentation, and the expansion of the targeted research endeavor of universities—need to be more fully developed, diversified, and implemented. It is particularly important to increase the research support involvement of specific industries, such as chemicals, petroleum refining, machinery, and electrical equipment, which have historically benefited from the numbers of doctoral-level scientists and engineers produced by universities, particularly by public universities, and which also spend more on basic research activities both absolutely and as a percentage of total research dollars.[36]

Although National Science Board figures show that in the period 1980 to 1982 federal research support declined an average of 2.4 percent annually,[37] a reallocation of federal research and development funds to emphasize federal obligations to research, and particularly to basic research in the physical sciences, mathematics, and engineering, was evident in the FY 1984 budget. However, even though the improvement of the federal research funding situation for universities and colleges was given a high priority by the current administration, the actual budget figures translated into level funding in terms of constant dollars for the support of research in academic institutions.[38] Although statements by the president's science advisor reflect an understanding of the unique position university research occupies in the nation's research endeavor by virtue of its combination of the elements of both teaching and research,[39] this understanding has not been translated into policy. Although the data are not yet available, there is reason to assume that the failure to translate a theoretical appreciation into actual funding policy will also be reflected in a continuing imbalance in the federal funding of research at public and private universities. Certainly the federal government's own commitment to increase its support of basic research as its area of primary responsibility in the national research effort should be reflected in increased support of the sector historically most dedicated to the conduct of that research.

Finally, the states, through general institutional support of research at their state universities, as well as through fiscal policies that translate to important sources of indirect research support, have been notable and often silent partners in the nation's research effort, partners whose contributions have often been overlooked. That they have been beneficiaries of important direct and indirect results of university research, such as increased tax revenues from research expenditures and new industrial development, is also clear. Yet the support and encouragement of university research has generally remained outside any direct policy formulation by individual state governments. If *de facto* state support of research at this nation's public research institutions has resulted in such undeniable mutual benefits, what more could be achieved—and, in fact, *is* being achieved in some states, such as North Carolina and Texas—by the development of reasoned and expanded support of university research?

ACKNOWLEDGMENTS

I would like to acknowledge two members of the staff of the Graduate School at the University of Massachusetts/Amherst for their assistance in preparing this paper. Ms. Suzanne Lorimer did much of the research and compiled an exhaustive bibliography of relevant documents. In addition, she assisted in writing the early drafts of this paper. Her thoroughness and carefully reasoned arguments were most valuable to me in this project. Mr. Michael Weinberg also reviewed the early drafts and provided some useful suggestions.

NOTES

1. National Science Board (U.S.), *University-Industry Research Relationships: Selected Studies* (Washington, D.C.: National Science Foundation; for sale by the Superintendent of Documents, U.S. Government Printing Office, 1982), p. 12.

2. See, for instance, Bruce S. Old Associates, *Return on Investment in Basic Research. Exploring a Methodology* (Concord, Mass., November 1981); National Science Foundation, *How Research Reaps Unexpected Rewards* (Washington, D.C.: The Foundation; for sale by the Superintendent of Documents, U.S. Government Printing Office, 1980); Maya Pines, "Unpredictable Payoffs of Basic Research," in U.S. Congress, House, Committee on Science and Technology, Subcommitte on Investigations and Oversight, *University/Industry Cooperation in Biotechnology*; hearing, June 16, 17, 1982 (Washington, D.C.: U.S. Government Printing Office, 1982), pp. 240–255; and the Transportation Research Board (U.S.), *Research Programming and the Value of Research* (Washington, D.C.: 1981).

3. See, for instance, Walter Hahn's overview of previous analyses of the economic impact of research and innovation in *Research and Innovation: Developing a Dynamic Nation: Studies*, Prepared for the use of the Special Study on Economic Change of the Joint Economic Committee, U.S. Congress (Washington, D.C.: U.S. Government Printing Office; for sale by the Superintendent of Documents, 1980), pp. 1–137; Rachel McCulloch, *Research and Development as a Determinant of U.S. International Competitiveness* (Washington, D.C.: NPA Committee on Changing International Realities, 1978); and the *Seminar on Research, Productivity, and the National Economy*: Seminar before the Committee on Science and Technology, U.S. House of Representatives, Ninety-Sixth Congress, Second Session, June 18, 1980 (Washington, D.C.: U.S. Government Printing Office, 1980).

4. See, for instance, Francis W. Dresch and Robert W. Campbell, *The System*

of *Financing Research and Development in the United States* (Menlo Park, Calif.: Stanford Research Institute, Strategic Studies Center, September 1977); Jurgen Schmandt, *Financing and Control of Academic Research* (Austin, Tex.: Lyndon B. Johnson School of Public Affairs, 1977); and Robert R. Trumble and Jamie E. McDonald, *Rationale for Stable Funding of Research and Development* (Washington, D.C.: National Science Foundation, Division of Science Policy Research and Analysis, January 1983).

5. Although we recognize the valuable contributions made to the conduct of research and education in this country by non-Ph.D.-granting institutions and by the historically black institutions, our focus in this paper is on the role and status of research in the nation's Ph.D.-granting research universities.

6. John H. Powel, Jr., and Robert D. Lamson, *Elements Related to the Determination of Costs and Benefits of Graduate Education* (Washington, D.C.: The Council of Graduate Schools in the United States, March 1972).

7. Joseph L. McCarthy and David R. Deener, *The Costs and Benefits of Graduate Education: A Commentary with Recommendations* (Washington, D.C.: The Council of Graduate Schools in the United States, March 1972).

8. Ibid., p. 13.

9. We will not consider in this study the output and the benefit accruing to the individual researcher or faculty member in terms of the appreciation of his/her marketable teaching or research value since this has no direct bearing on a consideration of research cost allocation. See, however, a good discussion of the manner in which academic faculty—and teaching and research assistants as well—pay for this experience in Powel and Lamson, pp. 211–213.

10. All of the statistics used in this discussion were taken from: National Research Council (U.S.). Office of Science and Engineering Personnel, Survey of Doctorate Recipients, *Science, Engineering and Humanities Doctorates in the United States: 1981 Profile* (Washington, D.C.: National Academy Press, 1982), Tables 1.5A and 1.5B, p. 20.

11. *Science Indicators 1982*, Report of the National Science Board 1983 (Washington, D.C.: National Science Board, National Science Foundation; for sale by the Superintendent of Documents, U.S. Government Printing Office, 1983), p. 88.

12. *A Century of Doctorates; Data Analyses of Growth and Change. U.S. Ph.D.'s—Their Numbers, Origins, Characteristics, and the Institutions from Which They Come.* A report to the National Science Foundation, to the National Endowment for the Humanities, and to the United States Office of Education from the Board on Human Resource Data and Analyses, Commission on Human Resources, National Research Council (Washington, D.C.: National Academy of Sciences, 1978), Table 45A, p. 110.

13. See *Academic Science/Engineering, Graduate Enrollment and Support, Fall 1981. Detailed Statistical Tables* (Washington, D.C.: National Science Foundation, 1983), Tables C–2 and C–3, pp. 85–86.

14. National Science Board (U.S.), *University-Industry Research Relationships*, pp. 34–35.

15. Ibid., pp. 34, 82.

16. *National Patterns of Science and Technology Resources 1982* (Washington, D.C.: National Science Foundation; for sale by the Superintendent of Documents, U.S. Government Printing Office, 1982), p. 10.

17. Ibid.

18. National Science Board (U.S.), *University-Industry Research Relationships*, pp. 34–35.

19. Ibid., p. 35.

20. Roland W. Schmitt, "National R and D Policy: An Industrial Perspective"; paper presented at the National Conference on the Advancement of Research (San Antonio, October 10, 1983), p. 1.

21. *National Patterns 1982*, p. 10.

22. *Research and Development in Industry, 1981. Detailed Statistical Tables* (Washington, D.C.: National Science Foundation, 1983), Table B–28, p. 34.

23. Ibid.

24. *National Patterns 1982*, p. 10.

25. *Science Indicators 1982*, p. 108 and Table 4–5, p. 109.

26. Ibid., p. 108.

27. National Science Board, (U.S.), *University-Industry Research Relationships*, pp. 6 and 137–61.

28. Howard R. Bowen and Paul Servelle, *Who Benefits from Higher Education—and Who Should Pay?* Prepared by the ERIC Clearinghouse on Higher Education (Washington, D.C.: American Association for Higher Education, August 1972), p. 26.

29. See, for instance, the Southern Regional Education Board, *Sites for High Technology Activities*, draft based on a report to the Southern Regional Education Board by Battelle Institute (Atlanta, June 1983), and also Southern Regional Education Board, *Universities and High Technology Develoment*, draft based on a report to the Southern Regional Education Board by Battelle Institute (Atlanta, June 1983).

30. For the standard model used in these economic impact studies, see John Caffrey and Herbert H. Isaacs, *Estimating the Impact of a College or University on the Local Economy* (Washington, D.C.: American Council on Education, 1971); also see Rebecca A. Dorsett and William C. Weiler, "The Impact of an Institution's Federal Research Grants on the Economy of its State," *Journal of Higher Education* 53(4): 419–428 (July–August 1982).

31. See McCarthy and Deener, p. 10, and Powel and Lamson, p. 51.

32. *National Patterns 1982*, p. 10.

33. Ibid.

34. Ibid., p. 11.

35. Statistics in this discussion were derived from *Academic Science/Engineering R&D Funds, Fiscal Year 1981. Detailed Statistical Tables* (Washington, D.C.: National Science Foundation, 1983), Table B–30, pp. 51–52.

36. Willis H. Shapely, Albert H. Teich, and Jill P. Weinberg, *AAAS Report VIII: Research and Development, FY 1984; Budget Analysis Colloquium Proceedings,*

A report prepared for the Executive Officer and the AAAS Committee on Science, Engineering, and Public Policy (Washington, D.C.: American Association for the Advancement of Science, 1983), Table 3–12, p. 149.

37. *Science Indicators 1982*, p. 54.
38. Shapely, Teich, and Weinberg, p. 131.
39. Ibid., p. 130.

CHAPTER 12
THE STATE RESEARCH UNIVERSITY: COSTS OF EDUCATION AND EQUITABLE OPPORTUNITY [1]

CHARLES E. BISHOP

Public support of higher education in the United States is almost as old as the republic itself. From the opening of the first state university in the 1790s to the present, public commitment to investment in higher education has been strong, though the particulars of policy and the scale of that commitment have changed through time.

One of the most difficult tasks has been to determine which activities and goals of public higher education provided at the state level fall most clearly within the national interest and, therefore, which have a legitimate claim to major support from the federal government. In recent years, two missions of the state research university have generated the most concern as to responsibility for funding. These are insuring equitable opportunity, especially on the undergraduate level, and strengthening research programs on the graduate level. The debate has questioned not so much the general social value each endeavor represents, but the appropriate delineation of federal, state, and private responsibilities for realizing that value in as equitable and efficient manner as possible. There has been strong traditional support, for example, for the ideal of equitable opportunity for all qualified undergraduate students, but far less agreement as to who should bear which costs in realizing that ideal. Likewise, there is strong national agreement that research is increasingly vital to our social and economic well-being and that the development of scientists is crucial to our future, but there is no clear consensus as to who should bear the costs of that research.

The wide-ranging social benefits of low-cost, high-quality undergraduate education for all qualified students and a vigorous graduate education and research effort both indicate significant federal responsibility and, therefore, each warrants considerable federal investment. The activities of research, graduate, and undergraduate education are so closely intertwined—both economically and academically—that extrication of any one activity weakens the quality and efficiency of the others. The most distinguishing characteristic of the multi-product state research university is the profound interdependency of operations, and given this interdependency of all operations, investment in one concern advances, either directly or indirectly, the cause of the other.

Federal support in the form of special aid to deserving students is more economical in insuring equal access than other means, including lowering tuition for all students. Moreover, such support is academically expedient as well. With federal aid programs, state institutions are not forced to sacrifice needed tuition revenues for the sake of insuring equitable access. Instead, they are free to maintain tuition levels that allow for the largest number of potential students while at the same time protecting the institution's larger academic interests, enriching graduate education and research as well as undergraduate education. On the other end of the spectrum, federal investment in research not only promotes the creation and application of new knowledge, but in the case of the multiproduct state research university, advances the cause of undergraduate and graduate education as well. Strong research and graduate programs effectively lower the cost and enhance the overall intellectual environment for undergraduate education. A two-fold federal investment in equitable access and in research in the comprehensive state research university is not only warranted, but given the structure of the institution, advances two of its most important ends in a mutually supporting way.

INDIVIDUAL OPPORTUNITY: COSTS AND BENEFITS

Concern over providing wider accessibility to higher education was a major factor underlying the creation of public universities in this country. The public universities, and particularly the land-grant universities, were created to provide low-cost, geographically accessible, opportunities for postsecondary education. The mission of the state research universities reflects deeply rooted social values that qualified students should have equitable access to higher education and that knowledge created through publicly sponsored research should be freely available to all who can use it.

In order to formulate a rational public policy to enhance accessibility, due consideration must be given to the matrix within which individuals make decisions with regard to investment in higher education, decisions that obviously involve choices among alternative uses of resources. Theoretically, individuals can gauge the return from private investment in education by comparing the direct costs they would incur plus the income they would forego as a result of college attendance with the discounted income stream they might expect throughout their lives. By comparing the additional earnings associated with various levels of education in relation to the additional cost of obtaining that education, one can estimate the rate of return from additional levels of higher education. These returns can then be compared with the returns from alternative uses of their resources. This economic calculus is complex and its strict application is difficult, insofar as neither the costs nor the returns can be known with certainty. From a public policy standpoint, however, it is necessary to identify as clearly as possible which major variables most affect individual enrollment in the state research university.

Numerous studies have disclosed that a variety of factors influence individual enrollment in higher education. These include academic ability, opportunity costs, tuition charges, other direct costs of education, parental education, family income, and social mores of ethnic group, neighborhood, or region.[2]

Enrollment in higher education is particularly responsive to tuition charges. Changes in tuition exert a substantially greater effect upon enrollment than changes in the opportunity cost, i.e., income potential foregone by attending the university. Indeed, Bishop estimated that if tuition were increased to cover full cost, enrollment in higher eduation would decrease approximately 50 percent.[3] Similar results were obtained by Hopkins.[4]

Family income and individual ability are also significant factors in determining individual enrollment, particularly as they correlate with changes in tuition. The probability of enrolling in higher education increases directly with increases in family income. Since tuition elasticity increases as family income decreases, changes in tuition exert greater influence upon low-income families. On the other hand, at prevailing tuition levels, modest increases in tuition have little effect upon attendance of those from high-income families. Tuition elasticity increases as ability of the student decreases. At prevailing tuition levels, students of exceptional ability are quite likely to attend college even if tuition is increased modestly. On the other hand, increases in tuition greatly discourage students of moderate to low ability.

It should be emphasized that much of the expenditure for undergraduate higher education is made by parents and likely represents in large part consumption rather than investment. In a decision-making context, people may forego current consumption in order to provide education for their children. Therefore, the revelant criterion may be the definition of a combination of expenditures on the education of their children and the purchase of other goods which maximizes the satisfaction of parents.

Costs and returns are not, of course, the only factors affecting individual enrollment. The value of higher education cannot and should not be measured solely in monetary terms, a point that obviously applies to both private and public decisions. It is impossible to capture in quantitative terms either the costs or benefits of many of the most significant products of higher education: more comprehensive literacies, better citizenship, greater social mobility, enhanced creativity, among many others. Many researchers have studied these factors in depth; Bowen, for example, stresses that education is the primary means of enhancing the quality of individual and collective life and places greater relative emphasis on education's social and cultural roles than its economic ones.[5] Whatever their emphases, most analysts would finally concur that the social, cultural, and economic benefits of education are ultimately inextricable from one another.

THE CASE FOR PUBLIC INVESTMENT

Still, we must more clearly elucidate why the potential of denied opportunity to deserving individuals is a matter of general public interest, or more precisely why equitable opportunity warrants federal investment. An important reason for the legitimacy of public expenditure to subsidize higher education is that the existence of a public system of higher education provides a kind of social insurance. Families want to know that no matter what happens to the financial situation of the household it would always be feasible for their children to obtain all the education for which they would be qualified. A second reason is that the taxes paid to support higher education are generally regarded as an acceptable mechanism for smoothing out what otherwise would be a large, lumpy expenditure at an early point of the life cycle.

In order to make a particular case for social investment in higher education, one must determine which ends of public higher education serve the general public interest, i.e., which ends constitute public benefits, which transcend the interests of particular individuals or states. The best means of determining what constitutes a public benefit is an analysis of general public values. We contend that insuring equitable opportunity and pursuing research are the two functions (perhaps the only functions) of the state research university that can be most appropriately discussed in this context. In each case, there is a strong tradition of public value and commitment. The national interest in equitable opportunity springs from adherence to such deeply rooted democratic ideals as freedom and individual rights, as well as from more practical realizations that exclusivity of opportunity is likely to yield unwanted political and economic consequences.

The national interest in research and graduate education can be described similarly, in more or less pragmatic terms. On one hand, there remains a persistent faith in the pursuit of knowledge for its own sake, despite the many trials of the twentieth century. This belief is mingled with a powerful interest in seeking the most advantageous economic and political uses of knowledge, which is more and more recognized as the nation's most important commodity in an increasingly competitive international market and as our best hope for defense in a troubled political arena.

Social investment in higher education is justified when the social benefits from such investments are greater than the private benefits, in other words, when the society derives benefits that are external to the individual student. It must also be assumed that these externalities are of such large order that market price alone cannot be taken as the primary indicator of the social value of education. If a society desires these benefits, and public consensus holds that they are derived primarily via education, then that society should be willing to subsidize education in order to encourage and insure individual participation to a greater extent than otherwise would be the case. This willingness is based on two grounds: (1) a commonly felt sense of public responsibility, and (2) an acknowledgment that private decisions and initiatives alone cannot produce or insure socially desired outcomes.

In addition to the direct returns from investment in higher education, the indirect effects for both the individual and the society are highly significant. For example, when the productivity of the human resource is increased, the productivity of other resources with which the human resource is combined also increases. In a very real sense, as the quality of the human resource increases society gains from an increase in total resource productivity. The distribution of such benefits is pervasive; they permeate the entire society. It seems reasonable, therefore, that the entire society should share the costs.

CHARLES E. BISHOP

INSURING EQUITABLE ACCESS IN THE STATE RESEARCH UNIVERSITIES

The state research universities were developed by the state governments with the assistance of the federal government. A major objective was and remains the provision of low-cost, geographically accessible, high-quality education. The legacy of state control over these universities has made possible greater diversity among institutions, allowing them to reflect the particularities of state and regional needs. The tradition of state control also reflects the persistence of concern over federal intrusion and control. The deep commitment to academic freedom in the American universities spawned distrust of bureaucratic control, especially from the federal level. There remains a general belief that state control is more likely to be consistent with the important goals of academic freedom.

Although their relative importance as a funding source has declined, state governments continue to be the major source of both capital and operating funds for the state research universities. In contrast, during the last twenty years, gifts and grants and the federal government have become increasingly important as funding sources. Indeed, federal support of certain aspects of the state research university is increasingly crucial. Institutionally derived funds from tuition, fees, and other charges, and income derived from endowments and gifts are also key funding sources for state universities. The particular mix of these various sources of funding has significant impact on the realization of equitable access.

Public expenditures for capital and operating costs constitute a form of subsidy to higher education. As a result, tuition charges assessed students can be kept at levels that encourage greater enrollment. But while lowering tuition may be a primary factor in stimulating enrollment, it may not be the best means of insuring equitable opportunity. Furthermore, it is also likely to come at some cost to either improving or maintaining academic quality.

Moreover, reduced tuition, scholarships, and other forms of aid to highly able students from high-income families are likely to have little effect upon decisions concerning college attendance. In contrast, subsidies are likely to be quite effective in encouraging moderately able students from low-income families to attend college, i.e., those students most likely denied opportunities without special assistance.

Aid specifically targeted to students from low-income families is far more efficient in promoting equity than is a reduction in tuition. If the least costly and most equitable means of assuring equitable opportunity is desired then aid targeted to students on the basis of financial need appears to be the best choice. Moreover, if the public desires that equitable opportunity not come at the expense of quality, then need-based aid to individual students appears a better choice than lowering tuition for all students, particularly to levels that necessitate reductions in academic services or changes in academic goals.

Given that insuring equitable access to higher education is a national policy, and given that the provision of need-based aid to students is an effective means of insuring such access, this type of aid should remain a principal form of educational assistance. It seems appropriate that this form of assistance to those whose financial means limit accessibility enables the federal government to fulfill a particular federal objective with limited intrusion into a state institution.

The federal government derives substantial benefits from investment in the state research universities. The increase in income resulting from increased education also generates an increase in government revenues, especially through the income and sales taxes. The federal government depends more heavily upon income taxes than state or local governments; the latter depend more heavily upon property and sales taxes. In addition, federal taxation is more progressive with respect to income than state and local taxes. The federal government, therefore, is more likely to capture benefits from increased income resulting from additional education than state and local governments.

The additional tax revenues are very important. In fact, Estelle James concludes that future discounted income taxes are sufficient to cover the social costs of investment at the undergraduate level.[6] Indeed, it is her view that investment in education at this level can be treated as a loan that is contingent on income. It should be emphasized, however, that most of the taxes are captured by the federal government while the investments are made largely at the state level. Without federal assistance, the net effect of public investment in higher education, therefore, is to transfer income from the states to the federal government. Also, inasmuch as there is extensive migration of people across state lines, there is a transfer of income from states of high enrollment in higher education to states of low enrollment. This, of course, provides additional rationale for federal aid to students. It is argued that if equitable access to higher education is desired, this can be assured by a reasonable program of student aid, and that since the federal government through the income tax mechanism recaptures a substantial portion of the increased earnings resulting from investments in education, the federal government should provide the student aid.

FEDERAL INVESTMENT IN GRADUATE EDUCATION AND RESEARCH

Just as we have argued that federally sponsored student aid can serve the larger interests of the public university, federal support of research does likewise. In each case, the argument for federal support is based on the nature of the benefits accrued. Through federal investment in research and graduate education, new knowledge is created and made readily transferrable not just among individuals, but among states and nations. Inasmuch as such pervasive benefits accrue more to the nation than to the individual states, and inasmuch as those benefits are consistent with established public values, they indicate federal responsibility and therefore warrant federal support.

Second, given the nature of the multiproduct state university, federally supported research programs further decrease the relative costs of undergraduate education while increasing the relative strengths of the university's academic programs and support systems as a whole. Thus, federal support of research programs indirectly serves the ends of equitable opportunity by providing lower cost, higher quality public education to a potentially greater number of deserving undergraduates.

As argued earlier, investment in research at the graduate level in the multiproduct state research university results in joint products with both graduate and undergraduate instruction. Fundamental complementarities of production in the institution enable all levels to operate more efficiently as a whole than separately.

Evidence of this interdependency is found in the scarcity of freestanding undergraduate institutions. James finds that as graduate enrollment increases relative to undergraduate enrollment in a comprehensive university, the relative cost of undergraduate instruction, particularly at the lower division, decreases. She concludes that "in contrast to the conventional wisdom . . . undergraduate education does not cost society more at the university than at the community college. On the contrary, introductory instruction is much less faculty intensive at the university where large lecture classes with lower cost supporting staff predominate yielding lower cost per full-time student."[7] As a result, she argues that the social costs of undergraduate instruction have been greatly overestimated in the multiproduct universities. She also concludes that if research is treated as an input into graduate education, the cost of graduate education has been greatly underestimated.

In a very real sense, then, the cost of undergraduate education in the state research university and the most efficient means of providing that education, depend upon the value society places upon research and graduate education. If society wishes to increase support of research, especially basic research, and graduate education to train research personnel, the relative costs of undergraduate education can be decreased as research-oriented pograms are expanded. If there is a general commitment to excellence on all levels in the public university, then a desired quantum of education will be accompanied by a certain quantum of research activity. The "cost" of such education will necessarily encompass the "cost" of the by-product research. If society is interested in high-quality, low-cost undergraduate education for all academically qualified students and high-quality research, then public investment in either can serve the interests of both.

CONCLUSION

Since the publication of the Carnegie Commission report in 1973 ("Higher Education: Who Pays? Who Benefits? Who Should Pay?") a great deal of research has been done on the demand for higher education and the costs of providing such education. Although there have been significant extensions and refinements in the analysis, the basic conclusions of the 1973 report remain intact. Most recent studies, including this one, reinforce the general spirit of the commission's recommendations.

In summary, the most appropriate divisions of federal, state, and private responsibilities appear to be the following. Except where there are special philanthropic interests or overriding national interests, investment in the physical plant of the state research universities should be made by the state. Because of its growing significance and the pervasive nature of its effects, the cost of basic research should be borne largely by the federal government. Since graduate education is intertwined with research, the costs of graduate education should be shared among graduate students and the federal and state governments. The direct costs of undergraduate education should be borne by the students, with need-based financial assistance provided by the federal government. Opportunity costs must be borne by the individual student. Finally, because public service programs are designed in response to local needs and conditions, the costs of these programs should be borne by the users or, where justified, by the local or state governments.

This appropriation of responsibility is from the vantage of the multiproduct state research university, where if adequate support in one area enhances the whole, inadequate support in one area will jeopardize the whole. This interdependency constitutes both the unique strength and vulnerability of the multiproduct state university. The division of federal, state, and private responsibilities described above, therefore, is particularly crucial to the well-being of the state research university and the public values it serves.

NOTES

1. In the preparation of this essay I have benefited greatly from the assistance of Dr. Carla Cooper and Dr. Irwin L. Collier of the University of Houston.

2. For example, John Bishop, "The Effect of Public Policies on the Demand for Higher Education," *The Journal of Human Resources*, vol. 13, no. 3, p. 291.

3. Bishop, p. 294.

4. T. Hopkins, "Higher Education Enrollment Demand," *Economic Inquiry* 12 (March 1974): 53–65.

5. H. R. Bowen, *Investment in Learning* (San Francisco: Jossey-Bass, 1977).

6. Estelle James, "Product Mix and Cost Disaggregation: A Reinterpretation of the Economics of Higher Education," *The Journal of Human Resources* 13, no. 2 (1978): 178.

7. James, p. 172.

CHAPTER 13
ACCOUNTABILITY AND AUTONOMY
DAVID A. WILSON

Accountability is a persistent demand levied on universities by external sponsoring authorities and agencies. The shrill tone of such demands may be somewhat muted by parallel expectations that education and research will contribute substantially to the solution of the nation's problems. Universities are expected to contribute to economic growth, international competitiveness, the national defence, health care, and improvement of declining public schools. So for the time being, they are relieved from some more carping public demands to explain themselves.

Yet, not too many years ago, accountability was a central and often bitter term in debates about higher education. The agitation and unrest in campus life was directed not only at the issues of civil rights and war, but also to demands for change on campus. Free speech, student power, ethnic equality, curriculum reform, and reconstitution each had its day on the streets, in faculty senate meetings, and president's office sit-ins. Because of the sensational character of that time, public attention was drawn to university life and increasing expectations for an accounting from university presidents were heard. The market for accountability was enriched by increasing costs, prospective decline in enrollment and continuing demands for open access. A rather bewildering array of new regulations also added a heretofore unknown dimension of complexity to university relations with governments. While regulators have relented somewhat in the search for demonstrated compliance, we should observe that auditors continue their ineluctable scrutinizing of the books and justification of indirect cost rates is still in demand. The effects of the application of scientific discovery are also of serious concern to environmentalists and others. Universities, as the home of most fundamental scientific research, are frequently charged with liability for technological dislocation. It is not difficult to foresee a concerted demand for an accounting of the consequences of rapidly developing technology, including the various social effects.

Institutions that dispose of much public money, employ large numbers of expensive people and charge substantial prices for their services should reasonably expect to account for their activities, their diligence, their excellence, their performance.

State research universities—members of NASULGC—constitute a unique category of public corporations or quasicorporations that claim a substantial degree of institutional autonomy in the name of academic freedom, scientific creativity, and managerial flexibility. They draw their resources from state and federal governments, local authorities, and private sources in a variety of forms, entailing in each case undertakings, obligations, and expectations. They house and institutionalize the efforts and talents of a great many, quite independent faculty entrepreneurs and professional research workers who, in turn, must perform services that satisfy the variety of clients. The internal obligation for accountability may match in complexity those of the world outside.

Accountability is the fraternal twin of institutional autonomy. Universities have sought and defended autonomy for their activities from the very beginning. They were formed by clerics, theologians, and scholars to escape the loving attention of bishops by acquiring charters from the pope or the king. Freedom to speak and teach truth is the ultimate justification for institutional autonomy. And the notion of a self-governing corporation that pursues its worthy purpose has served learning well.

Since at least the time of the Dartmouth College case, the constitutional foundation of the University of Michigan, and the emergence of the land-grant colleges and research universities, the United States has affirmed the appropriateness of the learning corporation. It seems unlikely that our contemporary state research universities could have come into existence without the freedom and flexibility of the form.

The American tradition of higher educational institutions, in contrast to most of the world and also to the tradition of schools in this country, is shaped by the pattern of academic freedom embedded in a corporate structure of self-government. This pattern has permitted the growth of the large, varied, complex, and multipurpose institutions of intellectual activity that are a rich medium of productive and creative research, scholarship, and teaching. The freedom to seek knowledge, to preserve it from generation to generation, and to place it at the service of society is protected by autonomy. In addition, the organizational agility that permits a reasonably efficient disposition of money and talent depends equally on relatively autonomous governance. This is particularly the case when re-sources come from many directions. Along with the development of these great institutions, especially those substantially supported from public funds, requirements for lucid accountability have grown.

FINANCIAL

Accountability has many faces. Financial accounts are the most obvious. State supported research universities receive money from governments, private corporations, and individuals on a variety of terms: (1) restricted and unrestricted gifts; (2) conditioned grants; (3) performance contracts; (4) student fees; (5) fees for services (such as health care coming from individuals and insurance sources); (6) appropriations variously speci-fied; and, (7) income from endowed wealth in the form of securities, real estate, and productive enterprises that produce income. Each of these funds entails its own accounting requirements to assure and document the appropriate expenditure of the money. The exigencies of such a pro-cess are difficult and complicated.

While state governments have from time to time raised issues about university accounting practices, the principal arena of controversy about financial matters has been with federal funds. Aside from very rare in-stances of alleged fraud, the issues raised by federal auditors have conse-quences for the practices of project funding and the complexity of faculty activity. Transfer of costs from one project to another, the possibility of double payments and the indeterminate character of university adminis-tration, particularly departmental administration, have all revealed ac-counting to be a judgmental, if not creative, art. Unfortunately, *de gustibus* does not rule, rather *disputandum ad nauseum* has prevailed. These argu-ments have often gone to the very essence of academic mores. The fac-ulty's reaction to the vulgar concern about money is confirmed and com-pounded by their indignation at the requirements of effort reporting.

PERFORMANCE

Performance accounting includes another set of expectations without dis-tinct indices or standards. Lacking the clarity of cost accounting or profit-and-loss statements, universities must develop techniques of evaluation that are cumbersome and often contentious in order to satisfy their cli-ents and themselves. Faculty assessment, teaching evaluations, personnel assessment, program review, research reporting, and quality assurance involve the wit, talent, and energy of many souls. They labor to produce information that assuages the anxiety that money properly expended, nevertheless, may buy less than it ought.

Faculty

Evaluation of faculty performance is one of the most difficult assessments undertaken in academic life. The system of tenure for regular faculty is a definitive characteristic of university life providing the security that permits initiative and imagination to realize themselves in teaching and research. At the same time, this assurance of lifetime tenure stimulates in the minds of some responsible observers concern that it encourages laziness and malingering. Such concern takes on weightier significance as the amount of money expended in support of faculty grows. There is confidence within academia that deep and genuine assessment is an integrated element of the tenure system. The methods are sufficiently complex and mysterious, however, to keep alive these outside concerns. Doubts about faculty tenure are perennial and important enough to enliven demands for accountability. The issue of teaching evaluation with the lack of clarity and plenitude of sensitivity has been a particular source of contention and dissatisfaction. State governments view universities as primarily institutions for teaching the young so that the tension between teaching and research coupled with the technically unsatisfactory character of assessment procedures often lead to skepticism.

Programs

In addition to assessment of faculty performances, universities are expected to account for the breadth, structure, and quality of the programs they encompass. The review of academic programs is difficult and can consume a great deal of effort. The standards for such reviews are often vague and the process is largely judgmental. This combination of standards with personal, if expert and collective, judgment not infrequently leaves an unsatisfying impression of subjectivity and arbitrariness. Nevertheless, academic program review is a mature art of considerable utility to the experienced administrator. Its utility is especially great when reviews of individual program quality are brought together in a context of constrained resources so that the relationships among programs become clear. The processes are complex, however, and the effects usually incremental so that expectations of any crisp accounting are often disappointed.

Research

One response that faculty spokesmen offer to financial auditors' requirement of effort reporting is that they should worry less about input—
money and effort—and assess research projects by results. There is a certain irony in such a dispute, however, since the auditors are assuming the
significance, efficacy, and quality of effort, requiring only that they see
some documentation. The assessment of research output is much more
complex and rich in difficulty than counting input. The competitive proposal system with its formal scientific review does provide reasonable assurance of quality and significance so that success in acquiring support is
a valid measure of individual and institutional research output. It leaves
behind some doubt, however, because of its apparent ingrown and eso-
teric character. Continuing endeavor on the part of researchers and research administrators to explain and defend the system against suspicion
of favoritism and irrelevance is necessary.

COMPLIANCE

Much public money carries with it the requirement that supported activities be conducted in compliance with a number of public policies.
Among these policies are affirmative action in employment, in student recruitment, and in financial assistance, protection of human and live ani-
mal subjects in research, occupational health and safety standards, the
handling and disposition of toxic and radioactive waste materials, competitive purchasing, veterans' preference, and the like. They add up to
tens, if not hundreds, of public concerns that must be accommodated in
the course of the central enterprises of teaching, research, and public
services.

In complying, universities have developed rather elaborate schemes of
accountable self-regulation. They maintain complicated record keeping, reporting and review procedures associated with recruitment, appointment, and promotion of faculty and other employees. They require
prior review of research projects by internal committees. They accept the
growth of staff and costs to administer compliance and reporting in an
accountable fashion. Frequent, and often regular, encounters with governmental compliance agencies and quasijudicial review boards are the
stuff of this class of accountability requirements. Such encounters are

often, perhaps too often, enlivened by accompanying litigation, making universities accountable to courts of law as well as bureaucrats and politicians.

GENERAL STEWARDSHIP

Clearly, the size, importance of purpose, salience in society, and valuation of education and research in modern America all lead to expectations of responsible general stewardship that put the leadership of these institutions on the spot.

In a world of simple rationality, institutions would be able to articulate their mission and goals sufficiently clearly to be of use in evaluating their effectiveness. Universities fall substantially short of that ideal. The contemporary state research university—not at all unlike independent universities of similar size—have accumulated such a complex of missions that overall evaluation is no simple matter. For this reason, these institutions are enmeshed in a web of subordinate evaluations without any broadly accepted technology for settling the balance among accounts. Financial solvency, continued growth, and standing in various national ratings of academic programs or of research awards are commonly offered by university leaders as plausible indicators of effective stewardship. Yet, those who make themselves generally responsible often exhibit uneasiness about the push and shove of competing expectations and requirements.

RESPONSIBILITIES

Who are these responsible parties? In the corporate structure of American universities, they are the boards of trustees or regents who formally have responsibility. The historical role of these boards was to embody and articulate the public interest in the integrity and effectiveness of the institutional effort. In the affairs of the state research universities, the trustee boards should play the dual role of holding the administrators and faculty accountable for performance of their obligations, and also assuring effective accounting for this responsibility to other authorities outside the university.

To accomplish such a task is difficult, however obvious the need may be. Difficulty arises from the complexity of university activity, the risk of disruption of activity by demands for information and assurance, the skill required to transform a large number of audit and review reports into a credible assurance of responsibility, and the delicacy required to protect morale and enthusiasm. Yet a number of assessment techniques are known. Their peculiarity and complexity rises from the nature of such activities as teaching and fundamental research for which no crisp bottom line can be found. A central function of leading institutional administrators—presidents, vice-presidents, and faculty leaders—is to see that these techniques are implemented on reasonable and reliable cycles and to produce explanations and reports that support the confidence of trustees. In turn trustees can exert their role as surrogate for the public interest by, in effect, certifying the accounting to appropriate public authorities.

STATE GOVERNMENT

The multiplicity of clientele, constituents, and support groups is the source of difficulty with accountability. At the core of this difficulty is the historically changing relationship between the universities and state governments. Although this relationship varies from state to state, typically, state government provides 20 to 40 percent of the support for a research university budget; usually funding the central teaching function in the form of faculty salaries and support costs. Insofar as this is the case, these funds constitute the central columns for the architecture of the university programs. Because of the centrality of this support, the state governments continue to have a special standing with public research universities. This is true even though the states provide less than half the funds expended and the universities, in many respects and in many cases, have great similarity in their missions and program structure to their private or independent counterparts. Thus, the effectiveness of university accountability to their state government patrons is crucial.

In the 1980s, state higher education programs have emerged from the organizational turbulence that characterized the period of rapid growth, expansion, and reorganization. New campuses are no longer so new, multicampus university and college systems have found their footing. Coordinating boards are routinized. Governors' budget offices and state legislative committees have developed their methods. These equilibriums of fatigue are often awkward and unbalanced. In more than one state they have left the streams of accountability in a confused condition.

The pattern of distribution of authority from state government to institutional administrations varies substantially among the several states. In some states, for instance Michigan and California, the research universities retain a great range of authority to manage their own affairs, while in other states government agencies involve themselves in detailed planning, budgeting, program review, and even preauditing of expenditures. These patterns have evolved over time. They are not likely to change easily or rapidly, although that kind of rigidity may itself vary as a function of historical roots and bureaucratic interest.

EXCELLENCE AND AUTONOMY

There is some reason to think that general excellence is positively correlated with general autonomy. It behooves the leadership of higher education in the states—leaders in government as well as universities—to accept such a correlation and to seek, for their own research universities, an optimum situation. By encouraging comprehensive management of resources combined with authentic, but economical, accountability, the states will get better results in a complex of endeavors than is likely with inflexible coordination and micromanagement.

It is to be expected that state governments will use their special influence to assure that state expectations are met. Those expectations are largely a matter of accessibility, high-quality undergraduate education, agricultural research and extension, as well as appropriate professional education, scientific research, scholarship, and service in support of the state's economic needs. Some tension is inevitable between these expectations and the need for research universities to respond to their own intrinsic imperative and also to national and international opportunities. This kind of tension is not unmanageable, so long as universities have the internal flexibility to deal with it. Insofar as state government and state political leaders see a benefit to the interests they represent in successful and prosperous research universities, they need to cooperate in discovering and instituting a method of supporting the institution that does not tangle it in a web of detailed and rigid requirements while, at the same time, demanding from them a credible accounting for their performance and stewardship of resources.

Thus, it is necessary to articulate both standards and processes for evaluating the success at meeting them. In fact, to accomplish this goal, institutional leadership, principally in universities, needs to discover the techniques for sustaining credible practices of accounting for performances. Such techniques must be satisfying to university presidents, their faculty and students, and their state, federal, and public patrons.

These state research universities are immensely valuable. They require, for continued success, that degree of accountable autonomy that permits the release of their considerable energy, the management of their substantial and various resources and the accomplishment of their complicated missions.

Recognizing that governmental demands for increased accountability may be thin disguises for specific program objectives of particular persons of influence, it is, nonetheless, proper to ponder the clarity and credibility of accountability processes in universities. Because of the mutual stake in better quality and greater effectiveness on the part of university leaders and public authorities any organized effort to improve the situation should be joint. But given the recognition by university leaders of the relationships between autonomy and excellence, as well as accountability and autonomy, the initiative to advance understanding of accountability as a set of processes and standards should be expected from the university community.

In recent years, the Sloan Commission, the National Commission on Research, and the National Academy of Science's Committee on Government-University Relations in Support of Science have addressed the issues of accountability in the realm of nationally supported scientific research. A number of specific recommendations have been forthcoming to improve existing difficulties and, perhaps, move toward a set of standards that would be mutually agreeable. In addition, both the National Commission on Research and the National Academy Committee recommended the establishment of a permanent government-university forum for examining issues of contention on a regular basis. Accountability will certainly be one such issue.

University and state educational leaders should consider the desirability of developing a mutual effort to examine contentious issues of accountability and establishing a standing forum among state universities and state governments for the airing of difficult issues. The objective of such a process should be to find mutually acceptable standards of accounting and evaluation that are consistent and supporting of university autonomy and flexible management while meeting reasonable expectation of accountability.

REFERENCES

Robert Berdahl. *The Statewide Coordination of Higher Education.* Washington, D.C.: American Council for Education, 1971.

Carnegie Foundation for the Advancement of Teaching. *The States and Higher Education: A Proud Past and a Vital Future.* San Francisco: Jossey-Bass Pub., 1976.

Paul L. Dressel, ed. *The Autonomy of Public College.* San Francisco: Jossey-Bass Pub., 1980.

John K. Folger, ed. *Increasing the Public Accountability of Higher Education.* San Francisco: Jossey-Bass Pub., 1977.

Lyman H. Glenny. *The Autonomy of Public Colleges.* New York: McGraw Hill, 1959.

Eugene C. Lee and Frank M. Bowen. *The Multicampus University.* New York: McGraw Hill, 1971.

John Millet. *Conflict in Higher Education, State Government Coordination versus Institutional Independence.* San Francisco: Jossey-Bass Pub., 1984.

Malcolm Moos and Frank Rourke. *The Campus and the State.* Baltimore: Johns Hopkins Press, 1959.

National Commission on Research. *Accountability: Restoring the Quality of the Partnership.* Washington, D.C.: 1980.

University of Maryland. *The Post-Land Grant University.* The University of Maryland, 1981.

CHAPTER 14
THE RATIONALE FOR PRIVATE
SUPPORT OF A STATE UNIVERSITY
JOSEPH M. PETTIT

One approach to this subject would be a philosophical one; namely, what theoretical arguments could be developed if there were not already a tradition of private support to public universities and we were considering the desirability and feasibility of starting such a tradition? In many nations public higher education is fully supported (and controlled) by the government; even the students pay little or no tuition. Philanthropy has no role. But that is not our situation. Private support of state universities has been with us for a long time, and the amount of support is growing. One could ask, of course, *why* do we have it, and do we really want more?

A pragmatic, current approach is probably better. We can start where we are, look backward, and then ahead. It is well known that gift support of *private* universities is high, but it is not as well known that it is also high in many of the public institutions—and growing rapidly at an average rate of 15 percent a year in recent times. National data[1] show that in 1981–1982, private philanthropy to 258 reporting public universities and four-year colleges reached $1,216,681,000, up 17.4 percent from the prior year, and exceeding $1 billion for the first time. This is clearly a well-established activity, hardly needing a theoretical rationale. Perhaps the best rationale is success itself: it works.

One could ask, nevertheless, what *has* brought about this impressive level of private support to institutions that are believed by some people to be fully supported from public funds? To answer that to the fullest extent, one would need to investigate the myriad of reasons why each institution sought each particular gift and why an individual or corporation responded favorably. There is certainly no single rationale operating on both sides of all such transactions. Time and resources do not permit such an encyclopedic coverage here. Even the reader may not have the time nor desire to know that much about the subject.

Instead let me offer some data and viewpoints deriving from my own institutional experience. These may provide a sufficient basis for generalization and discussion. I know the public sector well, as an alumnus of the University of California at Berkeley, and a former faculty member there, and now for twelve years as president of another state institution, the Georgia Institute of Technology. I have worked on the other side of the street also, being an alumnus of Stanford University, and later a professor there and dean of the engineering school, as well as a one-time member of the research faculty at Harvard.

PRIVATE SUPPORT TODAY

Private support is not uniformly distributed throughout public institutions. This should not be surprising; neither is research support uniformly distributed. Indeed, this NASULGC study is concerned with the *leading* state universities, and it should not be surprising that those leading in research tend also to be those leading in private support. Specifically, the national data show that, for public institutions, the top one hundred in support from the private sector brought in 96 percent of the total private dollars, averaging $11.7 million to each institution. The top ten ranged from $25.3 to $63 million. But even the average for all 258 reporting institutions was $4.8 million, not a trivial sum. Incidentally, on the average, this sum is composed of 31.4 percent from business, 19.3 percent from foundations, 18.3 percent from alumni, 18.2 percent from nonalumni individuals, and 12.8 percent from all other sources.

Corporate support provides the best testimonial to our success in conveying a message of the need and appropriateness for private support of leading public universities. Corporate support of all higher education has been growing, and by 1981–1982 it had reached $823,001,000.[2] Remarkably, 46.5 percent of this went to public institutions. This percentage has been increasing; five years earlier it was only 40.7 percent. In one recent capital campaign, a major chemical company contributed more than $1 million; it was their first grant to a state university.

Looking further at 1981–1982, several categories are of interest. The top ten institutions in *corporate* support averaged $3,688,444 from this source. The top ten in *foundation* support averaged $2,329,150. In support from *nonalumni individuals*, the top ten averaged $2,031,073; while the top ten in *alumni* gifts did well to average $2,119,300. Evidently it is almost as easy to tell our story to nonalumni as to our own graduates.

Gifts from alumni included special gifts for capital purposes, bequests, and such, as well as gifts for current operations made through the annual alumni fund. Looking at the latter alone, it is interesting to note the percent of alumni who contributed. In 1981–1982 the top ten averaged 33.7 percent participation, while the highest was 45.1 percent. The average for the top one hundred was only 14.4 percent, and still lower for *all* public universities and four-year colleges. Evidently the best of the publics is better than the average of the privates, though on average alone the publics are behind. The best include a mixture of large and small state universities. They have shown that private support from alumni can be successfully achieved.

THE FOUNDING PHASE

The present state of both research and private support in our state universities was not always this way. Steady evolution has occurred. Let us go back to beginnings to heighten the contrast with the present.

While beginnings were different with every state university, the situation in Georgia was perhaps representative. The University of Georgia was chartered in 1785, and qualified under the Morrill Act of 1862 to become the land-grant university for the state. Agriculture continues there, but "the mechanic arts," i.e., engineering, were soon discontinued. Thus in 1885, two Georgians in the legislature became concerned with the immediate economic needs of the state, and the need for an industrial foundation in addition to that of traditional agriculture. They were concerned that an engineering education was nowhere available in the state. These men felt it would be the proper province of the state government to establish a public engineering college and to support it in parallel with the University of Georgia. Then sons of even the poorest of citizens would have access to a technical education and a better hope for their future.

THEN AND NOW

Given the economic and political circumstances of Georgia in the period of reconstruction after the Civil War, we should not wonder that the founders of Georgia Tech had only modest aspirations for the school. In their minds was an undergraduate engineering college of small size and reasonable quality, serving a limited economic need in Georgia. They were even concerned that the engineering program be of a very practical nature. They would leave for later generations the consideration of graduate education and research, even though by 1885 programs of this kind were being established at a few leading state universities. The first Ph.D. in engineering had been awarded at Yale in 1863, but for the newly chartered Georgia Tech that kind of event was to be far in the future.

The founders thought that they would do well to provide young people with the fundamentals of education in engineering, science, and commerce. They could scarcely have envisaged all that such a modest state institution might become, and has become. Growth alone would have been difficult for them to imagine: a student body of 11,000, with more than 700 coming from distant nations, together with a full-time instructional faculty of 600.

It would probably not have occurred to the founders that not only would teachers be teaching, but that they would be doing research on the frontiers of their disciplines, making important new contributions. Nor would they have seen the possibility or need for increasing the research on the campus through the addition of a research institute, the Engineering Experiment Station. Its research faculty would grow to 600 full-time engineers and scientists, with a support staff of 800 full- and part-time employees. This research institute would cover a wide range of activities, from technical assistance to help small industry in the state to research in the highly sophisticated technology of electronic defense to help in the national security. The founders could certainly not have dreamed that faculty research could ever be held in such high regard by the U.S. government and by industry and that these sponsors would willingly invest more than $80 million each year in new grants and contracts.

The founders would have seen no need for a professor to have earned the Ph.D., so how could they have foreseen a day when it would be essentially a requirement? They could not have imagined that more than 95 percent of the faculty in engineering, for example, would indeed have earned the doctoral degree. They would have seen no need for a new state university to be a cosmopolitan institution, so how could they have foreseen an engineering faculty with degrees from seventy-five different institutions?

The founders did see the need for undergraduate instruction, but they could not have foreseen that in addition to a large high-quality undergraduate student body, there would be—by 1984—more graduate students than the total enrollment was at any time during the first thirty-five years. They could picture the graduates seeking jobs from a limited assortment in the local economy, but certainly could not have dreamed of more than 600 employers journeying to the campus every year to hire them—and paying a high premium for those with advanced degrees.

The same kind of story could be told about the founding phase of any of the nation's leading state universities. But today we must look squarely at ourselves, not as we were but as we are today—the diversity of our activities, the quality of our faculty and students, the quality of all our endeavors—and realize that these things were not in our original charters. We must ask ourselves how we got here, how we can move ahead from here. We must look squarely at the role of state government, with its proper but limited role of providing low cost instruction for in-state students. We must realize that because of the many competing demands state government will never be able or willing to provide the resources needed for our institutions to rise to their full potential, even though this would result in great benefit to the state and its people.

What we are today provides interesting speculation on what kind of state university we would seek to create if our particular institution did not already exist. What kind of institution would we think was needed in our state? Certainly Georgia continues to need a flow of practically educated young people for industry and business, but now those needs are being well supplied by dozens of postsecondary schools of all kinds. In 1984 we should—as the founders did in the nineteenth century—want to add something that otherwise would not exist, something we have actually shown to be possible and desirable: an institution with a level of education and research, one that could rank with the very best private universities and yet would provide low-cost accessibility to all residents of the state who had the ability to benefit from it. Such an institution should reach toward the highest levels of the intellectual life so that it could be a contributor to new knowledge, to new ways of doing things, and to offer new levels of attractiveness to the highest quality of faculty and students available anywhere in this nation. To do less would be to turn our backs on our own potential.

QUALITY

Not only do the leading state universities differ from the other public institutions in the variety of things they do, but there is one aspect we have relentlessly and successfully pursued. Its name is "Quality." Is this just an abstraction, something we merely brag about? No, but its pursuit has required the continuing search for the resources necessary to compete successfully for *people*—for people of the highest quality in a highly competitive market. We have wanted the best new faculty coming out of our nation's institutions, and to retain those who were best among us. We have sought to compete for the brightest students, at both the undergraduate and graduate levels. Outstanding students *seek* outstanding faculty; outstanding students *attract* outstanding faculty.

While it is easy to say that the most important thing is high-quality people, what has been needed to attract them? Certainly, an attractive professional position for themselves—in terms of salary, prestige, and the like—but also excellent facilities and working conditions. Thus, the physical conditions of the campus become important: offices, classrooms, laboratories, buildings, and even the landscaping. We must have excellent teaching and research laboratories, with modern equipment to provide modern instruction. We must have an excellent library, providing a totally modern, information-access facility. All of this has required us to seek and attract adequate resources, both public and private.

THE EVOLVING STATE UNIVERSITY

Today's leading state universities were founded, as Georgia Tech was in 1885, as totally state institutions—state controlled and state supported, except for the very small fees charged to the students. Now Georgia Tech is among the state *assisted*. Only 27 percent of our annual expenditures are covered by state appropriations. Why is this? Are we being singled out for some kind of "benign neglect" in our own state? Not at all. We have merely joined the ranks of the leading state universities in the nation. These are the major public research universities, and all of them have state appropriations of not more than 20 to 40 percent of their total revenues. The state appropriation *does* undergird the support of undergraduate teaching, but the scope and quality of the total activities of a major research university have far outgrown the simple though important role of classroom teaching.

Yet, why haven't we just *asked* for more from the state officials? We have—every year. Why won't they appropriate adequate funding for all the worthwhile things we are doing? In the first place they haven't *asked* us to do all these things. They haven't even asked us to be *excellent* in the basic teaching work we are supposed to do. *We* have reached for excellence because in everything we have done we believed that it was important.

Actually there are several real problems. As mentioned before, the state budget must cover many functions, not just higher education. While we happen to believe that a higher priority should be given to public higher education, there are other powerful claimants. Secondly, in Georgia as in some other states, we have a university system with thirty-three institutions, incorporating essentially all of public higher education in the state, including the junior colleges, the senior colleges, and all university and professional level education. The Board of Regents of the system must, in some sense of the word, award funding equitably among the institutions. Yet this can only provide for adequacy, not excellence.

The state does have an important financial role. We should recognize it and *build on it*. Basically the state appropriation assures low tuition fees for state residents. Our $66 million instruction budget is offset by $21 million in student fees, with the rest coming from $41 million in state appropriation and other sources, such as research overhead.

At times we chafe under the limited state assistance—and the total state control that comes with it—and we talk loosely about "going private." But it is sobering to calculate what endowment would be needed to generate our state appropriation. At 9 percent yield Georgia Tech would have to accumulate $456 million in endowment to provide us the $41 million mentioned above. This would put us in the top ranks of the nation's private universities. Although we—or our descendants—might well be able to get there, it is probably wiser to build on the state support we already have. The states have usually permitted us to do so. In Georgia the Board of Regents is on record stating that the initiative and success of an institution in gaining additional private support will not cause a reduction in the level of state support.

INSTITUTIONAL INITIATIVE

It has been left to the individual institution to strive for quality and to seek the necessary resources. Not all have striven to do so, and many have had only limited success. Those institutions that are now the leading public research universities have not been content to sit back, nor are they now, for they see even greater potential ahead. Every year they have sought the strongest possible support—research contracts from the federal government and private support from individuals, foundations, and corporations—and with gratifying results.

PRIVATE DOLLARS FOR A PUBLIC UNIVERSITY

This brings us now to an important question: how can we successfully compete for private assistance from our individual and corporate friends when the private universities say they need that money because they do not have the benefit of tax support? The distinction between private and public universities is no longer simple. Tax support *does* go to private universities. In several states there are annual appropriations of substantial amounts going to privately controlled universities, this in addition to programs of tuition assistance to individual students. And far greater is the state and federal tax supported research going to the major private universities.

The distinction between the great private research universities and the great public ones is not significant, not compared to the distinction between those institutions that are great research universities and those that are not.

ECONOMIC IMPORTANCE

This is a critical time in our history. The nation is being challenged in the international arena in technology, manufacturing productivity, and industrial management. In the past we faced successfully such a challenge in agriculture and won it through a mutual investment of resources from the federal, state, and private sectors. We need to broaden our scope into these new arenas of challenge and opportunity. It is time for increasing support from the private sector to flow into the public research universities. The private sector has much to gain from having at least one strong public university in every region, and each region has much to gain. It is a good investment. We are key to the economic development of our individual regions, and we are key to the economic and technological development of the whole nation.

THE FUTURE

If we are doing so well, can anything else be needed? We are *not* doing as well as we could be, not as well as we should be. We have serious impediments in the soliciting, accumulating, and spending of our private support. All of these impediments derive from the institutional setting, and could be dramatically improved by a major rearrangement. Our current organization and its jurisdiction as a branch of state government was appropriate for the nineteenth century, but is no longer.

State support is still appropriate, as discussed above, in order to provide substantially tax-subsidized higher education opportunities for in-state residents. But if that provides only 20 to 40 percent of our necessary revenues, is it any longer appropriate to have 100 percent state control?

Three other questions arise immediately. Does the state really want us to do so many things that require private and federal support? Do they really want us to spend so much money and effort on quality? Do they like it that we must pay such high salaries compared to other state employees?

The answers seem to be in the affirmative. The state leadership is proud of our Nobel Laureates, proud of the growth in high-technology industry in the vicinity of our universities, and proud of all those achievements that attract favorable notice to the state and those that provide new and better employment opportunities. They are proud of the favorable attention and large grants from the federal government and from major corporations.

Yet because the state controls every detail of our budgets, pooling state appropriations with private support for current operations, what is our credibility with the prospective donor that his money will not sometimes merely substitute for state money? What is the credibility that we can achieve quality when the state sets faculty raises as though they were for average state workers?

How can we hope to achieve quality when there are such severe constraints on gifts that become "state money," constraints on accumulating and on spending them for purposes necessary in the conduct of a competitive enterprise including such complex businesses as research and development contracting?

It would seem that a new organizational and jurisdictional arrangement might better accomplish not only those immediate teaching functions for which the subsidy of state appropriations for current budget expenses and for capital outlay are intended, but also all those extra dimensions made possible by the outside support—and which actually improve the teaching environment itself. If the state would relinquish total direct control, the obtaining and utilization of outside support would be greatly facilitated, and the state would see a much higher multiplier on its own money.

Various arrangements could be postulated, such as a state-chartered corporation or authority. The governing board could be responsible to the people of the state through a suitable appointment or election process, drawing upon the nation's long and diverse experience in selecting state boards of regents. The new organization would be free to set its own budgets, utilizing *all* sources of funds with the flexibility of a private university. It would be accountable to the state for the amount of teaching done, and the state appropriation could be based on a suitable formula. It would be free of civil service constraints on salaries and raises, and would be limited only by the total financial support it could generate from all sources.

THE UNIVERSITY IN SOCIETY

There is a missing concept that holds us back. Strangely enough our federal leaders were able to grasp this concept following World War II, but we have yet to awaken the state leaders and those of the private sector. The concept at the federal level was, first, that basic research is in the national interest, even though its applications may not be immediately evident. Second, that a vital group of research performers is to be found in the universities—an important national resource. During the war they moved temporarily to wartime projects but returned immediately thereafter. They would not work in the bureaucratic atmosphere of government laboratory establishments, nor would they work in industry—in spite of higher salaries. They preferred the freedom to direct their own research. They preferred the stimulation of ever brighter young students to work with on new research. They preferred the mutual reinforcement of teaching and research.

This national resource is also a state resource. The state would be well advised not to make the university a bureaucratic establishment comparable to those of the federal laboratories. They would do well to realize that the more tightly they seek to control this resource through political constraints the more likely they are to lose the worth that is there.

This resource represented by the university is also an economic resource, and important element to the corporate world, a source of technological innovation as well as flow of new employees and future leaders. It should be regarded as an important target of investment capital rather than of charity. And past corporate constraints, such as proprietary and legal, should be minimized, lest, again, the worth that is there be not fully accessible.

Finally, the state and federal tax structure could be of help in creating this new kind of organization, providing incentives for contributions, research contracting, and such.

New legislation is needed at both state and federal levels. It could be as significant for the twenty-first century as the Morrill Act was for the nineteenth.

NOTES

1. "Voluntary Support for Public Higher Education 1981–1982" (New York: Brakeley, John Price Jones Inc., pp. 8–19).

2. Anderson, Gene M., "Public Higher Education: The Corporate Sector fuels a Boom in Private Support," *News from New York* (New York: Brakeley, John Price Jones Inc., October 1983).

CHAPTER 15
FINANCING PUBLIC UNIVERSITIES AND COLLEGES IN THE YEAR 2000

DURWARD LONG

There have been several major works since the end of World War II that have focused on the finance of higher education, including the reports of a variety of government-sponsored committees and commissions. The most recent and notable reports and recommendations were issued by the Carnegie Commission on Higher Education, the Carnegie Council on Policy Studies, and the Carnegie Foundation for the Advancement of Teaching, most of them in the seventies.[1]

The various reports by the several Carnegie-sponsored organizations have been generally well received by the higher education community and by many persons of responsibility in several levels of government, although without enthusiasm by some of both groups. Some of the recommendations have been implemented in concept but key proposals, such as an increased level of public funding for all of higher education and the reduction in the gap between publics and privates, have not been accomplished.

Many of the concerns about financing higher education that generated the many reports of the seventies are still with us, some of them intensified by recent trends. New concerns have also emerged, especially in the general public, where they have surfaced in the political arena. At the heart of many of these concerns is a nervousness and uneasiness that rationalized and agreed upon public policy for the financing of higher education with long-term goals or priorities really does not exist at the federal or state level. At the root of this concern are the questions of who is going to pay how much for higher education and how that answer affects access under whatever policies or practices are implemented. As the costs become higher and higher in current dollars to all who share the cost, the concern becomes more intense and short-term pragmatic political responses become common.

Predictions of the future have not established for themselves an outstanding record of achievement or precision. In some cases, readings from the crystal ball have been inaccurate even about general directions. Nevertheless, explorations into probable futures and into preferred futures can be helpful. I intend here an exploration, especially in identifying issues, presenting relevant information, and stimulating discussion about financing public higher education for the remainder of the century. The condition of public higher education in the year 2000 will depend in good measure upon our assessment of the present situation, the judgment about the kinds of trends that, if unchanged, will dictate an undesirable future, and the intervening actions that can and should be taken to modify as much as possible the negative results of extrapolated current and recent trends. The leadership of the higher education community and the representatives of the body politic at the state and national levels will determine the state of health of the nation's institutions of higher learning in the year 2000 by the kind of action or inaction taken over the next fifteen years.

The content of the reauthorizing bill for the federal Higher Education Act will be important in continuing or modifying the recent trends of finance for colleges and universities. The act expires in September 1985, but contains a provision for an automatic extension of two years. Reauthorization hearings were begun but then suspended for 1984, partly because of differences within the academic community but also because of political conditions not directly associated with higher education. The political environment and broad economic issues within that environment lead one to speculate that reauthorization will not occur prior to 1987. I hope to provide a basis of discussion within higher education, government, and other publics that may lead to concerted action to influence funding to maintain and improve the financial health of public colleges and universities by action on financial issues in the various states.

THE FEDERAL GOVERNMENT AND HIGHER EDUCATION

Federal involvement in and assistance to higher education is historic, originating in a major way with the Morrill Act of 1862.[2] The current complex of relationships of the federal government and colleges and universities, however, began by defense-related research contracts to a small number of universities during World War II as an addition to land-grant support. Following that small beginning, the federal government initiated a significant support program for the veterans of World War II that totalled about $1 billion. Research contracts to universities were expanded and continued to expand even further in the 1960s, reaching about $1.5 billion in fiscal year 1964. By fiscal year 1968, federal support for higher education and its programs reached $4.7 billion, with research support constituting a little more than half, student aid (grants, loans, and work-study) about one-quarter, and the remaining funds devoted to GI benefits, social security benefits, and categorical support, including funds for libraries and construction.

In the mid-1970s, student aid began to replace research and development as the major form of federal support. By fiscal year 1981, student financial assistance constituted more than 60 percent of a total of $15.5 billion the federal government budgeted for higher education. The 60 percent included $6.1 billion for programs in the Department of Education, $1.8 billion for Social Security benefits, and $1.6 billion for GI benefits. Research had fallen to about 35 percent of the total but had doubled in dollars since 1968 to more than $5 billion. The Department of Education's Categorical Programs had declined from $803 million to $420 million.

The pattern of support for higher education has been erratic and divorced from general long-term policy except in the most admirable intent of increasing total funds available to colleges and universities until recently. For example, although the need for federal fellowships continues and there is now interest in increasing them again, they fell from 51,000 in fiscal year 1968 to a few more than 9,000 in fiscal year 1982. Federal support for college libraries reached $37 million in fiscal year 1968 and although the need continues, fiscal year 1983 funded the program at $3 million despite increases in cost of more than 400 percent for periodicals and a nearly 300 percent increase in the price of books over the intervening years. Another excellent example is the inattention that science and engineering education received following the end of the National Defense Education Act's infusion of funds and more recently the decrease in undergraduate science education from $70 million in fiscal year 1981 to $15 million in fiscal year 1982. At the present, however, there is renewed interest in this need as the nation lags in this important field. The phase-out of social security and GI benefits decreased student aid by about $3 billion, a decrease that affected mostly low income students at a time when professed interest was being given to increased support for low income students to attend college in greater numbers. Despite a wealth of resources available to the federal government by which a coherent and sustained program of support for national priorities could be developed and pursued, decisions about funding are made year to year, budget to budget, and primarily from short-range political considerations rather than programmatic directions that support national priority needs over the long term.

The absence of coherent and integrated policy to accomplish common goals and objectives at the federal level has been described by a Twentieth Century Fund Report, as follows:

> Federal assistance to higher education has served a confusing variety of goals with an unsystematic proliferation of programs. These federal programs represent an obvious political resolution of the conflicting objections of state and private institutions, high- and low-income families, students, parents, and administration. The only consistent result has been to increase the resources available to higher education—surely a defensible federal goal, but one that might be achieved more efficiently if it were consciously accepted as the only agreed purpose of federal aid. Instead, a number of other goals have been translated into other programs having so little intelligible relation to one another that they tend to cancel out.[3]

FUNDAMENTAL ISSUES FOR GOVERNMENT

The fundamental issues for the state and federal government revolve around long-term government goals, the role of higher education in meeting those goals, and the methods by which those goals are to be achieved. The goals of an educated citizenry, the creation and testing of new knowledge, and the dissemination of new knowledge should be fundamental in government's support of higher education. Within these goals, priority should be given to access to colleges and universities by citizens and to the maintenance of knowledge creation, testing, and dissemination. In seeking to support these objectives as priorities, governments must answer the following questions. What is the optimal level of participation in higher education to achieve an educated citizenry and the development of human resources to be sought as a matter of policy? What is the level and scope of research (knowledge creation) and public service (knowledge dissemination, economic development, and so forth) desired as a governmental policy objective. And, of course, who should pay what portion of the costs of these college and university missions and what incentives are to be established to assure the realization of the objectives?

The federal system of government and the division of powers between the federal and state governments complicate the resolution of this issue at the national level, especially in light of the fact that the responsibility for education is reserved to the states. Nevertheless, there are several specific aspects of the national interest directly related to higher education that can and should be strongly influenced, if not determined, by the federal government. This assumption has been at the heart of federal involvement in higher education since the Morrill Act.

In assessing the larger picture of financing higher education as it affects the national interest, it is necessary to examine the changing policy assumptions on which actions responding to these issues are based, the financial needs of colleges and universities, and the share of cost borne and to be borne by the student and his family, government, and philanthropy.

ASSUMPTIONS UNDERLYING POLICY AND PRACTICE

As mentioned above, beyond the policy determined by the federal government for its role in the financing of higher education, there are fifty states, each with separate authority to establish policy and to determine proportionate responsibilities of the citizens and their government for financing colleges and universities. Within the states as well as in the federal government, it is difficult to obtain much more than pragmatic, short-term financing for specific programs rationalized by diverse policy assumptions and objections. Long-term policies with coherent philosophical foundations are difficult if not impossible to secure in statutory mandates. The philosophy and social objectives are usually restricted to rhetorical form and like any governmental policy that must derive political support from diverse constituencies with varying objectives and interests, some of them contradictory, public policy regarding the financing of higher education represents a number of compromises that are often reconsidered as financial, social, and political conditions change. These are the realities within which the higher education community must work in promoting its activities for the long and short run.

The actions and programs developed by states and the federal government for higher education are founded upon certain assumptions that merit and receive reassessment upon renewal of funding whether in the reauthorization process for federal legislation or the states' annual or biennial appropriation process. Historically, at least for much of the past century, there have been several assumptions, remarkably consistently held, underlying public policy for financing college and university education, assumptions that are undergoing questioning and modifications as financial pressures on publicly funded services mount.

Assumption One: The Beneficiaries of Higher Education

A basic assumption about college and university education is that both society and individuals benefit by the acquisition of higher education and that the benefit, while unquantified and unquantifiable, is sufficient to justify investment of public funds by a variety of subsidies for the higher education industry, public and private. This view also encompasses the benefit of higher education as an economic enterprise with the attendant benefits of providing substantial employment, of consuming a considerable quantity of goods and services, of supplying the personnel needed by a complex society, and of creating knowledge that revitalizes segments of the economy. This assumption emphasizes financial subsidies and other approaches to finance that seek to minimize the direct monetary costs to the student and his family, who pay only a fraction of the real cost and repay to the society benefits that go beyond the subsidy. The latter approach assumes that such a subsidy and pricing system constitute an incentive that will encourage socially optimal levels of participation in an equitable fashion.

Assumption Two: The Public Nature of Private Colleges and Universities

Another assumption that influences the action of government in determining methods of financing higher education has to do with the role of private colleges and universities. In the early history of the United States, government, mostly colonial and state, provided modest assistance to private institutions, a practice that continued well into the nineteenth century. Such support was given on the assumption that the private institution served a public purpose and interest, an assumption that waned, then disappeared, as a basis for governmental policy and action in the late nineteenth century and for much of the twentieth.

Changing Assumptions and Views About Higher Education

The assumptions briefly described above are not as universally held today as they once were, having been eroded by a number of factors that in turn are influencing the finance of higher education. The increasing costs of all public enterprises and the consequent absolute increase in taxes have influenced a reconsideration of the benefit assumption to place a greater emphasis upon value to the individual. As a result, the low or no tuition principle is under seige on the grounds that the primary recipient and beneficiary of higher education (i.e., the student and his family) should bear a higher percentage of the costs. The societal benefit is not as heavily emphasized in these "new" assumptions despite the fact that in terms of economic value, the relative lifetime earnings of a college graduate as compared to a high school graduate have decreased over recent years and are continuing to decrease, and despite the findings presented in Howard Bowen's *Investment in Learning* (1977) and other similar but briefer works that stress the benefits of higher education to the society. In addition, more sophisticated economic analyses of costs and benefits of higher education have led to questions about whether the subsidies provided through a policy of low direct charges for higher education is an equitable approach for all segments of society. Likewise, there have been challenges to the assumption that low direct charges guarantee the greatest opportunity of access although empirical studies confirming the challenge are few.

In addition to these challenges to assumptions supporting the low tuition policy and practice, assumptions that have been held nearly sacred in the past, a change has occurred in the manner in which private universities and colleges are viewed. The newer view is that private institutions serve a public function equal to public institutions in providing, at a subsidized price level also, higher education to students who not only benefit themselves but who also benefit society as a result of the education acquired. This view argues persuasively that private institutions enhance the diversity of opportunity, invest funds of their own generation, contribute to the development of human capital as certainly as public institutions, and deserve the recognition as institutions serving a public function. The provision of public financial support to students who exercise the option of attending nonpublic institutions is a natural outgrowth of the growing support of the modified concept of the role of private colleges and universities.

There was also once a rather strong view that higher education is a nonmarket industry, and, as a consequence, the financial and economic practices and principles that are applied for evaluation purposes in market enterprises, such as return on investment and pricing in relation to cost, are inapplicable to colleges and universities as a test of the achievement of public policy. As other ways of thinking about higher education are changing, so is this one. We hear of full return on investment, full cost pricing to users, competitive pricing, competitive marketing for student recruitment, level of diminishing return, investment return on human capital, economy of scale, critical mass, and much of the language and concepts that apply to competitive market enterprises and industrial production. Their use often confuses the larger social purpose of higher education as derived from philosophical goals and in which economic principles are used merely in the evaluation of means used in carrying out the philosophy and purpose but not as a primary means of assessing the relative value of the function in economic terms.

FINANCIAL NEEDS OF COLLEGES AND UNIVERSITIES

The financial needs of colleges and universities have grown considerably over the past decade from a variety of causal factors. The increase in enrollment from approximately 9.2 million in 1972 to about 12.4 million in 1982 following an even greater increase in the previous decade, the growth in new knowledge, and the changing techniques and methods of producing that new knowledge have been fundamental in driving instructional budget needs higher, in both research and instructional activities. As importantly, there has been an inflation of prices of goods and services for major components of higher education purchases as measured by the Higher Education Price Index (HEPI) that averaged 7.5 percent annually during the same decade.[4] Equally important in this ever-upward cost progression has been the increased demand upon public colleges and universities, especially the latter, to provide more public service to a greater number and diversity of groups within the society—at subsidized prices. These trends have been accompanied by the distribution of students into instructional programs that on the average require specialized and more expensive faculty, facilities, and support services than previously. There have been increased support programs needed to serve formerly underrepresented groups such as minorities, working adults, women, and underprepared students from all groups in society; these are "social costs" for which there is little or no financial recovery. Programs of regulation by state and federal regulatory procedures and policies, designed to influence or assure results in keeping with governmental or political objectives, have also required greater investment of resources by colleges and universities, especially those in the public sector, to comply with the resulting bureaucratic practices. Accounting to the complex of constituents to whom public institutions must be responsible and accountable for various aspects of their operation has added still another cost component that is far from negligible.

Financial needs of colleges and universities in the future decades will be determined in the main by: (1) the increase or decrease in the costs of goods and services within the Higher Education Price index; (2) the number of students enrolled at various levels and the distribution of those students among different curricula and degree programs; (3) the degree to which efforts are made to catch up in areas such as faculty salaries, deferred maintenance, and equipment obsolescence that were underfunded in the recent past; (4) the expansion or shrinkage in mission responsibilities and their components, and changes in methods, techniques, and essential equipment required for more effective instruction, research, and service; (5) the support level by institutions for maintaining and improving quality; and (6) the amount of subsidy provided to public service functions.

Increase In Prices

There was an average annual price increase of 7.5 percent in the previous decade and the future trend is likely to continue to be inflationary, even if at a lower rate. The Council of Economic Advisors is projecting a 1984–1989 annual average Consumer Price Index (CPI) increase of 4.2 percent, a conservative projection when compared to the last fifteen years. If one considers that the CPI over the 1971–1980 decade was slightly less than the HEPI on average,[5] it seems reasonable to use 5 percent as the average annual price increase through the year 2000 to estimate revenue needs. Accepting that rate for discussion purposes and extrapolating it to the year 2000, a total increase of $64 billion will need to be added to public institutions just to maintain the current level of operation for *status quo* enrollment, mission, and quality—with no allowance for addressing those components of operation that have been underfunded in recent years, components that will need more than the average increase in the years ahead (see table 1).

Using a 5 percent annual increase just to meet the extrapolated increase in the cost for goods and services, public institutions will need an additional 44.5 percent in total revenue in 1990 over 1982 and 135 percent in the year 2000 over 1982. The combined total of dollars needed is almost $100 billion for public and private institutions. From where will these additional dollars come?

Table 1
Current Fund Revenue Needed
(with average annual increment of 5 percent)

	FY 1982	FY 1990	FY 2000
Public	$47,585,403	$68,736,694	$111,964,834
Private	24,259,978	35,843,037	58,384,530
TOTAL	$71,845,381	$104,579,731	$170,349,364

Enrollments and Their Implications

Enrollment as well as price changes will have a significant effect upon the financial needs of colleges and universities. Throughout much of its history, higher education in the United States has been a remarkable growth industry. For example, while the college age (18–24) population increased at an average rate of 1 percent during the eighty years preceding 1960, college enrollment increased at an annual rate of 4.4 percent during the same period. Enrollment as compared with the college age population growth during the 1960–1970 decade was even greater, with the population increasing at an annual rate of 4.2 percent while enrollments grew at a rate of more than 8 percent. The growth pattern, both in the traditional college-age pool and in the percentage of increase in enrollment, came to an abrupt halt in the 1970s. The growth rate of the college-age population declined from 4.2 percent to 1.8 and the enrollment rate decreased to 1.7 percent.

We are told that the decades of the 1980s and the 1990s portend more serious decreases in both the college-age population and college enrollment.[6] After growing from 16 million in the college age population in 1960, we have seen it increase to 30 million in 1980, and are told that it will drop to less than 24 million in the mid-1990s by which time the eighteen-year-old portion of the population will have declined 25 percent from 1980 levels (from 4.3 to 3.3 million). The projections for 1995 to 2000 are more encouraging in that the eighteen-year-old cohort is expected to approach 3.8 million and the eighteen to twenty-four age group will increase to about 25 million. Both are below the highest levels of the past. What effect will these fluctuating numbers of college-age people have on enrollment in colleges and universities during that period? Of equal importance, what effect will enrollment during the next sixteen years have upon the financial needs of colleges and universities and their sources of revenue?

There are different opinions about the effect that the declining college-age population will have upon actual enrollments in the years ahead. One view is that while the effect upon the major regions of the country and individual institutions within the regions will be markedly different (at least ten states will have steady increases), the overall effect will be that of enrollment decreases in most institutions for more years than there will be increases. According to this view, the net effect will be that most institutions will have fewer full-time students in the year 2000 than they have now. This opinion is based primarily on the premise that the source from which most full-time students are drawn is the very one that is shrinking (high school graduates) and that part-time enrollment from the older population will also decrease.

Another opinion suggests that the population from which college and university enrollments come is no longer dominantly the eighteen to twenty-four age group and that it will be less so as the median age of the general population of the United States increases. This view suggests that in the year 2000 the pool from which colleges and universities may draw enrollment will really be 190 million adults with about 165 million beyond age twenty-four. If the enrollment possibilities of these larger numbers materialize, they will do so because of a continuation of the trend of increasing participation of people beyond the age twenty-four and the success of institutions in providing opportunity for enrollment by appropriate educational and delivery conditions.

Factors Influencing Enrollment

The number of students who will enroll in institutions of higher learning through the remaining years of the twentieth century will be influenced by many factors that operate directly and indirectly on the higher education industry. For example, the degree to which efforts are made in the K–12 systems to reduce drop-outs, to effect qualitative improvement, and to generate aspirations for higher education will be fundamental in increasing the pool of high school graduates beyond the number now projected and will likewise influence the college enrollment rate. Consequently, it is of vital interest for the higher education mission that colleges and universities develop and implement effective cooperative relationships with K–12.

Similarly, actual and perceived differences in the level of employment and unemployment for high school and college graduates and the immediate and lifetime wage differences of college graduates as compared to high school graduates do and will have direct and indirect effects upon enrollment in higher education. When there is high unemployment for high school graduates and the perception exists that college graduates have a competitive advantage in securing employment, more high school graduates, recent and otherwise, will be influenced to enroll in higher education. On the other hand, the perception of high unemployment of college graduates generally influences a reluctance to enter higher education. If the public and student perceptions are positive or negative about employment opportunities in specific fields of study, the distribution of enrollment is affected. By providing a more accurate picture regularly, higher education needs to combat the negativeness often created by the media. Despite the recent decline in relative lifetime earnings of the college or university graduate when compared to the high school graduate, it is still higher. Also, college graduates have a definite comparative advantage in the job market. Data from the Bureau of Labor Statistics as reported by the American Council on Education (1984) indicate the following:

1. In 1983, 87 percent of college graduates were in the labor market compared to 75 percent of high school graduates.
2. High school graduates were more likely to be unemployed than college graduates in 1983 (10 percent vs. 3.5).
3. Between 1970 and 1983, the unemployment rate for college graduates increased by only 2.2 percent, from 1.3 to 3.5 percent.
4. High school graduates experienced a significantly greater increase in unemployment rates from 1970 to 1983, 7.1 percent from 2.9 percent to 10 percent.
5. Among workers with a college degree, 68 percent held positions in managerial and professional occupations (e.g., engineers, lawyers). In comparison, only 12 percent of high school graduates were employed in managerial and professional jobs.

In addition to the foregoing influences on enrollment in higher education, the familial and parental environment is important in the college-going rates. As the number and percentage of K–12 students and high school graduates increase from families of origins and backgrounds previously underrepresented in relation to those groups traditionally attending college, the retention of previous rates of participation of the college age pool becomes more difficult. This is especially so if those origins and backgrounds are accompanied by low or inadequate economic resources and/or cultural and linguistic barriers. In view of the fact that the college-age population will include a continuing increase in numbers and the relative proportion of young people from the underrepresented segments of our population, the problem of maintaining or increasing the past participation rates becomes obvious.

Enrollment Distribution: Influenced by Cost?

Although all of the factors briefly described above are influences upon the number and nature of college enrollments, perhaps none of them is as influential alone as each is when taken together with the system of financing for college and university education and the relative shares of cost borne by the student and his or her family, the taxpayer, and other sources. While there are conflicting views about the elasticity or inelasticity of demand in relation to price and cost to the student, there is reason to believe that at some level of price and cost, enrollment is influenced. This direct level of immediate cost to the student and his or her family is a matter of the highest importance for public policy to decide, in each state, and at the federal level. Such policy is likely to influence the number and distribution of enrollments in the years ahead.

Since 1950, for example, enrollment in public colleges and universities has more and more increased over private ones. The division of enrollment in 1950 was about 50/50. By 1981–1982, it had reached 78 percent public and only 22 percent private. It is projected to reach 80 percent public by 1990 (which is now the case in 41 states) and will probably increase slightly above that proportion by 2000.

Another change that is of concern is the trend of enrollment away from four-year institutions and to the two-year colleges. As recently as 1970, nearly 75 percent of all students enrolled were in four-year institutions. In 1981–1982, it had dropped to about 62 percent and is projected to be at 58.7 percent in 1990. With the continuance of recent cost trends, it is likely to be down to half in 2000.

These two trends in enrollment shift to public and two-year institutions are also related to the increase in part-time and independent students that include high percentages of women and students over twenty-four. It also likely reflects the increasing role of tuition and other costs in the private institutions in comparison with public ones, and perhaps more importantly, the increasing costs of public four-year institutions as compared to public two-year colleges. It is highly likely that the pricing system has become much more influential in channeling enrollment than it has been in the recent past. The data seem to suggest this effect although there are few studies that provide reliable conclusions about the effect of the level of tuition on the choice of a private versus a public institution or of a four-year versus a two-year institution.

The distribution of enrollments among the several types of institutions seems to indicate that cost has become or is becoming a significant factor. The overall costs of a college education may be influencing an increasing number of students from upper income families to attend public institutions and larger numbers of students from low- and middle-income families to attend lower cost two-year institutions or simply not go to college. With government assistance shifting to the lowest income students and the relatively higher costs to students from middle-income families, *choice* for the latter is becoming less and less.

Changes in Enrollment, 1972–1982

A review of the changes in enrollment during the 1972–1982 decade suggests trends that are likely to be continued if present policies and practices continue. During the decade between fall 1972 and fall 1982, the changes in enrollment in the more than three thousand institutions of higher education were significant in changing the landscape from that of the past. Overall, there was a 34.8 percent increase in enrollment during that period but the various groups that increased more than the average were as follows:[7]

60.8 percent increase in women

85.3 percent increase in blacks and other nonwhites

77.4 percent increase in the above 35 age group

69.8 percent increase in the 25–34 age group

65.9 percent increase in part-time students

These figures represent the changing composition of enrollment that in turn affects other aspects of higher education. Additional data about the enrollment only confirms the change. In the decade, fall 1982 increases over fall 1972 included the following:[8]

22.7 percent increase in age 18–24

18.9 percent increase in full-time

34.1 percent increase in public institutions enrollment

27.3 percent increase in private institutions enrollment

10.9 percent increase in universities

24.3 percent increase in other four-year institutions

73.1 percent increase in two-year institutions

While these data are encouraging in terms of the percentages of the overall increases of college attendance by certain segments of the population, other data comparing 1981 with 1969 diminish any assessment of great success with participation rates. For example, the percentage of high school graduates attending college in 1981 (33 percent) was less than in

Table 2
Projected Enrollments in Full-time Equivalent (FTE) Students
(in thousands)

	1982 (Actual)	1990 (Projected)	2000 (Projected)
Public			
NCES	6,713	6,349	
Carnegie Commission		6,855	7,910
Leslie and Miller			7,807
Constant Participation Rate of High School Graduates		6,133	5,087
Private			
NCES	2,193	2,079	
Carnegie Commission		2,244	2,590
Leslie and Miller			2,556
Constant Participation Rate of High School Graduates		2,008	1,666

1969 (35 percent). More significantly, the participation rates for low-, middle-, and high-income groups remained about the same in 1981 as in 1969. And while college-going rates for women increased by 5 percent, it declined for men by 11 percent. College attendance by dependent students also declined by 6 percent while independent student participation increased 3 percent. The rates for blacks increased only one percent while college going for whites decreased by 2 percent.[9] These data sober any great enthusiasm for the effectiveness of current and recent policy to increase access for all citizens.

Projected Enrollment

The figures above reflect a changing pattern when compared to the years before the seventies. The uncertainties of the conditions applicable to each of the enrollment influencing factors briefly described above lead one to be influenced by his or her own assumptions about them in "projected" enrollments or in suggesting enrollment "possibilities." Depending upon the assumptions about the conditions discussed, the projected number of enrollments may be dramatically lower than the present, show a modest growth over current numbers, or suggest an even greater growth. These differences are reflected, from different sources, in table 2.

Financial Impact of Enrollment Changes

Whatever the numbers are, what impact will the different numbers have upon the finances of higher education? Suppose the enrollments turn out to be the lowest suggested above, will the resource needs of colleges and universities decrease significantly below their current level or below the inflated price level extrapolated above? The National Center for Education Statistics thinks so, as expressed by its projections. The distribution of the decreases among institutions and programs within institutions will likely influence the answer. Even if the decrease is continuous and concentrated in specific institutions or programs within institutions, the likely result will be a modest restraint on the increased revenues needed for inflation and other purposes as contrasted with a decrease in the base level. The nature of curricula is such that decreases scattered among several programs does not permit much, if any, cost saving. Only the planned, gradual elimination of programs and personnel where continuous decline is expected will accomplish that, and in the doing, may stimulate even additional decreases in enrollment in related programs.

The reality of college and university operations, of course, is that resource needs are influenced by the nature and diversity of programs and the aggregates of students to be served by them. The exact number of the aggregate often has little to do with realizable economies. Reduction in the aggregate does little if anything to lessen the fixed costs or need for increases to maintain purchasing power. Despite the fact that support formulas for the past twenty-five years have been developed on a per full-time equivalent student basis, costs are not generated in that simplistic a fashion, nor can cost reductions be achieved on that basis.

It is certain, however, that a reduction in enrollments in a given institution accompanied by increased funds to meet price increases will produce a per student cost that will be higher than may be politically tolerable within the context of past and present formula funding. The costs per full-time equivalent student according to the various projections, assuming a 5 percent increase in revenues and expenditures, appear in table 3.

According to the lower enrollment estimates and a 5 percent cost increase, the average cost per full-time equivalent student will increase from slightly less than $7,000 in the public sector to $11,209 by 1990 and to $22,009 in 2000 while average costs per FTE in the private sector will increase from slightly more than $11,000 to $17,850 in 1990 and $35,045 in 2000. These numbers are shocking to us at this time although they may not be quite so startling in 1990 and 2000 if per capita income increases at the same rate of costs per student (5 percent annually). One

Table 3
Projected Revenues and Expenditures per FTE Student, 1982, 1990, 2000
(according to enrollment projections and costs)

	1982	1990	2000
Public Institutions			
Revenues Per FTEs			
NCES	$ 7,089	$11,073	n/a
Carnegie Commission		10,256	$14,478
Leslie and Miller			14,669
Constant Participation Rate		11,464	22,511
Expenditures Per FTEs			
NCES	6,930	10,826	n/a
Carnegie Commission		10,027	14,155
Leslie and Miller			14,342
Constant Participation Rates		11,209	22,009
Private Institutions			
Revenues Per FTEs			
NCES	11,404	17,813	n/a
Carnegie Commission		16,503	22,291
Leslie and Miller			23,601
Constant Participation Rates		18,443	36,209
Expenditures Per FTEs			
NCES	11,037	17,241	n/a
Carnegie Commission		15,973	22,542
Leslie and Miller			22,842
Constant Participation Rates		17,850	35,045

Note: See Appendices E and F for revenues and expenditures on which the calculation is made.

can readily see the impact of such numbers, however, both on tuition and student financial aid under our present system. Such projected increases in the "per student" analysis argues persuasively that institutions and state governments should begin to work toward alternative methods of funding by which funds "freed" by enrollment decline can be used for needs other than direct instruction, as outlined below.

Meeting Previously Underfunded Needs

Beyond the need to maintain purchasing power in relation to inflation and to respond to enrollment patterns, colleges and universities will be facing critical needs for the remainder of the century that have been previously underfunded. First and foremost among these needs are faculty salary improvements. The recent decade's trend of reduction in the purchasing power of faculty salaries must be reversed if the nation prevents significant "brain drain" from higher education. The data in table 4 indicate that, on the average, faculty at all ranks lost economic ground in the 1972–1982 decade.

In addition to the need for increased funds for faculty salaries, there will be serious requirements for more funds for physical plant, not only to redress deferred maintenance that has consistently become more commonplace and severe but also to respond to increasing maintenance costs for buildings that have been put into service in the last two decades. One must recall that the latter have been constructed by the lowest bidder, and have more complicated engineering, electrical, and other support systems than buildings constructed earlier—support systems that will need replacing in the eighties and nineties.

A third component of cost that will demand more than inflationary increases is instructional and research equipment. Much of the equipment that colleges and universities have at the present is equipment that was purchased as part of new capital projects funded by the state government and/or as part of a federal research contract or grant. A recent survey of university research instrumentation in computer and physical sciences and engineering by the National Science Foundation indicated that one-fourth of the 1982 research equipment inventory with an aggregate purchase price of $904 million is obsolete, that only 16 percent of all academic research equipment inventories is state-of-the-art and 31 percent of all instrument systems in use in 1982 is more than ten years old. Funding for regular replacement of high-cost laboratory and support equipment simply is not available to most colleges and universities within current budget restraints of the state and federal governments. Continuing investments in computers, computer support, and telecommunications will be a critical need in the foreseeable future. Libraries, too, are falling behind and must be assisted in developing more effective cooperative purchasing and utilization to coordinate differentiated strengths. Similarly, there is need to meet the extraordinarily high inflation in the cost of periodicals, books, newer microfilm, microforms, video-cassettes, microfiche, and other learning and research materials.

Table 4
Annual Percentage Change in Average Salaries of
Instructional Faculty, 1971–1972 to 1981–1982

	All Ranks Current Dollars	All Ranks Constant Dollars
1971–1972 to 1972–1973	+4.2	+0.1
1972–1973 to 1973–1974	+5.1	−3.6
1973–1974 to 1974–1975	+5.8	−4.8
1974–1975 to 1975–1976	+6.0	−1.0
1976–1977 to 1977–1978	+5.3	−1.3
1977–1978 to 1978–1979	+6.0	−3.1
1978–1979 to 1979–1980	+7.1	−5.5
1979–1980 to 1980–1981	+8.7	−2.6
1980–1981 to 1981–1982	+9.0	+0.3
1971–1972 to 1981–1982	−2.2	
1971–1972 to 1976–1977	−2.1	
1976–1977 to 1981–1982	−2.4	

Source: National Center for Education Statistics, *The Condition of Education*, 1983 Edition, A Statistical Report. Washington: Government Printing Office, 1983, p. 100.

When one considers the needs created by inflation, faculty salary improvement, maintenance of library and plant, and equipment replacement that will face all universities and most colleges in the next two decades, it is clear that more than a 5 percent increase in revenue is needed in several parts of the budget and as a result the overall increase needed will exceed 5 percent.

Modification of Mission and Program

Central to the financial needs of a college or university is its mission and the degree to which the mission is advanced through programs and activities. Recent years of financial pressures have influenced institutions and those political authorities that govern them to revise the number and breadth of programs designed to implement mission or, in rare cases, to reduce the scope of mission of an institution as a means of reducing the demand for increased funding. In some instances of program termination or mission contraction, there have been modest reallocations of resources to underfunded programs. Unfortunately, there have been few studies to trace the impact of such contractions and terminations on continued budget needs. There is little doubt that this method of responding to financial needs will be considered and used over the next decade and after as an alternative to increased revenues. Given the difficulties of immediate reduction in personnel, the effects of program termination and mission contraction as means of reducing financial demands in the short term have not been significant in achieving that goal.

Assuming that there will be greater success in the future in reducing the factors that drive the fund needs of colleges and universities, there will certainly need to be new program initiatives that are likely to need new funding or the reallocation of old funds to them. With exponential increases in knowledge, rapid development in the applications of new knowledge, and new social and economic needs to which higher education must respond, funding for new initiatives will be necessary. Resources needed will likely have to be provided in part, if not all, from selected contractions or terminations of current programs or missions.

A fact often overlooked is that institutions do close because of financial difficulty. Although, as table 5 shows, most of those that closed in the twenty years between 1961–1981 were private (204 out of the 240), public ones do close, merge, or go through retrenchment, mission change, "down-sizing," contraction, and other changes. Because of financial problems for which gradual response has been inadequate, impossible, or nonexistent, these changes are usually painfully wrenching to the institution and its personnel. If the financial trends that began in the seventies are continued to the year 2000, they will likely produce more closings generally and will perhaps include more public four-year institutions. They will certainly produce other changes in public and private institutions.

Beyond the important question of institutional survival, there is an important question whether the general role of higher education will include adaptations to the technological changes in American life and work and the development of a global economy. Both will require significant change in serving larger numbers of nondegree students at home and in internationalizing major centers of higher education. We should begin now in examining the cost/benefit questions of transnational education and its financing. Such a new mission and method of delivery will require significantly different financing and delivery.

The Support Level for Maintaining and Improving Quality

There is little agreement within the higher education community about the level of direct and indirect support required for instruction, research,

Table 5

Number of Closings of Institutions of Higher Education, by Level and
Control of Institution, Academic Year 1960–1961 to 1980–1981

Academic Year	All Institutions			Public Institutions			Private Institutions		
	Ttl.	4-Year	2-Year	Ttl.	4-Year	2-Year	Ttl.	4-Year	2-Year
1960–61 to 1964–65	25	4	21	6	0	6	19	4	15
1965–66 to 1969–70	70	29	41	11	0	11	59	29	30
1970–71 to 1974–75	98	48	50	17	0	17	81	48	33
1975–76 to 1979–80	43	29	14	2	1	1	41	28	13
1980–81	4	3	1	0	0	0	4	3	1
1960–61 to 1980–81	240	113	127	36	1	35	204	112	92

Source: U.S. Department of Education, National Center for Education Statistics, Digest of Education Statistics, 1982, 1962.
Note: Numbers exclude branch campuses of institutions.

and public service to be delivered at the appropriate level of quality. Neither is there agreement about the relationship of funds provided to the results achieved in specific institutions nor throughout higher education generally. Because of this uncertainty, intensified by observing many institutions that seem to continue as usual despite budget reductions, funding authorities have reconciled themselves to the view that colleges and universities can make fiscal adjustments to their operations without affecting quality in any significant way. College and university faculty and administrators on the other hand argue that the level of investment in direct and indirect inputs must be maintained at that of past levels at least in order to protect quality. Since higher education depends strongly on high labor intensity, specialized facilities, and extensive support services to professional personnel as crucial to quality, the level of funding provided in the years ahead for these input elements will influence greatly the financial needs of colleges and universities. Few can foresee a change within higher education by which new or different aspects of operation will be accepted as means to assess quality. Although the historic direct "cost per student" approach to assessing funding levels and needs requires reexamination as a quality indicator, it will likely continue to be a driving force for increased funds.

Subsidy To Public Service

One of the important elements of operations of institutions of higher learning is public service through dissemination of knowledge; public access to and use of facilities, specialized equipment, and other resources; and service as a neutral broker for public affairs activities. Many of the programs and activities within this mission were subsidized to reduce cost to the users and participants on the assumption that such subsidy makes participation of citizens and groups more equitable and in turn, enhances the chances of success. The subsidy is often drawn from overall institutional funding. As more and more public service functions are demanded by more and more nonuniversity groups and mandated by governing authorities without significant increases in funding for the function, institutions have had to reduce activities and/or to increase cost to users. Increased resource needs will be determined by the degree to which government mandates this function of service and by the degree to which institutions continue to perform them effectively.

SHARES OF COST IN FINANCING
HIGHER EDUCATION

From where will the additional funds for the needs described above come? The main sources that share in the funding of higher education are: (1) government (federal, state, and local); (2) the student and his or her family; and (3) philanthropy, including endowments and gifts. Although funding from institutional operations of colleges and universities themselves is increasing, that source is still minor.

The share of cost expected to be borne by the three major sources and the share of cost to be provided among the levels of government within government's portion is rarely the basis of appropriations or tuition levels established. Rather, it is the result of accommodating the different assumptions briefly cited above, the particular immediate economic conditions, and the national and state priorities at the time of action. The relative share of cost for each major source has changed in its portion of the total over the past fifty years, and especially over the recent thirty years, as reflected in table 6. What the shift shows, however, is a

Table 6
Percentage of Expenditures by Source of Revenue, 1929–1930 to 1979–1980

	1929–1930	1939–1940	1949–1950	1959–1960	1969–1970
Monetary Cost[a]					
Student and Family	64.6	63.7	21.3	47.9	38.8
Taxpayer	22.4	23.4	70.3	40.1	52.2
Philanthropy	13.0	12.9	8.4	12.0	9.0
Economic Cost[b]					
Student and Family	69.6	69.9	52.6	73.2	65.8
Taxpayer	19.2	19.4	42.3	20.0	29.2
Philanthropy	11.2	10.7	5.1	6.8	5.0
Educational Monetary Cost[c]					
Student and Family	35.1	38.1	25.2	31.3	29.9
Taxpayer	41.8	40.7	61.1	52.8	59.7
Philanthropy	23.1	21.2	13.7	15.9	10.4

[a] "Monetary Cost" is used to identify the percentage of total dollars spent by students (including room and board, books, tuition, etc.), taxpayers, and gifts in total dollars spent by the institutions.
[b] "Economic Cost" adds to monetary costs the "foregone" income by the student during college.
[c] "Educational Monetary Cost" is the percentage of educational costs paid by the student (in tuition and other educational fees), taxpayers, and gift funds.

decline in the percentage shared by the student and his or her family and an increase in taxpayer support in all groupings of cost. It also shows a decline of some significance in the percentage provided by philanthropy.

An examination of the data in table 7 reveals a few interesting shifts in "shares" of revenue that have occurred. Most notable is the statistic surrounding comparative percentages of revenue received by public and private institutions from government.

Institutions show a considerable decrease in the percentage of revenues received from the federal government over the eleven years, nearly 5 percent less for the private four-year and more than 7 percent less for the public four-year institution. The public colleges and universities (four-year and two-year) show an increasing reliance on state funds with the four-year institutions showing a 2.6 percent increase and the public two-year institutions experiencing a nearly 9 percent increase from state sources. The latter increase in state funds for public two-year colleges was offset by a more than 13 percent decrease from local governments, a change that may indicate a trend worth watching closely, a trend that may

Table 7
Percentage of Current Fund Revenue from Each Government Level,
1970–1971 and 1981–1982

	1970–1971			1981–1982		
	Federal	State	Local	Federal	State	Local
Private						
4-year	22.4	1.7	.8	17.3	1.8	.7
2-year	5.5	1.1	.3	4.3	1.9	.5
Public						
4-year	19.7	41.7	1.1	12.6	44.3	.7
2-year	6.8	40.8	30.9	5.7	49.7	17.3

Note: See Appendix G.

signify that community colleges are more and more becoming state-funded and state-controlled.

Tuition Trends of the Recent Past: The Student's Share [10]

The trends of the past decade contain troublesome signs for the financing of higher education for the remaining years of this century, although there were also some signs of strength with which the trends may be combatted. The trends during the past dozen years reflect the following:

1. Very few public institutions remain tuition-free any longer, especially with community colleges in California joining the tuition-charging group.

2. Tuition increases in recent years, on the average, were greatest for institutions in the low tuition category.

3. Tuition for public research universities, including fifty-one major institutions, ranged from $233 to $1,200 in 1972–1973, but had increased to a range of $453 to $2,216 by 1979–1980, reflecting nearly a doubling of tuition.

4. Tuition in fifty-one major private research universities ranged from $2,245 to $3,099 in 1972–1973 but increased to $3,301 to $5,745 seven years later, an increase of nearly 50 percent at the lowest but nearly 90 percent at the highest.

5. The rate of tuition increase in private institutions was more than those in public institutions but was not disproportionate to the price movement in other areas of the economy.

6. The "gap" between the amount of tuition charged by private versus public institutions continued to widen during the seventies and into the eighties.

7. Between 1970–1971 and 1981–1982 tuition as a share of current funds revenues declined slightly for public four-year institutions, and increased 3 percent for public two-year institutions, but increased by 1.5 percent for private four-year institutions and 15 percent for private two-year colleges.

8. Extrapolating tuition increases for public universities by an average annual rate of 5 percent produces an average tuition of nearly $2,700 for public universities, $2,100 for other public four-year colleges, and nearly $1,100 for public two-year institutions in 2000.

9. Extrapolating tuition increases for private universities by an annual rate of 5 percent of the 1982–1983 average produces an *average* tuition of nearly $13,000 for universities, $10,000 for other four-year colleges, and $7,000 for two-year institutions.

The reporting of increased revenues from tuition by public institutions during the past decade, especially the last half of it, obscures the amount of that increase that was generated by out-of-state tuition as compared to in-state tuition. Many institutions have begun to base their nonresident tuition on 50 to 100 percent of the direct instructional cost to the institution. In some cases, this approach increases the nonresident costs in a public university to the level on or above that of some of the private ones. The departure from low tuition to a sustained level of share of cost is clearly reflected in the most recent two years of experience by state universities and land-grant colleges,[11] perhaps as a pragmatic response to urgently increasing financial needs for which there was no other solution. An increase of 14.3 percent in the average undergraduate resident tuition in 1982–1983 was followed by another increase of 10.3 percent in 1983–1984, pushing the average tuition to $1,237 for the group of 146 surveyed by the National Association of State Universities and Land-Grant Colleges in 1983–1984. Only 29 of the state universities and land-grant colleges responding to the 1979–1980 annual survey had resident tuition above $1,000. In 1983–1984, only four years later, more than half charged $1,000 or above while 29 had tuition above $1,500. The nonresident tuition increased 16.9 percent in 1983–1984 over 1979–1980, driving the average to $2,968. Sixty-eight of this group of public institutions have tuition levels above $3,000 for nonresidents.

While tuition has increased in both the public and private sectors, the increase has been relatively less in the public institutions. As mentioned earlier, the share of revenue provided by the student and his or her parents was slightly less in public four-year colleges and universities in 1981–1982 than in 1970–1971, but higher in two-year colleges. In both cases, however, the cost to the student in constant dollars is less or approximately the same. The increase rate in disposable personal income has also been greater than tuition increases in the public sector. Between 1972–1980, personal disposable income per capita rose by 111 percent, wages of production and manufacturing workers increased by 82 percent, the CPI increased by nearly 70 percent, but average tuition increased in the publics by approximately 50 percent and in the privates by about 72 percent.

Student Charges: Tuition, Room, and Board [12]

Tuition is only a part of the total monetary expenses of students to attend college. The major components of expense, however, are tuition, fees, board, and room costs, commonly combined as "student charges" in the language of college finance. Tuition often contributes the smaller part of student charges but as tuition increases this becomes less and less the case. During the ten years of 1973–1974 to 1982–1983, total tuition, room, and board charges increased in the public sector from an average of $1,517 (all types of institutions) to $2,944, nearly doubling, and in the private sector from $3,164 to $6,920 or more than double, while price increases for the school year increased 110.5 percent during the same period. The total student charges at private institutions increased on the average slightly more than the price index while at public ones they grew slightly less than the CPI.

Eighty-one of the state universities and land-grant colleges studied in 1983–1984 had total student charges exceeding $3,000; for nonresidents only three were below $3,000 with sixty-eight above $5,000, of which nine had charges above $7,000. The high costs for nonresidents, many of whom are important to the enrichment of undergraduate as well as graduate instruction, not to mention their value to research, are gradually being priced out of the public universities unless both institutional and federal assistance is provided.

The rates of student charges (tuition, room, and board) to median family income remained almost constant at private universities but decreased slightly at all other types of institutions, even the private two-year college. (See table 8.)

Table 8
Average Student Charges as Percent of Median Income for All Families

	1970	1972	1974	1976	1978
Universities					
Public	15.0	15.0	13.6	13.8	13.0
Private	32.1	31.6	31.5	32.5	31.8
Other Four-year Institutions					
Public	12.2	13.1	12.0	12.1	11.5
Private	26.3	26.4	24.4	23.9	23.4
Two-year Institutions					
Public	10.3	10.8	10.3	10.0	9.6
Private	21.3	20.4	20.0	19.5	19.0

Student Financial Assistance: A Government or Institutional Share

One promise of the higher tuition advocates is that financial assistance to those who cannot afford to pay the increased levels will substitute for low tuition and at the same time the increase in tuition will raise more funds for the institution. Student financial assistance by federal and state governments and institutions, however, has probably not been sufficient to offset the negative effects the increases in tuition and student charges have created in the past five years. Recently, the federal government has shifted much of the needed increases to the states, and, as federal aid stabilizes with tuition increasing (recently) at rates even above inflation at private and public institutions, funding low- and middle-income students will be one of the most important issues in financing higher education. The centerpiece of the federal program, the Pell Grants (formerly Basic Educational Opportunity Grants) was funded at $2,441,328 in fiscal year 1980. The budget proposed by the president to Congress for 1985 included $2,800,000 for Pell Grants. When adjusted for inflation, that amount represents a decline in purchasing power of nearly one-third. The inflationary effect has been recognized by periodically increasing the maximums of the Pell Grants. That approach, however, simply reduces the numbers of students that can possibly be served by the limited budget, regardless of how many students there are with need. More students can be served only by reducing the amount of the grant to each and requiring self-help (work-study, loans, or work) as a substitute. Recognizing the limitations of level funding of Pell Grants, Congress appropriated $3,575,000 for this program in 1985; much of the increase was simply to fund the shortfall in funds of the previous two years.

The present limits of the Pell Grant restrict the award to a maximum of $1,900 or 50 percent of the instutitions' student charges, whichever is less. The practical effect the 50 percent limit may have on some low tuition institutions is to influence an increase in tuition in the hope that the Pell Grant will cover at least half of it. The current bill for reauthorization of the Higher Education Act includes a provision to raise the maximum to $3,000 or 75 percent of student charges, whichever is less. The proposal was opposed by private institutions on the grounds that it would divert students from private to public institutions, a speculation that needs more evidence. The 50 percent limit should be abolished or increased with need assessment prevailing. The bill for reauthorization also proposes *entitlement* for all students who qualify according to need as contrasted to the current ceiling in numbers of dollars, which restricts the number of students with need that can be helped. In the long run, entitlement should be a goal for the higher education community, but the current environment of huge deficits and debt service at the federal level leads one to question whether it is pragmatically possible to achieve it now, and whether, in fact, concerted effort to achieve entitlement now may produce negative reactions on other fronts.

It may be wiser at this point for public institutions to work to increase total dollars and increased maximum grants by the Pell program for the short term, with entitlement a long-term objective. Such a delay may also give time to consider more thoroughly the relative positions of private and public institutions in relation to public funding at the state and national level and other issues surrounding subsidies for attending higher education. While the key words for financial assistance are "access" and "choice" for students, choice should not be necessarily valued as highly as access. If a policy that provides a wide choice through the use of public funds limits access by low income students and others, the priority in funding should be given to access. The high expenditure per student by private institutions has been developed outside of public accountability review as have the tuition levels on which student assistance is based. When the four-to-one tuition ratio means that state and federal funds purchase substantially fewer places for low income students in private institutions than in publics, the policy and practice needs reconsideration. Access rather than choice should be dominant in governmental financial aid policy and tuition subsidies.

A recent study of student financial aid to students in public institutions in 1981–1982 indicated that roughly 3 million out of 9.7 million students in public institutions, or 31 percent, received assistance in meeting college attendance costs. Of that 3 million, however, less than one third, or about 800,000, received only nonneed-based aid. The remaining 2.2 million students, or 23 percent of all students enrolled, received combinations of need- and nonneed-based aid but qualified for need-based aid under at least one federal, state, or institutional program. More than half of all the aid recipients qualified for aid on the basis of income below $9,290, and one out of ten family-dependent aid recipients were from families earning less than the 1981 median family income of $25,407. The study reported that low-income recipients seemed reluctant to assume loans but as student income rose, loans became more frequent and larger, and they are currently increasing rapidly. Low-income students also tended to attend low-cost institutions. When the need-based recipients and the nonneed recipients are considered in relation to two types of institutions, two-year institutions (which have the lowest tuitions) and public research universities (which average the highest tuitions among the public institutional types), the former have the lowest percentage of enrollment receiving aid of any type while in the latter, roughly one half of all aid recipients receive nonneed-based aid. The breakdown by institutional type is shown in table 9. The data also indicated that *dependent* need-based aid recipients constituted the percent of recipients in the different types of institutions in the order shown in table 10. This reflects older and independent students enrolled in two-year colleges and younger, traditional full-time undergraduate enrollments in liberal arts colleges. The study also found that minority students accounted for about one third of the need-based recipients and that within the public sector they were concentrated in two-year colleges and comprehensive colleges and universities. A greater number of the minority students than the nonminority students were also likely to be independent. Slightly more than half of need-based recipients (55 percent) were women, many of whom were also independent and attending less than full-time.

Federal student assistance, at its present level of approximately $7.5 billion will need to be increased to more than $9 billion in 1989–1990 and to $12 billion in 2000, if an inflation increment of 4 percent annually is added. If the increment is 4 percent, it is likely to be at least 1 percent below the average inflation rate of the period. If one extrapolates by the same increment the estimated 1 billion in current dollars provided by the states, the programs will increase to nearly $2 billion. Institutional assistance, which provides approximately a quarter of the total student aid from all sources, will probably reach the $4 billion mark in the year 2000 if it keeps up with inflation. The total minimum cost under current sys-

Table 9
Student Aid Recipients as a Percentage of Total
Enrollment by Type of Public Institution, 1981–1982

	Need-based Aid %	Nonneed-based %
All Institutions	23	8
Special	10	14
Universities	23	50
Comprehensive Colleges	29	11
Liberal Arts	43	6
Two-Year	15	4

Source: Jacob O. Stampen, *Student Aid and Public Higher Education:
A Progress Report* (Washington: American Association of State Colleges and Universities, 1983), pp. 27, 28, 47, 68–71.

Table 10
Dependent Need-based Recipients as a
Percentage of Total Need-based Aid Recipients
by Type of Institution

Type of Institution	Percentage
Liberal Arts	93
Comprehensive	71
Universities	68
Special	58
Two-Year	52
All Public	63

tems will approximate $18 to $20 billion. It is likely that waiver of or reduction in tuition to needy students would cost less.

Our current system includes low, moderate, and high tuition accompanied by financial assistance to students according to need as established by the income level of the parents or student and the charges of the institution. This approach needs careful reexamination and restructuring to accomplish greater access for all students. Information about expenditures per full-time student equivalent, a factor that drives both tuition and student aid, reveals interesting differentials between public and private institutions and between different types of institutions.[13] Some of the findings are:

1. In constant dollars, the per FTE student expenditures between 1971 and 1982 remained nearly constant with a slight decrease in public institutions;

2. On the average, in 1980–1981 private *universities* spent more than 50 percent more per FTE for Education and General Expenditures than did public *universities*; the rates hold for expenditures for instruction although private institutions spent a lower percentage of their total expenditures on instruction than did the public institutions;

3. Private *universities* on the average spent more than 50 percent more per FTE for research than did public *universities* in 1980–1981;

4. In four-year public and private *colleges*, public institutions spent nearly 50 percent more than privates per FTE for research and about 20 percent more for instruction in 1980–1981;

5. In operation and maintenance of plant, institutional support, and student services, private institutions of *all types* (universities, four-year and two-year) spent more per FTE than the analogous public institutions;

6. Per student costs in private institutions and the absence of substantial public institutional support are driving forces that set tuition about four times, on average, the tuition in public institutions.

The issues now being created by increasing tuition costs beyond the levels and policy of financial aid are tracking students by economic and social groupings more seriously than low tuition ever did. It is also creating divisive tensions between public and private institutions, two-year and four-year colleges and universities, and four-year and comprehensive graduate and research institutions. Moreover, the amalgam of increasing tuition and financial aid is not improving access, is driving students to more narrowly occupational curricula, and is producing college graduates with significant debts.

SCENARIOS OF REVENUE AND EXPENDITURE

In Appendix E, there are three extrapolations that are based on different assumptions about revenues and needed expenditures. "Scenario One" shows a straight 5 percent increment annually from 1980 to 2000 in both revenues and expenditures, and assumes that highs and lows in particular components of cost will even each other out (a fanciful thought, of course). Scenario One increases tuition, federal, state, and local appropriations, grants, endowment earnings, and all other categories of revenue by 5 percent. It also projects the same increase in each functional component, overlooking the need for investment above the inflation level. By applying such increments, tuition will average nearly $2,500 in public universities by the year 2000 and about $12,000 in private universities. The per student cost will average $15–22,000 for public institutions and $22–35,000 in private ones, depending upon enrollment. Both public and private institutions will have a minor positive balance of revenue over expenditures in 1990 and 2000.

"Scenario Two," in Appendix F, extrapolates variable estimates of revenue and expenditures based on different assumptions that will be readily discernible upon study. The assumption for tuition for both public and private institutions, however, is 5 percent annually. In Scenario Two there are sufficient revenues to take care of expenditures for public institutions but, in addition to the annual 5 percent tuition increase, it assumes a 6 percent annual increase in federal and state appropriations and a level of expenditures for most program areas that is likely to be below the estimated inflation increase except in research, libraries, student services, plant maintenance, scholarships, and hospitals. Private institutions, however, show a deficit with revenue increases similar to the publics except in federal appropriations and restricted contracts, which show a 5 percent increase annually. By this scenario, tuition costs will be about the same for public and private institutions as in Scenario One; FTE student costs will range from $16–25,000 in the public sector and $25–40,000 in the private sector. Total revenues of the public sector will total $130 billion in the year 2000 with $58.6 billion for the private institutions, a total of more than $188 billion for both.

INTERPRETATION OF RECENT TRENDS

What does all of the above say about financing higher education in the United States? I believe it says the following:

1. The low or no tuition philosophy that has been held so strongly in the public sector is giving way to one of expecting an increased share of the costs of higher education for those who can afford to pay accompanied by programs of student assistance for those who cannot afford to pay their share;

2. The federal government is striving to stabilize in current dollars the level of funding to higher education and by emphasizing student assistance to low-income students, neglecting other critical support needs that are in the national interest;

3. There are needs for the remainder of the century to maintain current levels of effort, to improve faculty salaries, to address deferred maintenance and additional capital needs, to replace and add equipment, to maintain libraries and other learning resources, to maintain public service, and to develop gradually greater differentiation of mission among institutions to reduce overall budget demands;

4. Access to higher education has not improved through the past fifteen years under policies in effect and has actually decreased for traditional participating groups;

5. The student, and if dependent, the parent and student, pay considerably more in current dollars but less than the percentage of cost in public institutions than has historically been the case;

6. State governments have increased their share of financial support as the local and federal governments have decreased their support of higher education;

7. The greatest change in the share of support by government has been for public two-year colleges for which the local governments decrease of 13.6 percent has been partially offset by an increase of nearly 9 percent by state government;

8. Student assistance programs at the state and national levels have overemphasized choice to the detriment of access;

9. Philanthropy has actually decreased in its share of support for higher education institutions;

10. A 50 percent higher expenditure per student by private instutitions and a four-to-one ratio of tuition by privates to publics are implicitly recognized in public financial assistance programs;

11. The historic view of social benefit from higher education has weakened as a basis for funding public institutions and increased as a basis for providing assistance to private ones;

12. There is evidence that long-term government policy for funding higher education is neglected in favor of short-term responses and that higher education will itself have to be more persuasive and united in its representation of long-term national benefits and interests; and

13. Despite the regular increases in tuition by public institutions in recent years, the tuition "gap" between public and private institutions has not lessened over the past decade and in most cases is greater.

EXTRAPOLATIONS OF TRENDS

Without policy changes or other intervention to modify or reduce the trends of the recent past, what will be the picture for public and private institutions in the year 2000 as affected by financial conditions?

1. Because of increased costs, insufficient program adjustment, and declining traditional enrollment, there will be fewer four-year and two-year public institutions and no tuition-free institutions;

2. The average resident tuition cost in public universities will be $2,500 with the highest above $8,000;

3. Total median undergraduate charges at public universities will be about $4,800 with the highest more than $15,000 per year;

4. Tuition for nonresident students will average about $4,000 with the highest exceeding $14,000 per year;

5. Student charges for nonresidents in public institutions will average around $11,000 with the highest public cost exceeding $20,000 per year;

6. All public institutions will depend upon tuition as a larger source of revenue to fund its operations;

7. Student financial assistance needs will have reached $18–20 billion from all sources just to maintain inflation in prices, yet will serve many fewer students due to the necessity to raise the grant maximum periodically;

8. Loans and work-study funds that require matching by the states and public universities and colleges will be the major source of federal support for students not at the poverty level, and more self-help will be required of students;

9. Because of cost, at least half, if not the majority, of students in higher education will be enrolled in two-year colleges and a good portion of them will be attending part-time;

10. There will be no substantial increase in minority students enrolled in colleges and universities and many fewer low-income students will enroll due to high expenses;

11. Increased taxes on the citizen to reduce the federal deficit will have reduced the per capita disposable income growth below the inflation level, thereby reducing the amount of disposable income available for higher education;

12. Substantial increases in government funding will not be available to meet current and previously underfunded needs without dramatic changes in the economy and political attitudes;

13. Primary methods by which higher education will cope with financial needs will be increased efficiency and mission and program contraction;

14. The need to serve an older population and a more technological and international society will not be met without reallocating current funds to design and deliver those programs;

15. The number of private colleges and universities will be fewer with the remaining ones charging tuition rates in the range of $10,000 to $30,000 per year;

16. Private institutions will be receiving far more dollars from the state and federal governments for student financial assitance and their average per FTE student costs will exceed $25,000 and perhaps reach $35,000;

17. Profit-seeking proprietary institutions that serve short-term technical educational needs will have increased in number and will be competing with traditional colleges and universities, public and private, for students and financial assistance funds;

18. Public and private universities will have reduced their investment in research and will be diverting funds from instruction and research to student assistance and plant operation and maintenance;

19. Public and private institutions will be marketing research more to outside clients to maintain research capability and instrumentation;

20. High tuition will limit nonresident enrollment to the wealthiest students and those receiving a majority of their support from graduate fellowships and assistantships funded by a matching of state and federal funds or contracts to outside clientele; and

21. Faculty salaries will have declined further in realtion to purchasing power, discouraging the "best and the brightest" from entering college and university teaching, research, and service.

QUESTIONS TO CONSIDER

The general outlines of the above are simply unacceptable to most of us in public higher education and I suspect the private sector as well. If so, which course should public universities pursue, beginning immediately, to assure a more encouraging picture for the year 2000?

1. Do we in the public sector forsake the low or no tuition principle in its entirety and develop an approach that establishes a policy that sets tuition at 35–60 percent of instructional costs on the basis of increasing the share to participants and in light of the relationship of its level to disposable personal income?

2. Do we adopt, through tuition, the concept of student responsibility for a continuing uniform share of the costs of instruction realizing the increase in dollars will be significant and that public attitudes are at the moment not fully prepared for this approach?

3. Do we advocate tuition-free lower division college education for students to be financed by public funding in public institutions, public financial aid to students at a level equal to the average direct instructional cost (or a portion) at public institutions, modest tuition at the upper division, and higher tuition (35 percent or above of direct instructional cost) for graduate and professional study?

4. Do we devise proposals that focus on a uniform low or no tuition principle for all public institutions for students at the freshman and sophomore levels, 35 percent of the instructional costs at the upper division, and a minimum of 50 percent for graduate and post-baccalaureate courses of study, adopting differential shares according to assumed value to the society and individual?

5. Do we advocate tying tuition increases of the future to increases in disposable personal income as contrasted to increases in the Consumer Price Index?

6. Can we unite behind a program of financial assistance that is more discriminating in its recognition of public over private institutions in its distribution of funds and in its recognition and protection of independence of the private sector, quality in the public institutions, and access for more people?

7. At what point do the needs in public institutions become of such crucial importance that they have to be given greater priority over the needs of private institutions even in student aid for those institutions and vice versa?

8. Do we really know whether tuition or financial assistance conditions influence enrollment choices between the privates and publics and among the several types of institutions and should we attempt to document answers to these questions?

9. Should any capitation grants and cost of education allowance from public funds to private institutions be based on the average costs of instruction in similar types of institutions in the public sector?

10. Do we develop new means of public funding for the tuition portion of a student's cost of going to college, such as state and national service that "banks" tuition credits on a two-years-for-one-of-service basis or a publicly-sponsored, tax-deductible College Annuity Plan for parents to invest in over a ten-year or fifteen-year period?

11. Should we develop a proposal that is explicit and distinctive for the sharing of support for research by federal and state governments?

12. Should we support and advocate federal *entitlement* for Pell Grants, knowing that the current political environment is too concerned about the national debt to give further guarantees and that pragmatically, the higher education community may need to settle for increased funds only?

13. Should we advocate new mechanisms that consolidate oversight and allocation authority for federal higher education funds?

14. How should federal, state, and local responsibility for the various aspects of higher education be apportioned as they relate to the national interest?

ALTERNATIVE PHILOSOPHIES

The answers to these questions are fundamentally related to our philosophy about the societal role of colleges and universities and our assumptions about methods most likely to advance that result. There are basically three philosophical approaches to the issue of financing, although several permutations and combinations of different aspects of each are possible. The first approach is the "Governmental Responsibility for Investment in Human Resources." This philosophy says that higher education is similar to lower education in importance today and in the future as a matter of social need for developing human capital for the general benefit of society. This view would support providing access at the lowest cost possible to the student regardless of his or her family's economic standing. It further argues that if, upon reliable analysis and conclusion, those who can afford to support higher education are not doing so because of the low or no tuition, let the government adjust the tax system to require a greater payment. This approach gives greater weight to foregone earnings as a student's share of the total economic cost.

The second broad approach we may call that of "Shared Responsibility." It advocates that the student and family work in partnership with government and philanthropy in financing college attendance. It assumes that the government (state and federal) and philanthropy will provide two-thirds to three-quarters of the total educational costs of the institutions and the student and family will provide one-quarter to two-thirds— whatever that cost in dollars may be. This approach includes the condition that financial assistance be provided to independent students for student charges on a self-help basis (i.e., the student will assume responsibility for a percentage of those costs by participating in work-study or working outside the institution by borrowing funds, etc.). Dependent students are expected to receive support from their parents for total student charges according to their ability to pay and to provide self-help as well.

The third broad approach is that of "Full Pricing to the User." This approach is predicated upon the assumption that higher education is primarily a consumer enterprise that benefits the consumer more than society, and if able to pay, the user should pay the full cost of instruction. Ironically, even though many advocates of this approach view higher education as a consumer item, they also advocate student financial aid according to need for those who cannot pay. Others who hold to full pricing and student assistance do so because they believe that the current system subsidizes the middle- and high-income segments of the population more and unequally in relation to lower income persons.

We are told that the concept of full or "higher" pricing of tuition accompanied by expanded student aid was defeated with the adoption of the Higher Education Amendments of 1972. The trends since 1972 have been moving, however, slowly and progressively toward the practice of high tuition and expanded student assistance, including "self-help" as a fundamental part (40 percent or $500, whichever is greater, of the educational costs) of the aid package. What was seemingly won by low or modest tuition advocates in concept is about to be lost by pragmatic responses of institutions and government that see few other sources than tuition for needed revenue.

It is time we paused on this path to reconsider whether broad access, which is assumed to be federal and state policy, is enhanced more effectively and efficiently by low tuition or student assistance. There are studies by Van Dyk (1975) and Bishop (1977) that seem to make the case that low tuition stimulates college attendance of numbers of low-income families. Lavin, Alba, and Silberstein (1979 and 1980) suggest that in relation to the CUNY experience of substituting student aid for free tuition, the evidence is that it produced questionable benefits for both students and taxpayers. Others, such as McPherson (1978) and Carlson (1974 and 1975), have studied the effect of tuition rates on college enrollment, concluding that low-income students are sensitive to tuition levels in their choice of institutions.

Reductions in tuition will likely have a positive impact on enrollment of students as the experiment in Wisconsin (for which the author was one of the architects) that decreased tuition more than $300 in two selected two-year liberal arts campuses demonstrated. The campus located in a rural community experienced an increase of 4 percent in enrollment while the campus located in a community that was growing more rapidly had a 12.2 percent increase. Comparable decreases in enrollment occurred in those two campuses two years later when the tuition was raised to its former level.

There is sufficient evidence that supports the view that low-income per-

Table 11
Increases in Minority Full-time Student
Enrollment, 1970–1978

	1970	1978	Percentage Increase
American Indian/ Alaskan Native	28,456	38,706	38.1
Black/Non-Hispanic	365,929	632,148	77.2
Asian/Pacific Islanders	60,571	127,572	129.6
Hispanic	108,744	209,621	98.1

Note: See the expanded discussion of this hypothesis in Jacob Stampen, *The Financing of Public Higher Education* (1980), pp. 29–36.

sons or those from low-income families are more likely to enroll in higher education if tuition is low. While the correlation of the increase in enrollment of minorities during the 1969–1978 period is not solely related to low tuition but also with opportunity to attend part-time, the availability of student aid, the "climate" of equal opportunity, and other factors, the increases shown in table 11 are encouraging. The progress for the most part was prior to the last six years of higher increases in tuition levels.

We have made gains in the seventies but we must continue the progress until the participation of formerly underrepresented groups is more closely similar to other population groups. At the same time, we must not pursue policies that reverse the participation of previously highly represented groups who have been the traditional mainstream of higher education, most of whom clearly reflect the success of a broad access policy and approach.

The issues concerning the financing of higher education are complex and interrelated in ways that are not yet completely understood. New action in one direction threatens continued success in another, and the full range of causal and influencing factors is unknown. For this reason the subject needs the continuous individual and collective thought and wisdom of the leadership of the higher education community, the body politic in the states, government's knowledgeable professionals, and public statesmen. To stimulate such thought, discussion, and debate, a list of recommendations appears below. Not all of them are supported with equal fervor by the author and some of them are given as if by a "devil's advocate." Refinements and alternatives will be welcomed in the quest to maintain a vital higher education system, public and private, through democratic and equitable approaches.

RECOMMENDATIONS FOR DISCUSSION

General Philosophy and Policy

1. Policy regarding the financing of public higher education should be viewed as social policy to achieve desired social results, few of which can be evaluated or justified by economic principles alone.

2. The central policy of state and federal government should declare and affirm the objective of maximum development of human capital through higher education and affirm by action the maximum participation of its citizens from all ethnic, social, economic, and age groups in higher education.

3. Policy and practice for financing higher education should be based upon the principle of societal as well as personal benefit from college attendance, and to the greatest degree possible strive to maintain low immediate monetary costs for college attendance to the student and parent as a means of encouraging optimal participation by all segments of the society.

4. Policy and practice should support access over choice when support of choice unduly limits access.

5. Reduction in the tuition gap between public and private institutions should not necessarily be pursued only through the raising of tuition in public institutions at a faster rate than private institutions.

6. Public institutions should pursue endowments and gifts for their functions as aggressively as private institutions pursue public funds in recognition of the shifting relationships of each to "public" and "private" revenue sources.

Shares of Cost by Student

7. If and when tuition increases become necessary, increases at the freshman-sophomore level should be avoided if at all possible, stabilizing the level of tuition at that level.

8. Higher education at the freshman and sophomore years should require the lowest share of cost in tuition by the student in all types of public instituions with upper-division tuition set as a minor portion of average instructional costs (not to exceed 20 percent) at that level.

9. The share of cost to be borne by students in the form of tuition for graduate, nonprofessional study should not exceed 25 percent of average instructional cost for that program level; and not exceed 60 percent for postbaccalaureate professional programs that have high earning potential.

10. Student assistance through low tuition and subsidized living costs according to need is preferred over high tuition and financial assistance.

11. If regular tuition increases are to be levied to meet essential costs, such increases should be made in relation to disposable personal income and its change and not according to inflation rates.

12. An expanded forgiveness of a portion of the annual loan repayment should be considered for students engaged in specific public service work of high priority and for work in a profession of high priority for states and the federal government.

13. The federal government, in using federalism as a means for different approaches to the same problem or need, should consider a partnership with a state or several states to experiment with reducing student aid by eliminating tuition for all institutions at the freshman-sophomore level.

14. The federal and state governments should encourage more minority, low-income, and other students who received loans on a need basis to complete their undergraduate degree by forgiving a certain portion of their loans upon graduation.

Federal and State Partnership in Financing Higher Education

15. The federal government should provide matching funds to states that establish a Public Service Program by which citizens eighteen to fifty-four may volunteer for public service at maintenance pay in return for tuition credits on a two-years-tuition-for-one-year-of-service basis, such credits to be utilized in the public institutions of the state in which the service was given or out-of-state public institutions or private institutions at the value of the level of tuition in the same type of public institution in the state of service.

16. The states and the federal governments should employ more creative tax credits and tax deductions policies to: a) encourage those who can afford it to establish College Annuity Savings for their childrens' college attendance costs; b) encourage unrestricted endowments or restricted endowments for programs of national priority in public institutions; and c) soften the negative effects of increases in tuition by tax credits for public and private institutions.

17. The federal and state governments should develop and implement

a plan for sharing in a more equal way the funding of student financial assistance to students with demonstrated need.

18. The federal government should take major responsibility for funding graduate fellowships and other graduate support in areas of national priority with state government sharing in that funding.

19. State government should assume or maintain responsibility for graduate fellowships supportive of the undergraduate programs and graduate programs having priority in the state's long-term needs, including the waiver of tuition for nonresident graduate students in the programs of high state priority.

20. Responsibility for research funding should reside with the state government for "capacity to serve" expenses for research directly related to undergraduate and graduate instruction with the federal government bearing responsibility for maintaining project funding for contract research by college and university faculty and for replacement of obsolete research instrumentation on a block-grant matching basis with states.

21. In their support for higher education, the state and federal governments should manifest in policy and practice the distinction between public and private institutions and while diversity and choice should be supported, unlimited diversity and choice nor costs in excess of public instructional costs should be advocated as a general approach.

22. The federal government should take advantage of the federal system by developing with the several states experimental methods of financing colleges and universities without increasing the demand for increased tax revenues nor increasing monetary costs to student and parent.

23. There should be a federal program providing for tuition waivers by public institutions to low income students for which the federal government provides block grants for states.

24. Construction of new physical facilities should be undertaken only if absolutely essential for program purposes and for which renovation is impossible or more expensive; state governments should emphasize renovation rather than new construction whenever practicable.

Federal Programs

25. The federal government should implement an effective means for the development of a coherent plan and program to respond to long-term and short-term national priorities in higher education to which categorical aid should be directed.

26. If the Pell Grants remain the centerpiece of federal student aid programs for low-income students, it should be funded at a higher level, the

one-half of student charges limitation should be removed, and students should be eligible to receive the maximum upon demonstration of need regardless of the percentage it contributes toward student charges.

27. The cumulation of maximum limits for undergraduate and graduate students to borrow under the Guaranteed Student Loan program should be adjusted upward regularly as a matter of policy.

28. The Trio program should be transformed into a part of a National Public Service Corps with the same ideas as suggested above (15).

29. The federal College Work-Study Program and the Cooperative Education Program should remain separate for this critical period of financing higher education with College Work-Study funds increased dramatically. States should be encouraged to increase matching funds for these programs.

30. The federal government should consolidate more of the responsibility for oversight of federal support for higher education.

31. The federal government should assist in the support of research facilities with an emphasis upon installed equipment, renovation, and cost-sharing with the state for any construction.

NOTES

1. For a summary of these major works, see Appendix A.

2. For a brief but excellent discussion of federal aid, see Charles B. Saunders, Jr., "Reshaping Federal Aid to Higher Education," *Crisis in Higher Education*, in *Proceedings of the Academy of Political Science*, Joseph Fromkin, editor, vol. 35, no. 2 (New York, 1983), 110–134.

3. Peter Passell and Leonard Ross, *State Policies and Federal Programs: Priorities and Constraints*. A Twentieth Century Fund Report (New York and London: Praeger Publishers, 1978), p. 60

4. See Appendix B.

5. See Appendix B.

6. See Appendices C and D.

7. National Center for Educational Statistics. *Digest of Educational Statistics, 1983–84* (Washington: Government Printing Office, 1984), p. 98.

8. Ibid.

9. See "Rating College Participation, 1969, 1974, and 1981," American Council of Education Policy Brief, April 1984, prepared by John B. Lee and Associates, Applied Systems Institute.

10. See Appendix H.

11. "1983–84 Student Charges of State and Land Grant Universities" (Washington: National Association of State Universities and Land Grant Colleges, 1984).

12. See Appendix I.

13. See Appendices J and K.

Appendix A
Major Reports on the Financing of Higher Education

The Carnegie Commission report *Quality and Equality* (1968) and its revision in 1970 urged increased financial support to higher education from the federal government and particularly in behalf of low-income students. In *The Capital and the Campus* (1971), the commission stressed the need for the states' continued financial support to public institutions and for expanded assistance to private institutions by the states. Another commission report, *Institutional Aid: Federal Support of Colleges and Universities* (1972) emphasized the importance of federal funds for direct institutional support. *Higher Education: Who Pays? Who Benefits? Who Should Pay?* (1973) contained a number of recommendations to be considered as a package to revise the shares of funding provided by various sources of revenue, to increase funding of low-income students, to improve funding for public and private institutions, and to lower the "tuition gap" between public and private institutions. A follow-up to that important work, *Tuition: A Supplemental Statement of the Carnegie Commission on Higher Education on "Who Pays? Who Benefits? Who Should Pay?"* was issued in 1974 to provide additional data and information to strengthen the rationale for the 1973 recommendations. *Tuition* seems to have been written in particular response to critics of the earlier report, and especially those who alleged that the commission's 1973 *Who Pays* had the main effect of serving primarily the interests of the private institutions. The Carnegie Council on Policy Studies issued *The Federal Role in Postsecondary Education: Unfinished Business, 1975–1980* (1975) and *The States and Private Higher Education: Problems and Policies in a New Era* (1977), focusing in the former on increased funding by the federal government, especially through student aid and urging, and in the latter, upon improved support to private institutions by state governments. A third work by the council that had influence was *Next Steps for the 1980's in Student Financial Aid: A Fourth Alternative* (1979), a report that "intended to be helpful" in the reexamination of the federal student aid program in advance of the Higher Education Amendments of 1979 or 1980. *The States and Higher Education: A Proud Past and a Vital Future* (1976), published also by the Carnegie Council for the Advancement of Teaching, emphasized increased support at the state level, especially for undergraduate instruction.

The *Report of the Commission on Postsecondary Education Financing* (1973) contained a number of public policy options concerning the increased level of funding responsibility to be assumed by government and the student, and a student aid program appropriate to each option. The *Report* also included an assessment of the financial impact of each option on enrollment. The Committee for Economic Development came on the scene in 1973 with its report *The Management and Financing of Colleges* urging that tuition in public universities be increased to 50 percent (as contrasted with the Carnegie Commission's 33⅓ percent) of the costs of instruction over a five year period for four-year institutions and ten years for two-year colleges.

Appendix B
Higher Education Price Index (EPI)
and
Consumer's Price Index (CPI) Changes

FY 1971–FY 1983	EPI	CPI
1971	6.4	5.2
1972	5.6	3.6
1973	5.3	3.9
1974	7.1	8.9
1975	8.6	11.2
1976	6.6	7.1
1977	6.5	5.8
1978	6.7	6.8
1979	7.7	9.3
1980	9.9	13.3
1981	10.7	11.6
1982	10.0	8.7
1983	6.3	4.3

Source: Research Associates of Washington, 1983.

Appendix C
NCES Enrollment Projections

Total Enrollment in all U.S. Institutions of Higher Education, with Alternative
Projections, by Sex and Attendance Status of Students and Control of
Institutions, Fall 1970 to 1990
(in thousands)

Year (fall)	Total enrollment	Sex		Attendance status		Control	
		Men	Women	Full-time	Part-time	Public	Private
1970	8,581	5,044	3,537	5,815	2,766	6,428	2,153
1971	8,949	5,207	3,742	6,077	2,871	6,804	2,144
1972	9,215	5,239	3,976	6,072	3,142	7,071	2,144
1973	9,602	5,371	4,231	6,189	3,413	7,420	2,183
1974	10,224	5,622	4,601	6,370	3,853	7,989	2,235
1975	11,185	6,149	5,036	6,841	4,344	8,835	2,350
1976	11,012	5,811	5,201	6,717	4,295	8,653	2,359
1977	11,286	5,789	5,497	6,793	4,493	8,847	2,437
1978	11,259	5,640	5,619	6,667	4,592	8,784	2,475
1979	11,570	5,683	5,887	6,793	4,776	9,037	2,533
1980	12,097	5,874	6,223	7,098	4,999	9,457	2,640
Intermediate alternative projections[a]							
1981	12,442	6,159	6,283	7,379	5,063	9,760	2,682
1982	12,620	6,238	6,382	7,459	5,161	9,906	2,714
1983	12,513	6,154	6,359	7,263	5,250	9,839	2,674
1984	12,351	6,039	6,312	7,025	5,326	9,730	2,621
1985	12,174	5,917	6,257	6,781	5,393	9,612	2,562
1986	12,120	5,865	6,255	6,669	5,451	9,584	2,536
1987	12,093	5,823	6,270	6,601	5,492	9,576	2,517
1988	12,098	5,802	6,296	6,585	5,513	9,591	2,507
1989	12,139	5,803	6,336	6,593	5,546	9,636	2,503
1990	12,101	5,770	6,331	6,536	5,565	9,616	2,485

Appendix C (continued)

Year (fall)	Total enrollment	Sex		Attendance status		Control	
		Men	Women	Full-time	Part-time	Public	Private
			Low alternative projections[a]				
1981	11,780	5,766	6,014	6,814	4,966	9,265	2,515
1982	11,779	5,730	6,049	6,747	5,032	9,279	2,500
1983	11,719	5,664	6,055	6,628	5,091	9,245	2,474
1984	11,593	5,564	6,029	6,460	5,133	9,163	2,430
1985	11,452	5,453	5,999	6,285	5,167	9,068	2,384
1986	11,305	5,342	5,963	6,106	5,199	8,970	2,335
1987	11,221	5,276	5,945	5,989	5,232	8,920	2,301
1988	11,170	5,223	5,947	5,925	5,245	8,890	2,280
1989	11,166	5,203	5,963	5,901	5,265	8,903	2,263
1990	11,099	5,157	5,942	5,819	5,280	8,858	2,241
			High alternative projections[a]				
1981	12,753	6,172	6,581	7,390	5,363	10,025	2,728
1982	13,128	6,279	6,849	7,490	5,638	10,339	2,789
1983	13,477	6,365	7,112	7,560	5,917	10,633	2,844
1984	13,745	6,410	7,335	7,561	6,184	10,869	2,876
1985	13,999	6,441	7,558	7,557	6,442	11,096	2,903
1986	14,239	6,459	7,780	7,540	6,699	11,312	2,927
1987	14,497	6,486	8,011	7,554	6,943	11,543	2,954
1988	14,796	6,535	8,261	7,640	7,156	11,802	2,994
1989	15,143	6,608	8,535	7,760	7,383	12,103	3,040
1990	15,409	6,654	8,755	7,812	7,597	12,336	3,073

Source: U.S. Department of Education, National Center for Education Statistics, Fall Enrollment in Higher Education.
Note: Because of rounding, details may not add to totals.
[a]For methodological details, see Volume II of Projections of Education Statistics to 1990–1991.

Appendix D

NCES Enrollment Projections to 1990
Total Enrollment in all U.S. Institutions, with Intermediate Alternative Projections, by Sex of Student, Fall 1970 to 1990

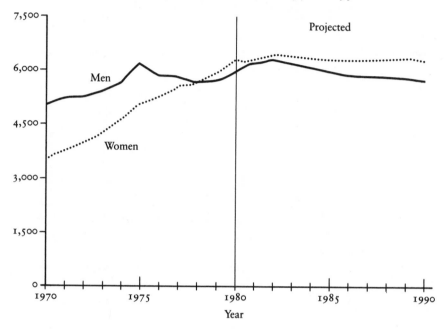

Note: Enrollment in thousands.

Appendix D (continued)

Total Enrollment in all U.S. Institutions, with Intermediate Alternative Projections, by Type of Institution, Fall 1970 to 1990

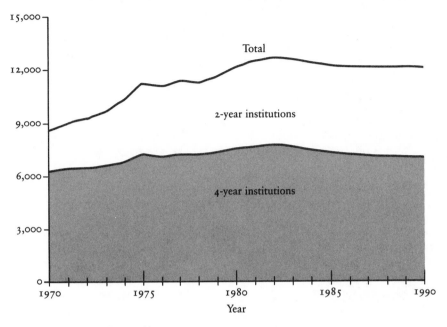

Note: Enrollment in thousands.

Appendix E

Revenues and Expenditures in Higher Education Institutions: Scenario One

Current Fund Revenues—Public Institutions, 1981–1982

Revenue Categories	Thousand $s	Increment
Total Current Fund Revenues	47,585,403	
Tuition and Fees	6,425,579	0.05
Federal Government	5,413,684	
Appropriations	1,109,629	0.05
Unrestricted Grants and Contracts	573,044	0.05
Restricted Grants and Contracts	3,654,136	0.05
Independent Operations (FFRDC)*	76,875	0.05
State Governments	21,605,158	
Appropriations	20,893,810	0.05
Unrestricted Grants and Contracts	63,570	0.05
Restricted Grants and Contracts	647,778	0.05
Local Governments	1,769,290	
Appropriations	1,610,488	0.05
Unrestricted Grants and Contracts	16,968	0.05
Restricted Grants and Contracts	141,834	0.05
Private gifts, grants, and contracts	1,278,091	
Unrestricted	138,200	0.05
Restricted	1,139,891	0.05
Endowment Income	244,634	
Unrestricted	115,135	0.05
Restricted	129,499	0.05
Sales and Services	9,632,606	
Educational Activities	1,075,159	0.05
Auxiliary Enterprises	5,130,667	0.05
Hospitals	3,426,780	0.05
Other Sources	1,216,361	0.05

*Generally includes only those revenues associated with major federally funded research and development centers.

Appendix E (continued)

Current Fund Expenditures and Transfers—Public Institutions, 1981–1982

Expenditures Categories	Thousand $s	Increment
Total Fund Expenditures and Transfers	46,523,700	
Educational and Gen. Expenditures/Transfers	37,459,681	
Instruction	16,459,179	0.05
Research	4,031,763	0.05
Public Service	1,830,017	0.05
Academic Support	2,025,111	0.05
Libraries	1,298,100	0.05
Student Services	2,099,925	0.05
Institutional Support	3,992,305	0.05
Operation and Plant Maintenance	4,136,844	0.05
Scholarships and Fellowships	1,106,812	
From Unrestricted Funds	378,811	0.05
From Restricted Funds	728,001	0.05
Educational and Mandatory Transfers	479,625	0.05
Auxiliary Enterprises and Transfers	5,079,370	0.05
Hospitals and Mandatory Transfers	3,908,231	0.05
Independent Operations and Transfers	76,418	0.05

Appendix E (continued)

Projected Revenues—Public Institutions
(thousand $s)

Revenue Categories	In 1990	In 2000
Total Projected Fund Revenues	70,305,313	114,519,946
Tuition and Fees	9,493,507	15,463,922
Federal Government	7,998,477	13,028,676
Appropriations	1,639,427	2,670,454
Unrestricted Grants and Contracts	846,647	1,379,099
Restricted Grants and Contracts	5,398,823	8,794,114
Independent Operations (FFRDC)*	113,579	185,009
State Governments	31,920,658	51,995,389
Appropriations	30,869,673	50,283,445
Unrestricted Grants and Contracts	93,922	152,989
Restricted Grants and Contracts	957,063	1,558,955
Local Governments	2,614,047	4,258,007
Appropriations	2,379,424	3,875,831
Unrestricted Grants and Contracts	25,069	40,836
Restricted Grants and Contracts	209,553	341,340
Private gifts, grants, and contracts	1,888,323	3,075,878
Unrestricted	204,184	332,595
Restricted	1,684,138	2,743,284
Endowment Income	361,436	588,741
Unrestricted	170,107	277,086
Restricted	191,329	311,655
Sales and Services	14,231,746	23,182,015
Educational Activities	1,588,500	2,587,498
Auxiliary Enterprises	7,580,332	12,347,562
Hospitals	5,062,915	8,246,955
Other Sources	1,797,119	2,927,318

*Generally includes only those revenues associated with major federally funded research and development centers.

256

Appendix E (continued)

Projected Expenditures and Transfers—Public Institutions
(thousand $s)

Expenditures Categories	In 1990	In 2000
Total Fund Expenditures and Transfers	68,736,694	111,964,831
Educational and Gen. Expenditures/Transfers	55,345,010	90,151,189
Instruction	24,317,704	39,610,977
Research	5,956,750	9,702,918
Public Service	2,703,769	4,404,154
Academic Support	2,992,011	4,873,671
Libraries	1,917,885	3,124,032
Student Services	3,102,546	5,053,720
Institutional Support	5,898,453	9,607,958
Operation and Plant Maintenance	6,112,003	9,955,808
Scholarships and Fellowships	1,635,265	2,663,675
From Unrestricted Funds	559,676	911,654
From Restricted Funds	1,075,589	1,752,021
Educational and Mandatory Transfers	708,625	1,154,275
Auxiliary Enterprises and Transfers	7,504,543	12,224,110
Hospitals and Mandatory Transfers	5,774,237	9,405,624
Independent Operations and Transfers	112,904	183,909

Appendix E (continued)

Current Fund Revenues—Private Institutions, 1981–1982

Revenue Categories	Thousand $s	Increment
Total Current Fund Revenues	25,065,910	
Tuition and Fees	9,499,761	0.05
Federal Government	4,228,717	
Appropriations	210,339	0.05
Unrestricted Grants and Contracts	601,525	0.05
Restricted Grants and Contracts	2,221,740	0.05
Independent Operations (FFRDC)*	1,195,113	0.05
State Governments	453,207	
Appropriations	268,799	0.05
Unrestricted Grants and Contracts	44,184	0.05
Restricted Grants and Contracts	140,224	0.05
Local Governments	180,934	
Appropriations	5,067	0.05
Unrestricted Grants and Contracts	24,221	0.05
Restricted Grants and Contracts	151,646	0.05
Private gifts, grants, and contracts	2,287,781	
Unrestricted	1,220,329	0.05
Restricted	1,067,452	0.05
Endowment Income	1,353,212	
Unrestricted	792,705	0.05
Restricted	560,507	0.05
Sales and Services	5,928,767	
Educational Activities	511,666	0.05
Auxiliary Enterprises	3,004,541	0.05
Hospitals	2,412,560	0.05
Other Sources	1,133,531	0.05

*Generally includes only those revenues associated with major federally funded research and development centers.

Appendix E (continued)

Current Fund Expenditures and Transfers—Private Institutions, 1981–1982

Expenditures Categories	Thousand $s	Increment
Total Fund Expenditures and Transfers	24,259,978	
Educational and Gen. Expenditures/Transfers	17,812,986	
Instruction	6,669,439	0.05
Research	1,925,071	0.05
Public Service	391,742	0.05
Academic Support	732,996	0.05
Libraries	640,387	0.05
Student Services	1,100,632	0.05
Institutional Support	2,535,147	0.05
Operation and Plant Maintenance	1,891,261	0.05
Scholarships and Fellowships	1,607,103	
From Unrestricted Funds	862,357	0.05
From Restricted Funds	744,746	0.05
Educational and Mandatory Transfers	319,208	0.05
Auxiliary Enterprises and Transfers	2,932,563	0.05
Hospitals and Mandatory Transfers	2,332,070	0.05
Independent Operations and Transfers	1,182,359	0.05

Appendix E (continued)

Projected Revenues—Private Institutions

Revenue Categories	In 1990	In 2000
Total Projected Fund Revenues	37,033,765	60,324,101
Tuition and Fees	14,035,474	22,862,308
Federal Government	6,247,741	10,176,912
Appropriations	310,767	506,206
Unrestricted Grants and Contracts	888,726	1,447,642
Restricted Grants and Contracts	3,282,522	5,346,882
Independent Operations (FFRDC)*	1,765,726	2,876,182
State Governments	669,593	1,090,697
Appropriations	397,139	646,897
Unrestricted Grants and Contracts	65,280	106,334
Restricted Grants and Contracts	207,175	337,466
Local Governments	267,322	435,439
Appropriations	7,486	12,194
Unrestricted Grants and Contracts	35,785	58,291
Restricted Grants and Contracts	224,050	364,954
Private gifts, grants, and contracts	3,380,094	5,505,818
Unrestricted	1,802,982	2,936,867
Restricted	1,577,113	2,568,951
Endowment Income	1,999,310	3,256,666
Unrestricted	1,171,186	1,907,739
Restricted	828,124	1,348,927
Sales and Services	8,759,489	14,268,285
Educational Activities	755,964	1,231,385
Auxiliary Enterprises	4,439,075	7,230,786
Hospitals	3,564,450	5,806,113
Other Sources	1,674,742	2,727,978

*Generally includes only those revenues associated with major federally funded research and development centers.

Appendix E (continued)

Projected Expenditures and Transfers—Private Institutions

Expenditures Categories	In 1990	In 2000
Total Fund Expenditures and Transfers	35,843,037	58,384,530
Educational and Gen. Expenditures/Transfers	26,317,893	42,869,075
Instruction	9,853,799	16,050,800
Research	2,844,207	4,632,913
Public Service	578,781	942,774
Academic Support	1,082,969	1,764,042
Libraries	946,143	1,541,168
Student Services	1,626,135	2,648,802
Institutional Support	3,745,567	6,101,134
Operation and Plant Maintenance	2,794,254	4,551,545
Scholarships and Fellowships	2,374,423	3,867,685
From Unrestricted Funds	1,274,094	2,075,365
From Restricted Funds	1,100,329	1,792,320
Educational and Mandatory Transfers	471,616	768,212
Auxiliary Enterprises and Transfers	4,332,731	7,057,563
Hospitals and Mandatory Transfers	3,445,530	5,612,405
Independent Operations and Transfers	1,746,883	2,845,488

Appendix E (continued)

Estimated Number of Full-time Equivalent (FTE) Students

Year	1982	1990	2000
Public Sector			
Enrollment Projections:			
NCES	6,713	6,349	
Carnegie Commission		6,855	7,910
Leslie and Miller			7,807
Constant Participation Rate of High School Grads		6,133	5,087
Private Sector			
Enrollment Projections:			
NCES	2,198	2,079	
Carnegie Commission		2,244	2,590
Leslie and Miller			2,556
Constant Participation Rate of High School Grads		2,008	1,666

Dollars per FTE Student—Public Institutions

	1982	1990	2000
Revenues on the basis of the following enrollment projections:			
NCES	$ 7,089	$11,073	
Carnegie Commission		$10,256	$14,478
Leslie and Miller			$14,669
Constant Participation Rate		$11,464	$22,511
Expenditures on the basis of the following enrollment projections:			
NCES	$ 6,930	$10,826	
Carnegie Commission		$10,027	$14,155
Leslie and Miller			$14,342
Constant Participation Rate		$11,209	$22,009

Appendix E (continued)

Dollars per FTE Student—Private Institutions

	1982	1990	2000
Revenues on the basis of the following enrollment projections:			
NCES	$11,404	$17,813	N/A
Carnegie Commission		$16,503	$22,291
Leslie and Miller			$23,601
Constant Participation Rate		$18,443	$36,209
Expenditures on the basis of the following enrollment projections:			
NCES	$11,037	$17,241	N/A
Carnegie Commission		$15,973	$22,542
Leslie and Miller			$22,842
Constant Participation Rate		$17,850	$35,045

References and Miscellaneous Information

	1982	1990	2000
Number of High School Graduates*	2,845	2,599	2,156

*McConnell, William R., and Kaufman, Norman. "High School Graduates: Projections for the Fifty States (1982–2000)." Western Interstate Commission for Higher Education (WICHE), Teachers Insurance and Annuity Association (TIAA/CREF), and The College Board, 1984.

Appendix F

Revenues and Expenditures in Higher Education Institutions: Scenario Two

Current Fund Revenues—Public Institutions, 1981–1982

Revenue Categories	Thousand $s	Increment
Total Current Fund Revenues	47,585,403	
Tuition and Fees	6,425,579	0.05
Federal Government	5,413,684	
Appropriations	1,109,629	0.06
Unrestricted Grants and Contracts	573,044	0.03
Restricted Grants and Contracts	3,654,136	0.08
Independent Operations (FFRDC)*	76,875	0.01
State Governments	21,605,158	
Appropriations	20,893,810	0.06
Unrestricted Grants and Contracts	63,570	0.01
Restricted Grants and Contracts	647,778	0.03
Local Governments	1,769,290	
Appropriations	1,610,488	0.03
Unrestricted Grants and Contracts	16,968	0.00
Restricted Grants and Contracts	141,834	0.01
Private gifts, grants, and contracts	1,278,091	
Unrestricted	138,200	0.03
Restricted	1,139,891	0.05
Endowment Income	244,634	
Unrestricted	115,135	0.01
Restricted	129,499	0.01
Sales and Services	9,632,606	
Educational Activities	1,075,159	0.03
Auxiliary Enterprises	5,130,667	0.05
Hospitals	3,426,780	0.08
Other Sources	1,216,361	0.01

*Generally includes only those revenues associated with major federally funded research and development centers.

Appendix F (continued)

Current Fund Expenditures and Transfers—Public Institutions, 1981–1982

Expenditures Categories	Thousand $s	Increment
Total Fund Expenditures and Transfers	46,523,700	
Educational and Gen. Expenditures/Transfers	37,459,681	
Instruction	16,459,179	0.045
Research	4,031,763	0.08
Public Service	1,830,017	0.045
Academic Support	2,025,111	0.045
Libraries	1,298,100	0.06
Student Services	2,099,925	0.06
Institutional Support	3,992,305	0.045
Operation and Plant Maintenance	4,136,844	0.08
Scholarships and Fellowships	1,106,812	
From Unrestricted Funds	378,811	0.05
From Restricted Funds	728,001	0.08
Educational and Mandatory Transfers	479,625	0.045
Auxiliary Enterprises and Transfers	5,079,370	0.045
Hospitals and Mandatory Transfers	3,908,231	0.08
Independent Operations and Transfers	76,418	0.05

Appendix F (continued)

Projected Revenues—Public Institutions
(thousand $s)

Revenue Categories	In 1990	In 2000
Total Projected Fund Revenues	73,962,747	130,643,482
Tuition and Fees	9,493,507	15,463,922
Federal Government	9,341,290	18,836,779
Appropriations	1,768,580	3,167,257
Unrestricted Grants and Contracts	725,915	975,569
Restricted Grants and Contracts	6,763,551	14,601,999
Independent Operations (FFRDC)*	83,245	91,954
State Governments	34,190,982	60,816,858
Appropriations	33,301,559	59,638,020
Unrestricted Grants and Contracts	68,837	76,039
Restricted Grants and Contracts	820,586	1,102,799
Local Governments	2,210,672	2,928,370
Appropriations	2,040,118	2,741,748
Unrestricted Grants and Contracts	16,968	16,968
Restricted Grants and Contracts	153,586	169,654
Private gifts, grants, and contracts	1,859,206	2,978,560
Unrestricted	175,068	235,276
Restricted	1,684,138	2,743,284
Endowment Income	264,904	292,618
Unrestricted	124,675	137,718
Restricted	140,229	154,900
Sales and Services	15,285,042	27,871,428
Educational Activities	1,361,979	1,830,386
Auxiliary Enterprises	7,580,332	12,347,562
Hospitals	6,342,731	13,693,480
Other Sources	1,317,145	1,454,947

*Generally includes only those revenues associated with major federally funded research and development centers.

Appendix F (continued)

Projected Expenditures and Transfers—Public Institutions
(thousand $s)

Expenditures Categories	In 1990	In 2000
Total Fund Expenditures and Transfers	72,261,278	127,920,624
Educational and Gen. Expenditures/Transfers	57,691,135	100,901,667
Instruction	23,406,609	36,349,747
Research	7,462,512	16,111,004
Public Service	2,602,468	4,041,554
Academic Support	2,879,912	4,472,415
Libraries	2,068,974	3,705,218
Student Services	3,346,961	5,993,898
Institutional Support	5,677,459	8,816,921
Operation and Plant Maintenance	7,657,010	16,530,909
Scholarships and Fellowships	1,907,155	3,820,760
From Unrestricted Funds	559,676	911,654
From Restricted Funds	1,347,479	2,909,106
Educational and Mandatory Transfers	682,075	1,059,242
Auxiliary Enterprises and Transfers	7,223,375	11,217,681
Hospitals and Mandatory Transfers	7,233,863	15,617,367
Independent Operations and Transfers	112,904	183,909

Appendix F (continued)

Current Fund Revenues—Private Institutions, 1981–1982

Revenue Categories	Thousand $s	Increment
Total Current Fund Revenues	25,065,910	
Tuition and Fees	9,499,761	0.05
Federal Government	4,228,717	
Appropriations	210,339	0.05
Unrestricted Grants and Contracts	601,525	0.05
Restricted Grants and Contracts	2,221,740	0.05
Independent Operations (FFRDC)*	1,195,113	0.05
State Governments	453,207	
Appropriations	268,799	0.05
Unrestricted Grants and Contracts	44,184	0.05
Restricted Grants and Contracts	140,224	0.05
Local Governments	180,934	
Appropriations	5,067	0.05
Unrestricted Grants and Contracts	24,221	0.05
Restricted Grants and Contracts	151,646	0.05
Private gifts, grants, and contracts	2,287,781	
Unrestricted	1,220,329	0.05
Restricted	1,067,452	0.05
Endowment Income	1,353,212	
Unrestricted	792,705	0.05
Restricted	560,507	0.05
Sales and Services	5,928,767	
Educational Activities	511,666	0.05
Auxiliary Enterprises	3,004,541	0.05
Hospitals	2,412,560	0.05
Other Sources	1,113,531	0.05

*Generally includes only those revenues associated with major federally funded research and development centers.

Appendix F (continued)

Current Fund Expenditures and Transfers—Private Institutions, 1981–1982

Expenditures Categories	Thousand $s	Increment
Total Fund Expenditures and Transfers	24,259,978	
Educational and Gen. Expenditures/Transfers	17,812,986	
Instruction	6,669,439	0.045
Research	1,925,071	0.08
Public Service	391,742	0.045
Academic Support	732,996	0.045
Libraries	640,387	0.06
Student Services	1,100,632	0.06
Institutional Support	2,535,147	0.045
Operation and Plant Maintenance	1,891,261	0.08
Scholarships and Fellowships	1,607,103	
From Unrestricted Funds	862,357	0.07
From Restricted Funds	744,746	0.08
Educational and Mandatory Transfers	319,208	0.045
Auxiliary Enterprises and Transfers	2,932,563	0.045
Hospitals and Mandatory Transfers	2,332,070	0.08
Independent Operations and Transfers	1,182,359	0.05

Appendix F (continued)

Projected Revenues—Private Institutions

Revenue Categories	In 1990	In 2000
Total Projected Fund Revenues	37,033,765	60,324,101
Tuition and Fees	14,035,474	22,862,308
Federal Government	6,247,741	10,176,912
Appropriations	310,767	506,206
Unrestricted Grants and Contracts	888,726	1,447,642
Restricted Grants and Contracts	3,282,522	5,346,882
Independent Operations (FFRDC)*	1,765,726	2,876,182
State Governments	669,593	1,090,697
Appropriations	397,139	646,897
Unrestricted Grants and Contracts	65,280	106,334
Restricted Grants and Contracts	207,175	337,466
Local Governments	267,322	435,439
Appropriations	7,486	12,194
Unrestricted Grants and Contracts	35,785	58,291
Restricted Grants and Contracts	224,050	364,954
Private gifts, grants, and contracts	3,380,094	5,505,818
Unrestricted	1,802,982	2,936,867
Restricted	1,577,113	2,568,951
Endowment Income	1,999,310	3,256,666
Unrestricted	1,171,186	1,907,739
Restricted	828,124	1,348,927
Sales and Services	8,759,489	14,268,285
Educational Activities	755,964	1,231,385
Auxiliary Enterprises	4,439,075	7,230,786
Hospitals	3,564,450	5,806,113
Other Sources	1,674,742	2,727,978

*Generally includes only those revenues associated with major federally funded research and development centers.

Appendix F (continued)

Projected Expenditures and Transfers—Private Institutions

Expenditures Categories	In 1990	In 2000
Total Fund Expenditures and Transfers	38,075,912	68,268,369
Educational and Gen. Expenditures/Transfers	27,842,131	49,627,380
Instruction	9,484,613	14,729,314
Research	3,563,172	7,692,621
Public Service	557,097	865,154
Academic Support	1,042,394	1,618,806
Libraries	1,020,680	1,827,882
Student Services	1,754,240	3,141,577
Institutional Support	3,605,234	5,598,818
Operation and Plant Maintenance	3,500,592	7,557,516
Scholarships and Fellowships	2,860,163	5,890,728
From Unrestricted Funds	1,481,690	2,914,708
From Restricted Funds	1,378,473	2,976,020
Educational and Mandatory Transfers	453,946	704,964
Auxiliary Enterprises and Transfers	4,170,400	6,476,503
Hospitals and Mandatory Transfers	4,316,499	9,318,997
Independent Operations and Transfers	1,746,883	2,845,488

Appendix F (continued)

Estimated Number of Full-time Equivalent (FTE) Students

Year	1982	1990	2000
Public Sector			
Enrollment Projections:			
NCES	6,713	6,349	
Carnegie Commission		6,855	7,910
Leslie and Miller			7,807
Constant Participation Rate		6,133	5,087
of High School Grads			
Private Sector:			
Enrollment Projections:			
NCES	2,198	2,079	
Carnegie Commission		2,244	2,590
Leslie and Miller			2,556
Constant Participation Rate		2,008	1,666
of High School Grads			

Dollars per FTE Student—Public Institutions

Year	1982	1990	2000
Revenues on the basis of the following enrollment projections:			
NCES	$7,089	$11,073	
Carnegie Commission		$10,256	$14,478
Leslie and Miller			$14,669
Constant Participation Rate		$11,464	$22,511
Expenditures on the basis of the following enrollment projections:			
NCES	$6,930	$10,826	
Carnegie Commission		$10,027	$14,155
Leslie and Miller			$14,342
Constant Participation Rate		$11,209	$22,009

Appendix F (continued)

Dollars per FTE Student—Private Institutions

	1982	1990	2000
Revenues on the basis of the following enrollment projections			
NCES	$11,404	$17,813	N/A
Carnegie Commission		$16,503	$22,291
Leslie and Miller			$23,601
Constant Participation Rate		$18,443	$36,209
Expenditures on the basis of the following enrollment projections:			
NCES	$11,037	$17,241	N/A
Carnegie Commission		$15,973	$22,542
Leslie and Miller			$22,842
Constant Participation Rate		$17,850	$35,045

References and Miscellaneous Information

	1982	1990	2000
Number of High School Graduates*	2,845	2,599	2,156

*McConnell, William R., and Kaufman, Norman. "High School Graduates: Projections for the Fifty States (1982–2000)." Western Interstate Commission for Higher Education (WICHE), Teachers Insurance and Annuity Association (TIAA/CREF), and The College Board, 1984.

Appendix G

Sources of Current Funds Revenues for Institutions of Higher Education by Control and Level of Institution, 1970–1971 and 1981–1982

Year and Source	Total	Public Institutions		Private Institutions	
		4-Year	2-Year	4-Year	2-Year
		Amount in Millions			
1970–1971:					
Total	$23,879	$13,260	$2,266	$8,115	$237
Government[a]	12,106	8,291	1,778	2,020	16
Federal[b]	4,601	2,616	153	1,819	13
State	6,595	5,528	924	140	3
Local	910	147	701	61	1
Private Sources	1,227	348	11	838	31
Students	8,146	3,485	437	4,043	181
Tuition and Fees	5,021	1,738	295	2,871	118
Auxiliary Enterprises[c]	3,125	1,748	143	1,173	62
Institutional[d]	2,401	1,136	41	1,215	9
1981–1982:					
Total	72,191	38,715	8,556	24,181	739
Government[a]	33,378	22,302	6,225	4,802	49
Federal[b]	9,592	4,882	491	4,187	32
State	21,849	17,142	4,255	438	14
Local	1,938	279	1,478	177	4
Private Sources	3,564	1,236	41	2,230	57
Students	23,896	9,583	1,935	11,792	586
Tuition and Fees	15,774	5,014	1,381	8,896	483
Auxiliary Enterprises[c]	8,122	4,569	554	2,896	103
Institutional[d]	11,353	5,594	355	5,358	46

Appendix G (continued)

Year and Source	Total	Public Institutions		Private Institutions	
		4-Year	2-Year	4-Year	2-Year
		Percentage Distribution			
1970–1971:					
Total	100.0	100.0	100.0	100.0	100.0
Government[a]	50.7	62.5	78.5	24.9	6.8
Federal[b]	19.3	19.7	6.8	22.4	5.5
State	27.6	41.7	40.8	1.7	1.1
Local	3.8	1.1	30.9	.8	.3
Private Sources	5.1	2.6	.5	10.3	12.9
Students	34.1	26.3	19.3	49.8	76.3
Tuition and Fees	21.0	13.1	13.0	35.4	49.9
Auxiliary Enterprises[c]	13.1	13.2	6.3	14.4	26.4
Institutional[d]	10.1	8.6	1.8	15.0	3.9
1981–1982:					
Total	100.0	100.0	100.0	100.0	100.0
Government[a]	46.2	57.6	72.8	19.9	6.7
Federal[b]	13.3	12.6	5.7	17.3	4.3
State	30.3	44.3	49.7	1.8	1.9
Local	2.7	.7	17.3	.7	.5
Private Sources	4.9	3.2	.5	9.2	7.7
Students	33.1	24.8	22.6	48.8	79.4
Tuition and Fees	21.9	13.0	16.1	36.8	65.4
Auxiliary Enterprises[c]	11.3	11.8	6.5	12.0	14.0
Institutional[d]	15.7	14.5	4.1	22.2	6.3

Source: U.S. Department of Education, National Center for Education Statistics, Financial Statistics of Institutions of Higher Education: Current Funds Revenues and Expenditures, 1970–71, 1974; and Higher General Information Survey, Financial Statistics of Institutions of Higher Education, for fiscal year 1982, unpublished tabulations (November 1983).
Note: Details may not add to totals because of rounding.
[a] Includes appropriations, restricted and unrestricted grants and contracts.
[b] Includes appropriations, restricted and unrestricted grants and contracts, and independent operations such as Federally Funded Research and Development Centers (FFRDC).
[c] Includes revenues generated by operations that were essentially self-supporting within the institutions, such as residence halls, food services, student health services, and college unions. Nearly all such revenues are derived from students.
[d] Includes endowment income, sales and services of educational activities, sales and services of hospitals, and other sources.

Appendix H

Estimated Average Undergraduate Tuition and Room and Board Rates Institutions of Higher Education Compared with Inflation Index[a]: 1973–1974 to 1982–1983

Year and Control of Institution	Total Tuition, Room, and Board				Tuition				Inflation Index[a] (1973–1974 = 100.0)
	All Institutions	Universities	Other 4-Year	2-Year	All Institutions	Universities	Other 4-Year	2-Year	
1973–1974									
Public	$1,517	$1,707	$1,506	$1,274	$438	$581	$463	$274	100.0
Private	3,164	3,717	3,040	2,410	1,989	2,375	1,925	1,303	
1974–1975									
Public	1,563	1,760	1,558	1,339	432	599	448	277	111.1
Private	3,403	4,076	3,156	2,591	2,117	2,614	1,954	1,367	
1975–1976									
Public	1,666	1,935	1,657	1,386	433	642	469	245	118.9
Private	3,663	4,467	3,385	2,711	2,272	2,881	2,084	1,427	
1976–1977[b]									
Public	1,789	2,066	1,828	1,490	479	689	564	283	125.8
Private	3,907	4,716	3,714	2,971	2,467	3,051	2,351	1,592	
1977–1978[b]									
Public	1,888	2,170	1,932	1,589	512	736	596	306	134.3
Private	4,158	5,033	3,968	3,148	2,624	3,240	2,520	1,706	

1978–1979[b]									
Public	1,994	2,289	2,027	1,691	543	777	622	327	146.9
Private	4,514	5,403	4,326	3,389	2,867	3,487	2,771	1,831	
1979–1980[b]									
Public	2,165	2,487	2,198	1,821	583	840	662	355	166.4
Private	4,912	5,888	4,699	3,755	3,130	3,811	3,020	2,062	
1980–1981[b]									
Public	2,371	2,711	2,420	2,020	633	915	721	385	185.7
Private	5,468	6,566	5,249	4,290	3,498	4,275	3,390	2,413	
1981–1982[b]									
Public	2,668	3,079	2,701	2,217	721	1,042	813	432	201.8
Private	6,184	7,439	5,949	4,840	3,972	4,887	3,855	2,697	
1982–1983									
Public	2,944	3,403	3,032	2,390	798	1,164	936	473	210.5
Private	6,920	8,537	6,646	5,364	4,439	5,583	4,329	3,008	

Source: U.S. Department of Education, National Center for Education Statistics, Projections of Education Statistics to 1986–1987, 1978; Higher Education, Basic Student Charges, 1974–1975, 1976; and unpublished tabulations (July, 1983).

Note: Data are for the entire academic year and are average charges. Tuition and fees were calculated on the basis of full-time-equivalent students (including undergraduate resident and non-resident students). Room and board rates were based on full-time students.

[a] Index constructed using Consumer Price Index data averaged on a school-year time frame with a base year of 1973–1974.

[b] Data have been revised since originally published.

Appendix I

Estimated Undergraduate Tuition and Fees and Room and Board Rates in Institutions of Higher Education, by Type and Control of Institution: United States, 1974–1975 to 1983–1984

Year and control of institution	Total tuition, board, and room				Tuition and required fees				Board (7-day basis)				Dormitory rooms			
	All	University	Other 4-year	2-year	All	University	Other 4-year	2-year	All	University	Other 4-year	2-year	All	University	Other 4-year	2-year
1	2	3	4	5	6	7	8	9	10	11	12	13	14	15	16	17
1974–1975:																
Public	1,563	1,760	1,558	1,339	432	599	448	277	625	634	613	638	506	527	497	424
Private	3,403	4,076	3,156	2,591	2,117	2,614	1,954	1,367	700	771	666	660	586	691	536	564
1975–1976:																
Public	1,666	1,935	1,657	1,386	433	642	469	245	689	720	655	699	544	573	533	442
Private	3,663	4,467	3,385	2,711	2,272	2,881	2,084	1,427	755	833	718	712	636	753	583	572
1976–1977:[a]																
Public	1,789	2,066	1,828	1,490	479	689	564	283	728	763	692	742	582	614	572	465
Private	3,907	4,716	3,714	2,971	2,467	3,051	2,351	1,592	791	882	759	772	649	783	604	607
1977–1978:[a]																
Public	1,888	2,170	1,932	1,589	512	736	596	306	755	785	720	797	621	649	616	486
Private	4,158	5,033	3,968	3,148	2,624	3,240	2,520	1,706	836	943	800	811	698	850	648	631
1978–1979:[a]																
Public	1,994	2,289	2,027	1,691	543	777	622	327	796	823	764	837	655	689	641	527
Private	4,514	5,403	4,326	3,389	2,867	3,487	2,771	1,831	889	1,000	851	858	758	916	704	700

	1	2	3	4	5	6	7	8	9	10	11	12	13	14	15	16
1979–1980:[a]																
Public	2,165	2,487	2,198	1,821	583	840	662	355	867	898	833	894	715	749	703	572
Private	4,912	5,888	4,699	3,755	3,130	3,811	3,020	2,062	955	1,078	911	924	827	999	768	769
1980–1981:[a]																
Public	2,371	2,711	2,420	2,020	633	915	721	385	940	969	904	1,000	798	827	795	635
Private	5,468	6,566	5,249	4,290	3,498	4,275	3,390	2,413	1,053	1,208	999	997	917	1,083	860	880
1981–1982:[a]																
Public	2,668	3,079	2,701	2,217	721	1,042	813	432	1,038	1,067	1,003	1,088	909	970	885	697
Private	6,184	7,439	5,949	4,840	3,972	4,887	3,855	2,697	1,175	1,326	1,124	1,118	1,037	1,226	970	1,025
1982–1983:																
Public	2,944	3,403	3,032	2,390	798	1,164	936	473	1,136	1,167	1,103	1,162	1,010	1,072	993	755
Private	6,920	8,537	6,646	5,364	4,439	5,583	4,329	3,008	1,300	1,501	1,234	1,179	1,181	1,453	1,083	1,177
1983–1984:[b]																
Public	3,160	3,670	3,260	2,560	870	1,270	1,020	510	1,210	1,250	1,180	1,240	1,080	1,150	1,060	810
Private	7,540	9,310	7,230	5,820	4,880	6,140	4,750	3,300	1,390	1,610	1,320	1,260	1,270	1,560	1,160	1,260

Sources: U.S. Department of Education, National Center for Education Statistics, *Higher Education Basic Student Charges, 1974–1975; Fall Enrollment in Higher Education,* and unpublished data; American Council on Education, *College Costs* (July 1983).

Note: Data are for the entire academic year and are average charges. Tuition and fees were calculated on the basis of full-time-equivalent students (including undergraduate resident and nonresident students). Room and board were based on full-time students. The data have not been adjusted for changes in the purchasing power of the dollar. Preliminary analysis indicates the 1983–1984 data compiled by the American Council on Education are comparable to prior years data compiled by the National Center for Education Statistics.

a Data have been revised since originally published.
b Preliminary estimates based on information collected by the American Council on Education.

Appendix J

Current Fund Expenditures per Full-time Equivalent Student in Institutions of Higher Education, by Type and Control of Institution, and Purpose of Expenditure: United States, 1980–1981

	Total				*Public*				*Private*			
	Total	University	4-year	2-year	Total	University	4-year	2-year	Total	University	4-year	2-year
1	2	3	4	5	6	7	8	9	10	11	12	13
Total current fund expenditures and mandatory transfers	$7,263	$11,532	$7,440	$3,090	$6,365	$9,725	$7,245	$3,061	$10,003	$16,977	$7,764	$3,514
Educational and general expenditures and mandatory transfers	5,678	8,676	5,720	2,863	5,145	7,604	5,655	2,851	7,305	11,902	5,829	3,030
Instruction	2,351	3,330	2,376	1,416	2,236	2,929	2,535	1,443	2,703	4,537	2,110	1,031
Research	642	1,710	390	10	574	1,495	449	11	847	2,358	292	2
Public service	233	535	160	58	259	631	176	61	156	246	134	14
Academic support	485	750	496	225	456	676	529	226	572	972	441	215

Libraries	200	294	216	89	179	246	220	90	263	439	209	80
Student Services	330	320	391	254	294	287	347	249	440	418	463	336
Institutional support	655	693	790	430	536	549	664	408	1,015	1,124	1,000	749
Operation and maintenance of plant	607	790	672	347	554	692	673	341	766	1,084	671	420
Scholarships and fellowships	284	445	330	72	160	268	178	64	661	979	583	180
From unrestricted funds	123	198	148	17	55	103	63	13	328	485	289	82
From restricted funds	161	247	182	55	105	165	115	52	334	494	293	98
Educational and general mandatory transfers	92	102	116	50	75	76	105	48	144	183	136	82
Auxiliary enterprises	826	1,345	914	227	701	1,278	772	209	1,208	1,549	1,150	484
Mandatory transfers	58	89	73	7	52	89	71	6	75	91	76	16
Hospitals	616	1,187	681	—	509	809	815	—	944	2,325	459	—
Mandatory transfers	7	17	4	—	4	8	5	—	14	44	3	—
Independent operations[a]	143	325	125	—	11	33	4	—	545	1,201	327	—

Sources: U.S. Department of Education, National Center for Education Statistics, surveys of "Financial Statistics of Institutions of Higher Education, fiscal year 1981," and "Fall Enrollment in Higher Education, 1980."

[a]Generally includes only those expenditures associated with major federally funded research and development centers.

Appendix K

Trends in Current Funds Expenditures and Mandatory Transfers by Institutions of Higher Education and per Full-time Equivalent (FTE) Student, by Control of Institution: 1970–1971 to 1981–1982

Control of Institution and Year	Current Dollars	Constant (1981–1982) Dollars[a]	Current Funds Expenditures Per FTE Student, in Constant (1981–1982) Dollars[a]
	All Institutions		
	Current Funds Expenditures (in Millions)		
Public and Private			
1970–1971	$23,375	$52,785	$7,834
1971–1972	25,560	54,658	7,646
1972–1973	27,956	56,771	7,827
1973–1974	30,714	58,258	7,816
1974–1975	35,058	61,256	7,848
1975–1976	38,903	63,756	7,519
1976–1977	42,600	65,559	7,887
1977–1978	45,971	66,318	7,881
1978–1979	50,721	67,909	8,134
1979–1980	56,914	69,357	8,172
1980–1981	64,053	70,485	7,992
1981–1982	70,339	70,339	7,803
Public			
1970–1971	14,996	33,863	6,837
1971–1972	16,484	35,251	6,596
1972–1973	18,204	36,968	6,780
1973–1974	20,336	38,574	6,852
1974–1975	23,490	41,044	6,904
1975–1976	26,184	42,911	6,579
1976–1977	28,635	44,068	6,940
1977–1978	30,725	44,325	6,930
1978–1979	33,733	45,164	7,193
1979–1980	37,768	46,025	7,200
1980–1981	42,280	46,526	7,004
1981–1982	46,219	46,219	6,816

Appendix K (continued)

	All Institutions		
	Current Funds Expenditures (in Millions)		Current Funds Expenditures Per FTE Student, in Constant (1981–1982) Dollars[a]
Control of Institution and Year	Current Dollars	Constant (1981–1982) Dollars[a]	
Private			
1970–1971	8,379	18,921	10,602
1971–1972	9,075	19,407	10,756
1972–1973	9,752	19,804	10,997
1973–1974	10,377	19,684	10,792
1974–1975	11,568	20,212	10,863
1975–1976	12,719	20,845	10,649
1976–1977	13,965	21,491	10,950
1977–1978	15,246	21,994	10,894
1978–1979	16,988	22,745	10,992
1979–1980	19,146	23,331	11,138
1980–1981	21,773	23,960	11,007
1981–1982	24,120	24,120	10,801

Source: U.S. Department of Education, National Center for Education Statistics, Higher Education General Information Survey, Financial Statistics of Institutions of Higher Education and Fall Enrollment in Higher Education, unpublished tabulations (November 1983).
Note: Details may not add to totals because of rounding.
[a]Dollars adjusted using the Higher Education Price Index, from National Institute of Education, Inflation Measures for Schools and Colleges, 1983.

CHAPTER 16
FUNDING GRADUATE AND GRADUATE PROFESSIONAL EDUCATION FOR THE TWENTY-FIRST CENTURY

LESLIE W. KOEPPLIN

During the academic year 1983–1984 approximately 450,000 graduate and graduate professional students were enrolled in the member institutions of NASULGC.[1] Total enrollment in these same institutions, including undergraduate and special students, was 2,206,608. By any reasonable measure, graduate and graduate professional education represents a substantial commitment of university, student, government, and private sector resources. It is particularly appropriate to review this commitment as part of Project 2000 in light of the pending reauthorization of the Federal Higher Education Acts. Because of the carry-over in its five-year cycles, this reauthorization will affect the funding of graduate and graduate professional education well into the twenty-first century.

BACKGROUND

The substantial development of graduate and graduate professional education in American higher education institutions dates from approximately a century ago and the importation of the graduate and research model from the German institutions of higher education and the concurrent development of the university's ability to confer academic training and respectability to professional education.[2] However, it was not until the period after World War II, and more directly since 1960, that graduate and professional education began to reach today's scope.

This growth came from the development of professional and graduate school programs within the university and the internal and external demand for the graduates. During the 1960s, almost all of this nation's research universities either greatly enlarged or became new hosts to a whole set of professional schools, including architecture, urban planning, medicine, nursing, public health, library science, engineering, the performing arts, law, management, and education. While the university was developing these schools, there was also a great demand for Ph.D. graduates from within and without the academy. The creation during the 1960s of a community college system, which now enrolls 4,330,000 students, the growth of the four-year public college enrollment from 750,000 to 3,000,000 and the increase in the enrollment from 1960 to 1980 in the private institutions and the member institutions of NASULGC caused a heavy demand for faculty with advanced training. The needs of the electronics, communication, and aerospace industries, and the development of American medicine, business, and law, also served as powerful reasons to expand these programs.

In 1945 there were fewer than 2,000 doctorates granted by all the United States universities; by 1960 the number had not yet reached 10,000; however, by 1973 it had reached its peak of 33,756.[3] Since 1973 there has been a decrease in the number of Ph.D.s awarded, and this year the number will approximate 30,000.

As a result, NASULGC member institutions now have on their campuses comprehensive programs in the graduate and professional areas which both represent an enormous investment and an extraordinary opportunity.

The relationship of this graduate education to research needs to be emphasized. American universities, as part of the research process, train through graduate education the scholars and the researchers of tomorrow. American universities cannot do graduate education or graduate professional education without a research capacity.

The National Commission on Student Financial Assistance recently has reminded us of the contribution research and graduate education have made to America's quality of life since World War II.[4] Among other accomplishments, the commission notes that since World War II the number of Nobel Prizes awarded to American scientists increased nearly fivefold while we can claim some 65 percent of the major technological innovations of the same period. The United States' international trade position, its developments in medicine and health care, its preeminent position in agriculture, and its expanded cultural and artistic programs would not have been possible without the research and graduate education accomplishments of our universities since World War II. The demands of a high-technology society can only increase the future responsibility and opportunity of this nation's universities.

The stake of the states in this research and graduate education effort has also been recently reviewed as part of the NASULGC Project 2000.[5] Richard L. Van Horn has emphasized the crucial role graduate education and research have played in the development of undergraduate education at the state universities. He has also noted the positive cultural and social developments and documented the growing importance of the state university graduate and research capacity to the economy of the state during a high technology era.

ISSUES IN THE FUNDING OF GRADUATE AND
PROFESSIONAL EDUCATION

The elements that make up the current funding of graduate and professional education among the NASULGC institutions include university and student resources, and government and private sector support.

The university supports graduate education through the appointment of quality research faculty and provision for their released time, the maintenance of libraries, computer services, and laboratories, the construction and maintenance of physical and support facilities, graduate assistantships, and direct graduate and professional fellowship support.

There have been substantial efforts to assess the specifics of the cost to the university of maintaining the graduate education programs. The Council of Graduate Schools in the early 1970s undertook several studies on the costs of graduate education.[6] For instance, it found in 1974 that the estimated total annual mean cost per enrolled graduate student for six fields was as follows: biochemistry—$18,000, chemistry—$8,100, economics—$4,100, English—$3,000, mathematics—$6,200, and psychology—$5,600.[7] It should be emphasized that these are 1974 dollars and that they are mean costs.

In fact, the range of costs in some of these fields shows the problem of trying to pinpoint the costs of the university's involvement in graduate education. For instance, the survey found that the costs, in 1974 dollars, for a year of graduate work in biochemistry ranged from $4,400 to $25,000 among the surveyed institutions. However, there can be little doubt about the grand scale of these costs. As noted above, approximately one in five students in a NASULGC member institution is a graduate or graduate professional student.

In understanding the university's commitment to graduate education one must also deal with the costs of research. A recent study of the benefits and costs of research has found that of the estimated $4.56 billion received by universities and colleges in 1982 in support of basic research activities, $3.15 billion or 69 percent came from federal sources, 21.4 percent came from the universities and colleges themselves, 6 percent of $275 million came fron nonprofit organizations and 3.5 percent from industry.[8]

The state is the major source of funds for the state research university's faculty appointments and equipment and facilities support, although endowment and other private support for these universities can play an important role. Thus, for most of the state research universities that belong to NASULGC, the state plays a vital role in supporting graduate education.

Graduate and professional students pay a significant part of the costs of their education themselves. During 1983–1984, tuition and fees for graduate students at NASULGC member institutions ranged from a median of $1,303 for resident students to a median of $3,104 for nonresident students and from $3,222 for resident medical students to $6,886 for nonresident medical students.[9]

Perhaps the largest single cost to the advanced student is foregone income, an income that ranges according to the field in which the student is enrolled. For instance, a graduate engineer in a four-year program could expect to lose perhaps $100,000–$150,000 in foregone salary, while a Ph.D. in the humanities could expect to lose perhaps $75,000–$100,000 income during the same four years.

Graduate and professional students work part-time to meet their costs. This part-time work, which can come through external and internal campus sources and which is often funded by federal research project support, is a major component of student support. The National Commission on Student Financial Assistance estimated that in 1981 some 27,000 graduate students were supported by federally funded research projects.[10] Graduate and professional students, as well as undergraduate students, are eligible for participation in the College Work Study program, which pays part of the costs of a position in a nonprofit organization.

It is also quite clear that graduate and professional students borrow. A recent study undertaken by the American Council on Education and funded by the Ford Foundation as a joint project of the National Institute of Independent Colleges and Universities, the American Association of State Colleges and Universities, the National Association of State Universities and Land-Grant Colleges, and the American Association of Community and Junior Colleges, surveyed student aid during 1983–1984 at a representative sampling of institutions of higher education.[11] The survey found at independent institutions that 68 percent of graduate students who received federal aid borrowed from the Guaranteed Student Loan program at a mean level of $4,585 and 14 percent borrowed from the National Direct Student Loan program at the mean level of $1,825. At public universities, 86 percent of graduate student aid recipients borrowed on the average $3,868 from GSL and $1,778 from NDSL. Considering that the maximum loan under GSL is $5,000, this survey indicates that almost all of graduate and professional students who receive student aid are borrowing close to the maximum to support their efforts.

The Educational Testing Service has also found extensive graduate professional borrowing. In a recent survey, it found that among its sample population private medical school students had borrowed approximately $31,000 by their fourth year in medical school and public medical school students borrowed approximately $21,000.[12] Law school students borrowed approximately $10,400 by the conclusion of their third year of law school and private law school students borrowed approximately $14,000. These are relatively large sums and there are many professional school students, including those in education, who cannot expect to have immediate high paying positions.

Finally, there are the federal fellowships. However, the number of federally funded fellowships has declined from 51,000 in 1968 to fewer than 10,000 new and continuing fellowships in 1983.[13] The Department of Education has an $11 million program for graduate and professional opportunity and will have in federal FY 1985 an additional $2.5 million for graduate fellowships in the arts, humanities, and social sciences. These two programs provide extremely important services. The GPOP program is a fundamental commitment to increasing minority and disadvantaged student participation in our graduate and professional programs while the new program for graduate fellowships in the arts, humanities, and social sciences will provide perhaps 100 to 150 fellowships in these areas. However, these are relatively small numbers, and there is no broad federal grant program for graduate and professional students.

This is in direct contrast to undergraduate education. The Department of Education provides in excess of $3.5 billion in direct grant support to undergraduate students. This grant support comes from the Pell and SEOG programs and is offered at the undergraduate level after the parent and student have made their contributions as part of a package that involves a College Work-Study program and two loan programs, the NDSL and GSL.

The private sector's support of graduate education is both long-standing and difficult to quantify. The National Science Foundation has noted that as early as the 1920s the University of Illinois chemistry department was the world's largest producer of Ph.D.s in any discipline and that some 65 percent of those Ph.D.s took positions in industry.[14] However, as noted above, a recent research study found that the private sector now provides only 3.5 percent of the costs of basic research.

In addition, there has been a trend of private and corporate philanthropy at graduate schools. For instance, the Ford, Danforth, and Woodrow Wilson Foundations have all had programs of support for graduate fellowships while the Andrew Mellon Foundation has undertaken an important new program in this area.

In summary, it is clear that the cost of graduate education among state research universities is being met by a large-scale combination of state, university, student, and federal resources. The university drawing on state resources conducts graduate education in tandem with its research mission and purpose. The student takes advantage of this offering at a substantial expense in foregone income and, if the student is needy, through part-time work and loans.

The federal commitment to graduate and graduate professional education, unlike its support of research and undergraduate education, is somewhat more difficult to characterize. As noted above, the federal government provides nearly 70 percent of all basic research funds at universities. It also provides a $3.5 billion undergraduate grant support program. However, its support for graduate education appears to come from a sense that graduate students reap such huge benefits from this education that they should expect to pay literally all of its costs through individual resources, part-time work, and loans.

TOWARD THE TWENTY-FIRST CENTURY

This federal government view of graduate education as of main interest (and cost) to the individual student needs to be reevaluated in light of recent research findings.

1. The Department of Defense alone currently employs 105,000 scientists and engineers, many with graduate training.[15]

2. There are 30,000 positions in the federal government requiring foreign language competence, half of them requiring advanced skills for analyzing foreign nations.[16] This is at a time when the most recent survey of our ability in language and area studies notes the lack of the very best people in foreign language and area study competence.[17]

3. The private sector is becoming in some instances a larger consumer of Ph.D.s than the universities. In chemistry 56 percent of all currently

employed doctoral scientists and engineers are employed in industry, compared to 34 percent in academic institutions; in engineering the percentages are 54 in industry and 33 in academia; and in computer science the percentages are 49 in industry and 40 in academia. In terms of recent graduates the statistics are even more striking. Physics and astronomy have become the only scientific fields in which academia maintains a higher overall employment of Ph.D. recipients than industry.[18]

4. A recent NSF survey has found that the number one reason for business cooperation with universities is access to graduate students who can be considered for future employment.[19]

These findings provide substantial evidence that graduate education is vital both to the national defense and economy. Given this crucial role, it is timely for the federal government to consider augmenting its current support of graduate education with a direct grant program. Such a program could be modeled after the existing Supplementary Education Opportunity Grant (SEOG) program funded at $412 million and currently available only to undergraduate students.

While the details of such a grant program obviously would need to be refined during the reauthorization hearings of the Higher Education Acts, three points should be emphasized:

1. A graduate grant program should supplement rather than supplant the undergraduate programs. It would be folly to tear dollars from the undergraduate grant programs to support graduate work, especially in light of the unmet need of undergraduate students.

2. The grant program should not be viewed as a mechanism for increasing graduate and graduate professional enrollment—although it could be used for those purposes in certain areas such as computer science and engineering—but should be seen as a way to balance the advanced student's current contribution to his or her education. This would create a mixture of student grant, part-time work, and loan funding similar to that of the undergraduate level.

3. The grant program should be administered on a flexible basis by the universities which could distribute it among both graduate and graduate professional students in cognizance of the unique needs presented by each student. In allocating the grant awards, the campus could take into account such individual factors as loan burden, part-time work, individual needs, and merit.

Such a federal grant program would distribute the costs of graduate and graduate professional education more broadly across the spectrum of those who benefit from a strong national economy and national defense.

NOTES

1. "1983–84 Enrollment at State and Land-Grant Universities," (Washington, D.C.: NASULGC, 1984).

2. Two excellent recent works on graduate education are: Jaroslav Pelikan, *Scholarship and Its Survival: Questions on the Idea of Graduate Education* (Princeton, N.J.: Carnegie Foundation for the Advancement of Teaching, 1983); and William G. Bowen, "Graduate Education in the Arts and Sciences: Prospects for the Future," *Report of the President* (Princeton: 1981). For a discussion of the university impact on the development of a profession, see: Paul Starr, *The Social Transformation of American Medicine: The Rise of a Sovereign Profession and the Making of a Vast Industry* (New York: 1982).

3. Bowen, "Graduate Education," p. 18–19.

4. National Commission on Student Financial Assistance, *Signs of Trouble and Erosion: A Report of Graduate Education in America* (Washington, D.C.: 1983).

5. See chapter 2 in this book, Richard Van Horn, "The Stake of the States in Research, Graduate Education and Professional Training."

6. Joseph L. McCarthy and William D. Garrison, *The Costs and Benefits of Graduate Education: Estimation of Graduate Degree Program Costs* (Washington, D.C.: The Council of Graduate Schools in the United States, 1974); Joseph L. McCarthy and David R. Deener, *The Costs and Benefits of Graduate Education: A Commentary with Recommendations* (Washington, D.C.: The Council of Graduate Schools in the United States, 1970).

7. McCarthy and Garrison, *The Costs and Benefits of Graduate Education*, p. 64–65.

8. See chapter 11 in this book, Samuel Conti, "Who Benefits? Who Pays?: A Consideration of the Distribution of University Science/Engineering Research Costs Among its Sponsors," p. 155.

9. "1983–84 Student Charges at State and Land-Grant Universities," (Washington, D.C.: NASULGC, 1984).

10. *Signs of Trouble and Erosion*, pp. 12–14.

11. "Who Gets Student Aid: A 1983–84 Snapshot" (Washington: American Council on Education, 1984).

12. "Talented and Needy Graduate and Professional Students: A National Survey of People Who Applied for Need-Based Financial Aid to Attend Graduate or Professional Schools in 1980–81" (Princeton: Educational Testing Service, 1982).

13. Association of American Universities, Association of Graduate Schools in the Association of American Universities, Council of Graduate Schools in the United States, National Association of State Universities and Land-Grant Colleges, "The Federal Role in Graduate Education: A Position Paper" (Washington, D.C.: 1983).

14. "The University-Industry Research Relationships" (Washington, D.C.: The National Science Foundation, 1982).

15. *Signs of Trouble and Erosion*, p. 18.

16. Ibid.

17. "Beyond Growth: The Next Step in Language and Area Studies" (Washington, D.C.: Association of American Universities, 1984).

18. See Conti, "Who Benefits? Who Pays?" p. 160.

19. "University-Industry Research Relationships," p. 19.

CHAPTER 17
PUBLIC AND PRIVATE UNIVERSITIES: MUCH ALIKE, USEFULLY DIFFERENT

ROBERT M. ROSENZWEIG

Of all the features that describe American higher education, none is so unusual in comparison with other nations than is the important role played by nongovernmentally owned and operated colleges and universities. They were the first institutions of higher learning in America; for many years they were the dominant institutions, by virtually any measure; and even after fifty years of vigorous growth of public institutions, the privates continue to constitute a significant proportion of the highest quality colleges and universities.

No feature of such enduring cultural significance and distinctiveness can be treated as a mere historical accident. A social arrangement that persists for so long clearly is connected to some central cultural theme. And, of course, that is the case here, for the existence of private higher education is but one expression of an historic American commitment to the mobilization of private energies for public purposes. As John G. Simon said, "Nonprofit organizations in our society undertake missions that are, in other countries, committed to business enterprises or to the state. Here, we importantly, if not exclusively, rely on the third sector to cure us, to entertain us, to teach us, to study us, to preserve our culture, to defend our rights and the balance of nature, and ultimately to bury us."[1]

As Simon goes on to say, that description is somewhat exaggerated. Few, if any, of the activities he lists are wholly "private," in the sense of being totally independent of the state. Many nongovernmental organizations use public funds through grants and contracts to fulfill their purposes, and virtually all depend on long-standing provisions of the tax code to exempt their own income from taxation and to allow donors to contribute money to their purposes without paying a tax on the money they give. Still, while truth is more complex than poetry, the essence of poetry is truth, and the truth is that we have, since the beginning of the Republic, depended on voluntary, nonprofit, nongovernmental associations for a large share of the society's communal activities.

This reliance on private associations generally fit the needs of nineteenth-century America. As the nation expanded across the continent, the pace of settlement frequently outstripped the reach of governments. If the customary community services were to be provided, it could only be through cooperative voluntary activities. It was a happy adaptation of theory to practice.

So, too, was the congruence—hardly coincidental—between the dominant political philosophy of the times and the growth of private associations. For different reasons and with different ends in mind, both the Jeffersonian and Jacksonian Democrats of the pre–Civil War period and the Republicans of the post–Civil War period advocated sharply limited governmental powers, a posture that left much need for private activity in the realm of social services and much room for private activity in the realm of business.

If the existence of large numbers of private colleges and universities is a distinctive mark of American higher education, it must also be said that the distinction between what is called "public" and what is called "private" has never been either neat or clean.[2] The early private colleges were closely bound to the communities or states in which they were formed. The original names of Brown and Princeton universities, for example, were the College of Rhode Island and the Providence Plantations and the College of New Jersey, respectively. Nor has it been uncommon for private institutions to have public parts grafted onto them, as Cornell and MIT, among others, still do.

Moreover, there was no sharp distinction between the early state universities and their private counterparts with respect to the social class of their student bodies or their commitment to the liberal arts and their disdain for practical and professional training. John R. Thelin points out that many characteristics now associated primarily with public institutions were begun in private colleges. He lists as examples extension programs, technical and professional education, tax-supported funding, free tuition, and open admissions. Similarly, the difference in size which we now associate with the difference in control was actually reversed as late as 1880, when two-thirds of the twenty-six largest American colleges were private.

The introduction of the land-grant colleges into the mix added a new emphasis, if not a wholly new element. The land-grant movement should probably be seen as a response to the unwillingness of existing institutions, both public and private, to meet emerging needs. Those needs had something to do with agriculture, but they had at least as much to do with the requirements of a growing industry and commerce for trained technicians and managers. And perhaps not least, they had to do with the need for opportunities for education and training of the middle class that industry and commerce both require and produce.

The growth of higher education in nineteenth- and early twentieth-century America was not much more planned than was the growth of industry and commerce. Markets were created and they were filled. The kind of institution that filled a market need was much more likely to be a function of local circumstances than of an overarching conception of what kinds of activities were most appropriate for what kinds of colleges and universities.

In this case, the analogy with nineteenth-century business is not far-fetched, for educators, like businessmen, yielded to the temptation to protect their markets from upstart newcomers. Thelin cites Yale's Lyman Bagg observing in the 1870s, "The blessing to this country of having all such money sunk into the sea, could be only equalled by that other blessing of having all but a half dozen of all the American 'colleges' founded in the present century, blotted from existence, or turned into preparatory schools for the other ones." Not to be outdone, Harvard's Professor Charles Eliot Norton observed in 1895, "Whatever is generous in the object of the founders would be far more effectively promoted if the means required for the foundation and carrying on of the new institutions were concentrated and applied in an already existing school of learning. The lamentable waste involved in the needless duplication of the instruments of study, of buildings, libraries, and laboratories, would at least be avoided."

Not much more needs to be made of all this than to conclude that in education, as elsewhere, America spawned a remarkably adaptive set of social institutions, and that, frequently, the differences among them have been less consequential than the similarities. Still, there are both public and private institutions of higher learning in this nation, and their existence amounts to something more than a distinction without a difference. Where money comes from does make a difference, as do the processes for recruiting those who hold an institution in trust. A college or university whose money and board of governors arrive through the processes of politics may be no more subject to pressure than is an institution that is governed by a church group, but the nature and substance of the pressures on them will be quite different. Moreover, the differences are both real and consequential. They may well affect such matters as admissions criteria, curriculum, faculty selection, student behavior, and student discipline, among others.

The contrast is, of course, strongest between public institutions and those that retain a strong religious identification. Those are strong and vital differences even in today's relatively homogenized world, and they constitute a large part of the educational diversity in which we take such great pride. Moreover, so entrenched is the value of that kind of diversity that even policy proposals that might undermine it are necessarily couched in its defense. It might be argued that private sectarian colleges—not to mention private liberal arts colleges, generally—are not performing an educational service that is fundamentally different from any public institution that offers a bachelor of arts degree. That argument is, indeed, implicitly what is at issue in the increasingly intense competition for students between public and private colleges and in the increasingly strident debate over federal and state student aid policies. But the competition and the debate are over the value of the differences that exist and whether those ought to be recognized in policy; few would dispute that there are recognizably different kinds of institutions involved.

More to the point here, though, is what is happening at the other end of the spectrum, the end that is occupied by an extremely important but relatively small number of research universities, whose functions, programs, financing, faculties, and ambitions look remarkably alike. Some are public and some are private, and important questions of policy may turn on whether that traditional classification still means anything to any but educational statisticians and professional taxonomists.

The transforming event in the twentieth-century history of American higher education was, of course, the Second World War. In an age that has come to be dominated by rhetorical hyperbole, descriptive words have tended to lose their force, but it is not hyperbolic to say that the war transformed universities. It was the war that confirmed the emergence of science as a key element of national power. As that happened, it became clear to policymakers that most of the people who conducted scientific research were to be found on university campuses, and they were called professors.

That lesson was not forgotten at war's end. While America's armed forces were rapidly demobilized, the growing reality of the cold war made it certain that science would not be. The support of university-based science and technology became a major preoccupation of government, initially through agencies of the Department of Defense, then through the new National Science Foundation, the Atomic Energy Commission, the National Institutes of Health, and others. The effect was to elevate research to a new level of prominence on university campuses. Moreover, the range of fields in which support was available was so broad, and the rate of growth in funding was so high, that a surprisingly large number of institutions were able to share in it and thereby develop their capacities. Far from being the exclusive preserve of a small number of already powerful universities, government programs of the 1950s and 1960s at least doubled and perhaps tripled the number of universities seriously and broadly engaged in high-quality research.

A second, seemingly unrelated, consequence of the war also helped to lay the foundation on which a large and varied university research establishment came to rest. That was the expansion of enrollment that was fuelled by the GI Bill. Enacted for other purposes, the GI Bill became the largest effort in American history to provide mass access to higher education without regard to the ability to pay. A society whose political system is based on a universal franchise does not easily or lightly turn away from such a commitment, and American society has not. Indeed, the commitment has been very substantially enlarged in the years since.

The enrollment surge that followed the Second World War and then the Korean War demanded an expansion of university faculties, which in turn produced support for the expansion of Ph.D. programs. It was a blending of social needs and responses that was ideally suited to broad institutional expansion: a surge in undergraduate enrollment, leading to an enlargement of graduate programs that produced increased numbers of scholars who could be employed in the growing institutions, and whose research—at least in the fields of science and technology—was needed and supported by the government. Small wonder that those times are nostalgically viewed as the Golden Age of universities in America. And small wonder, too, that they could not be sustained indefinitely, and that they are unlikely to be reproduced.

In the university world the responses of public and private institutions were not identical. The chief difference was, of course, that the publics necessarily expanded their enrollments, both undergraduate and graduate, much faster than did the privates. As a consequence, their faculties, facilities, and programs of research grew at a faster rate, as well. These were very good times for the major private universities; they were bonanza times for the publics.

What is so striking during all of this period is that government policy—at least insofar as it was aimed at universities—was substantially indifferent with respect to the differences between public and private. There were occasional debates at the margin. For example, fellowship programs were vexed by the question of whether a fellowship should carry with it a stipend, and both tuition and a cost of education allowance, or only one of those, and if so, which one? High-tuition privates and low-tuition publics differed, but never to the extent that programs were put in jeopardy over the difference. Similarly, the argument for full reimbursement of the indirect costs of research tended to be carried by the private universities because the publics could rely on state appropriations to meet a share of those costs. This difference rarely became a cause of conflict, if only because growing appropriations made conflict unnecessary. However, it is interesting to note that, even with the shrinkage of research funds and the tightening of state budgets, there has been no public-private conflict over the share of the total that goes to indirect cost reimbursement. Instead, all institutions have joined together in pursuit of the common goal of full reimbursement for all.

The fact is that from the institutions' point of view, the competition for federal funds for research and ancillary purposes—and it has been competitive—has been widely viewed as fair. Far more often than not, the principle governing the distribution of funds has been quality, an honest attempt by qualified persons to make judgments about the ability of the persons proposing to do the work and the likely importance of what they propose to do.

From the government's point of view, there has been no need and little reason to be concerned about the public-private difference. Periodically, concerns are voiced about the uneven geographical distribution of funds, and that may be mistaken as a public-private difference. In reality, however, the parts of the country that have fared best over the years are marked by strong sets of public and private universities, and that has been the source of their strength. Attempts to compensate for the concentration of funds by artificial preferences have never fared very well, and they have typically been short-lived.

The reality that underlies the enormously successful system for distributing funds for research and related purposes is that quality exists in our universities without regard to the method of their control. The system could not have been sustained for so long, nor could it have been so successful, if that were not the case. Nor should that underlying fact come as a surprise, for it has long been true. A look at the history of membership in the Association of American Universities is instructive. The founding members of the organization were the fourteen universities that, in 1900, offered the Ph.D. degree. Eleven of them were private. However, by the start of the First World War that difference had been erased, and the membership has remained nearly balanced between public and private universities. In recent years, the balance has been kept more or less by policy, but even so, it does no real injustice to the distribution of quality programs of research and graduate training.

What lessons can we learn from the record of recent history? The chief lesson has to do with the major item now on the agenda of American universities and of the government that depends on them, namely, the pressing need to rebuild the base. The nation's basic research capacity, which exists mostly in universities, has been sustained over the last fifteen years by drawing on capital put in place in the fifteen years before that. There are no regular programs in government for the construction and renovation of research facilities, nor have there been any since about 1970. Fellowship competitions designed to attract the best college graduates into careers of scholarship diminished to practically the vanishing point. As research grant budgets grew tighter, the pressing need to keep research groups in being drove out the important, but less urgent, need to improve scientific instrumentation. And funds for major pieces of equipment, the kind that is too expensive to buy from grant budgets even in more generous times, have been in even shorter supply. The consequences are evident. Faculties, facilities, and equipment are all aging together more or less gracefully. Unless the trend is reversed, it is inevitable that, as with steel and automobiles, the product will become less good, less competitive, more expensive.

Fortunately, our mixed system of state, federal, and private financing is readily adaptable to the task whose magnitude is beyond the capacity of any one of those. Furthermore, it can be done without debilitating and divisive arguments about who should have access to which source of funding. For the most part, state funds will, as they should, be devoted to each state's public universities. Beyond that, the governing principle must continue to be that quality and the promise of quality should dictate the flow of funds. Only a competition of that kind can provide the incentives that produce high-quality work and reduce extraneous divisiveness.

Thus far, I have emphasized the ways in which public and private institutions are alike. With respect to research universities, that is the proper emphasis. The major research universities, public and private, have more in common with each other than any of them has with a two- or four-year college, public or private. The typical comprehensive state university may have a greater variety of professional schools or display a wider range of doctoral programs than its private counterpart, but even those differences are neither invariable nor crucial. On the matters that are most visible, public and private research universities are more alike than they are different. Both are committed to research and graduate education as principal parts of their missions; both depend heavily on federal funds to support their research programs; increasingly, both seek private support for their activities; their faculties look very much alike in their training, interests, and abilities, and, indeed, faculty move freely from one kind of institution to another with few visible signs of culture shock and no apparent loss of momentum; and both kinds of institutions are well represented in anyone's list of the world's leading universities.

Is there, then, any difference that makes a difference? Do we, as a nation, maintain tax and expenditure policies that sustain these odd private institutions out of any reason more profound than inertia, or, to put it in a more dignified form, out of respect for tradition and the value of historical continuity?

The answer to that question can be put in the form of a paradox: The more alike public and private universities become in their functions, and even in the sources of their funding, the more important it is to retain a strong set of institutions whose distance from direct political control can enable them to act strongly on behalf of all universities when governments threaten important values in pursuit of some immediate purpose.

The most important word in that last sentence is the adverb: "when," not "if," governments threaten important values. It has happened before; it will inevitably happen again. For reasons of prudence as well as politics, governments respond to what appears to be urgent, and woe unto what seems to be less urgent if it stands in the way.

This is no hypothetical concern or nameless fear, and when it occurs, private institutions are in a better position to respond expeditiously. This is surely not because their leaders are braver or more virtuous. Rather, it is because their governing boards are nonpolitical, their core funding tends to be nongovernmental, their obligations to consult widely are less great, making their response time shorter, and they are less vulnerable to direct political retribution. Those elements could all be seen in two recent cases in point. The first involved an action by the Congress to require medical schools, as a condition of receiving capitation funds, to accept a specified number of American students who were in training in foreign medical schools. Both the number of students to be accepted by each school and the standards for their admission were to be established by the Secretary of Health, Education and Welfare.

The provision was broadly offensive to universities as an unacceptable intrusion into their admissions processes. The first strong response came from a group of private universities that announced that they would forego the federal funds rather than accept the offending provision and that they were retaining counsel to examine the possibility of constitutional challenge in the event that Congress failed to amend the law.

Eventually, the law was amended after efforts by public and private universities alike. However, the ability of a relatively small number of private institutions to act swiftly and pointedly established at the outset the seriousness of the issue for universities.

More recently, the university community has been vexed by the debate over proposed controls on scientific communication. At issue, specifically, is the wisdom of giving to the government the power to bar publication of scientific results that, while not classified, are deemed to be sensitive to the national security. It is not clear that the proponents of that approach understood how serious an issue that was to universities. That point was finally made unambiguously clear in a letter signed by the presidents of three leading private universities in which they indicated that their institutions would be forced to forego any research funding that carried with it such a grant of power to the sponsor. In this case, too, the key was the ability to act quickly and forcefully and in doing so to articulate an important interest of all universities. The existence of a set of institutions that is able to work with government, but not be of government, is a priceless asset to American higher education, indeed, to American society.

As this century lurches to a close and attention turns to the next, there is every reason to believe that the nation will need its research universities and that it will continue to need both its public and private research universities, no matter how they may converge in certain respects. That convergence, in fact, simplifies the task of formulating sensible policy. In the most fundamental sense what is needed from governments is identical for both kinds of universities: both require assistance in sustaining the investment in capital and people that high-quality research and graduate training demand; and both require respect for the independence that universities—which is in this case to say their faculties and students—need if they are to define the most important areas of inquiry and find the best ways to unlock their secrets. What is needed, in short, is to extract what is best from our recent past and use the result to enrich the future.

NOTES

1. "Research on Philanthropy," paper delivered at 25th Anniversary Conference of the National Council on Philanthropy, Denver, Colorado, November 8, 1979, p. 1.

2. In the discussion that follows I am indebted to John R. Thelin's wry and witty treatment of public and private higher education in eighteenth- and nineteenth-century America, which appears in his fine book, *Higher Education and Its Useful Past* (Cambridge, Mass.: Schenkman Publishing Company, Inc., 1982).

INDEX

Indians. *See* American Indians

Individualism, liberal education and, 59

Industry: basic research and, 47; faculty defections to, 96; knowledge-based, 95; pattern of development in high technology, 100; research supported by, 29. *See also* Business and industry

Institutions of higher education: control of, 120–122; current fund expenditures per full-time equivalent student, *280–281, 282–283*; differences between public and private, 301–303; enrollments in, 214–219, *250–251, 252–253*; financial impacts of enrollment changes in, 220–221; financial needs of, 212–226; modification of missions and programs of, 223–224; number of public and private, 123; prestige of, 124; private support of, 194–195; public parts of private, 296; pursuit of excellent by, 72; resources and spending of, 68; revenues and expenditures, *254–261, 264–273*; revenues and expenditures per student, 221; similarities between public and priate, 295–301; sources of current funds for, 274–275; support level of, 224–226. *See also* Community colleges; Enrollment; Higher education; Land grant institutions; State colleges; State Research universities; State Universities

Interlibrary loan programs, 49

International public service, 106–107, 112–113

International trade. *See* Foreign trade

International (world) community, 105; state university programs and, 89–90; technical assistance for trade with, 100–102

Involvement in Learning: Realizing the Potential of American Higher Education, 43

Ivy League universities, competitive advantage of, 125

James, E., 179

Janowitz, M., 66n.21

Jencks, C., 50, 62

Jobs: changing, 140; competition among college graduates for, 135; opportunities

for, 146; for scientists and engineers, 159–160. *See also* Careers

Kerr, C., 56

Kimball, B., 45

Klotsche, J. M., 151

Laboratory, establishing a research, 49

Lambert, Professor, 113

Land grant acts, 2, 9

Land-grant college movement, 43, 296

Land-grant institutions, 9, 10–12. *See also* State Colleges; State Universities

Language barriers, university help in overcoming, 100

Learning problems, 145

Leisure time, higher education and, 89

Liberal arts: college of (as an educational ideal), 40–44; professional schools and, 119–120

Liberal education, 17–18, 40–43; character formation and, 60–61; elite, 62; humanism and, 61; individualism and, 59; separation from research, 46; unifying theme of, 60

Liberal sciences, 63

Liberating Education (Gamson et al.), 66n.20

Libraries, 222; federal funds for, 207; problem of establishing research, 49

Lifelong learning, 19–20, 135

Lincoln, A., 9

Master's degree programs, business community and, 28

Megatrends (Naisbitt), 141

Minority students, 129–130, 131–132, 233; admission practices and, 80; in elementary and secondary schools, 144. *See also* Historically black colleges and universities; Racial/ethnic groups; *names of specific minority groups*

Morrill Act, 10, 87, 94. *See also* Landgrant acts

Morrill, J. S., 43, 106

Naisbitt, J., 141

NASULGC. *See* National Association

ABOUT THE CONTRIBUTORS

LESLIE KOEPPLIN, co-editor of this volume, is Director of Federal Relations at Rutgers, The State University of New Jersey.

DAVID A. WILSON, co-editor of this volume, is Professor of Political Science at the University of California, Los Angeles and Visiting Fellow, Center for Studies in Higher Education, University of California, Berkeley.

ALEXANDER W. ASTIN is Director of the Higher Education Research Institute at the University of California, Los Angeles.

CHARLES E. BISHOP is President of the University of Houston System.

EDWARD J. BLOUSTEIN is President of Rutgers, The State University of New Jersey.

JAMES T. BORGESTAD is Special Assistant to the President at the University of Minnesota.

BURTON R. CLARK is Allan M. Cartter Professor of Higher Education and Sociology and Chairman of the Comparative Higher Education Research Group at the University of California, Los Angeles.

SAMUEL F. CONTI is Vice Chancellor for Research and Dean of the Graduate School at the University of Massachusetts, Amherst.

DURWARD LONG is President of Sangamon State University.

C. PETER MAGRATH is President of the University of Missouri.

WALTER L. MILNE is Assistant to the Chairman and to the President at the Massachusetts Institute of Technology.

IVORY V. NELSON is Executive Assistant to the Chancellor in the Texas A&M University System.

BARBARA W. NEWELL is Chancellor of the State University System of Florida.

JOSEPH M. PETTIT is President of the Georgia Institute of Technology.

ROBERT M. ROSENZWEIG is President of the Association of American Universities.

RONALD W. ROSKENS is President of the University of Nebraska.

SHELDON ROTHBLATT is Professor of History and Chairman at the University of California, Berkeley.

DAVID S. SAXON is Chairman of the Corporation at the Massachusetts Institute of Technology.

RICHARD L. VAN HORN is Chancellor of the University of Houston, University Park.

HENRY R. WINKLER is President Emeritus and University Professor of History at the University of Cincinnati.